Praise for
IN THE PRESENCE OF MY ENEMIES

"A powerful story."—*Reader's Digest*

"Remarkably honest and unaffected. . . . Impressive."
—*Publisher's Weekly* **starred review**

"Recommend this awe-inspiring narrative to a broad audience, who are sure to be moved by the entire Burnham family's courage."—*CBA Marketplace*

"The issue . . . is not why an all-powerful God might choose to subject a man to evil, but how a man, with God's help, responds to evil. . . . The Burnhams, under torturous conditions, befriended their guards, comforted their fellow hostages and kept their faith in a God who seemed to have abandoned them."
—*USA Today*

IN THE PRESENCE OF MY ENEMIES

GRACIA BURNHAM

with Dean Merrill

Tyndale House Publishers, Inc.
Wheaton, Illinois

Dedication

This book is dedicated to . . . you.
If you prayed for Martin and me
while we were in captivity—
even once—then put your name
here. It is because of your prayers
that I came out alive and am
able to tell the story. Likewise,
I hope to become one
who earnestly prays and cares
for others who are hurting.
We truly need each other,
don't we?

TABLE OF CONTENTS

THE CAPTORS' ROSTER

Of the dozens of Abu Sayyaf who guarded the Burnhams at various times, these were the most prominent.

POPULAR NAMES	**"Moktar,"** "Abu Moktar" (see photo section)
OFFICIAL NAME	Khadafi Abubakar Janjalani
ROLE	Leader of the entire Abu Sayyaf (following the 1998 slaying of his older brother, the group's founder); late 20s, but looked younger; quiet; eventually "married" Reina
PRESENCE	Met the hostages upon arrival on Basilan May 31, 2001; left them late September 2001

POPULAR NAMES	**"Musab,"** "Abu Musab" (see photo section)
OFFICIAL NAME	Isnilon Totoni Hapilon
ROLE	Second-in-command of the Abu Sayyaf; knew little English; stern, headstrong; eventually "married" Ediborah
PRESENCE	From the beginning through early May 2002

POPULAR NAMES	**"Omar,"** "Abu Omar"
OFFICIAL NAME	Bakkal Hapilon
ROLE	Brother of Musab; eventually took Sheila for himself but did not formally "marry" her
PRESENCE	Met the hostages upon arrival on Basilan May 31, 2001; stayed through early May 2002

POPULAR NAMES	**"Sabaya,"** "Abu Sabaya" (see photo section)
OFFICIAL NAME	Aldam Tilao
ROLE	Spokesman to the media; negotiator with the government; known for his flair; very good English; eventually "married" Angie
PRESENCE	With the hostages the entire time

POPULAR NAME	**"Solaiman"** (see photo section)
OFFICIAL NAME	Jainal Antel Sali Jr.
ROLE	Prime liaison with the hostages for the first $3\frac{1}{2}$ months, due to his education, English fluency; late 30s; former engineer from a wealthy family
PRESENCE	From the beginning through late September 2001

POPULAR NAME	**"Mang Ben"**
ROLE	Early leader of the Burnhams' subgroup; tall, thin, stately appearance; late 30s
PRESENCE	From the beginning until killed in battle early July 2001

POPULAR NAME	**"Hurayra"**
OFFICIAL NAME	Jumadil Arad
ROLE	Friendly toward the Burnhams; mid-20s
PRESENCE	From the beginning through late September 2001

POPULAR NAME	**"Moghira"**
ROLE	Subgroup leader; eventually "married" Fe
PRESENCE	Met the hostages upon arrival on Basilan May 31, 2001; left New Year's Eve 2001

POPULAR NAME	**"Sakaki"**
ROLE	Gracia Burnham's first designated guard
PRESENCE	From the landing on Basilan until he went AWOL July 2001

POPULAR NAMES	**"Bro,"** "Kosovo"
OFFICIAL NAME	Alhamzer Limbong
ROLE	Classic warrior type; big, muscular, well-built, proud of his long, wavy hair; knew just a bit of English but willing to try using it
PRESENCE	From the beginning through late September 2001

POPULAR NAME	**"Zacarias"**
OFFICIAL NAME	Toting Craft Hanno
ROLE	Fun-loving; early 20s; Solaiman's assistant
PRESENCE	One of the original trio to abduct the Burnhams; left due to sickness late September 2001

The title *Abu* means "father of." *Mang* means "uncle."

Other resistance groups operating in the southern Philippines:

- Moro Islamic Liberation Front (MILF)
- Moro National Liberation Front (MNLF)

Moro is an ethnic label for Filipinos who are Muslim. It traces back several centuries to the Spaniards, whose name for Muslims in their own country was "Moors."

THE HOSTAGES' ROSTER

Captured at Dos Palmas Resort on May 27, 2001

MEN

NAME **Martin Burnham**   **CAPTIVITY** 1 year, 11 days

DESCRIPTION American missionary pilot from Kansas; age 41; husband of Gracia, father of three

CONCLUSION Killed by three gunshots June 7, 2002

NAME **Francis**   **CAPTIVITY** 20 days

DESCRIPTION Banker; age 50; husband of Tess

CONCLUSION Released June 15, 2001, after ransom was paid

NAME **Chito**   **CAPTIVITY** 38 days

DESCRIPTION Salesman for a cell-phone company; 30s; married, father of three

CONCLUSION Released July 3, 2001, after ransom was paid

NAME **Reggie**   **CAPTIVITY** 7 days

DESCRIPTION Former newspaper executive; VP of a construction company with many government contracts; late 40s

CONCLUSION Released June 2, 2001, after ransom was paid

NAME **Buddy**   **CAPTIVITY** 7 days

DESCRIPTION Publisher of a travel magazine; husband of Divine

CONCLUSION Abandoned June 2, 2001, after being wounded

NAME **R. J.**   **CAPTIVITY** 7 days

DESCRIPTION Buddy and Divine's 8-year-old son

CONCLUSION Released June 2, 2001

NAME **Guillermo Sobero**   **CAPTIVITY** 16 days

DESCRIPTION American contractor from California; age 40

CONCLUSION Beheaded June 11, 2001

NAME **Sonny Dacquer**   **CAPTIVITY** 6 days
DESCRIPTION Dos Palmas cook
CONCLUSION Left behind, then beheaded June 1, 2001

NAME **Armando Bayona**   **CAPTIVITY** 6 days
DESCRIPTION Dos Palmas security guard
CONCLUSION Left behind, then beheaded June 1, 2001

NAME **Eldren**   **CAPTIVITY** 6 days
DESCRIPTION Dos Palmas security guard
CONCLUSION Left behind June 1, 2001; survived a botched beheading attempt

WOMEN

NAME **Gracia Burnham**   **CAPTIVITY** 1 year, 11 days
DESCRIPTION American missionary from Kansas; early 40s; wife of Martin, mother of three
CONCLUSION Wounded by one gunshot during June 7, 2002, encounter, but evacuated

NAME **Tess**   **CAPTIVITY** 7 days
DESCRIPTION Wife of Francis; a "mother" to Gracia while on the boat; religious and caring
CONCLUSION Released June 2, 2001, in order to arrange ransom for her husband

NAME **Janice**   **CAPTIVITY** 7 days
DESCRIPTION Coworker of Chito; 20s; full of life
CONCLUSION Released June 2, 2001, in order to arrange ransom for Chito

NAME **Rizza**   **CAPTIVITY** 7 days
DESCRIPTION Girlfriend of Reggie
CONCLUSION Released June 2, 2001, after ransom was paid

NAME   **Divine**   **CAPTIVITY** 7 days

DESCRIPTION   Wife of Buddy, mother of R. J.

CONCLUSION   Abandoned June 2, 2001, after being wounded

NAME   **Angie**   **CAPTIVITY** 5 ½ months

DESCRIPTION   Sister of Divine; early 30s; single; worked in the family business (travel magazine)

CONCLUSION   Ransomed in late August but not released until November 15, 2001

NAME   **Letty**   **CAPTIVITY** 7 days

DESCRIPTION   Chinese-Filipino businesswoman

CONCLUSION   Released June 2, 2001, in order to arrange ransoms for her daughter and niece

NAME   **Kim**   **CAPTIVITY** 20 days

DESCRIPTION   Daughter of Letty; early teens

CONCLUSION   Released June 15, 2001, after ransom was paid

NAME   **Lalaine**   **CAPTIVITY** 38 days

DESCRIPTION   Niece of Letty; early teens

CONCLUSION   Released July 3, 2001, after ransom was paid

NAME   **Fe**   **CAPTIVITY** 5½ months

DESCRIPTION   Fisherman's daughter from Palawan; age 20; fiancée of Guillermo

CONCLUSION   Ransomed in late August but not released until November 15, 2001

Captured at Lamitan hospital on June 2, 2001

NAME   **Sheila**   **CAPTIVITY** 5½ months

DESCRIPTION   Nurse; married, mother of one son

CONCLUSION   Released November 15, 2001

NAME   **Reina**   **CAPTIVITY** 4 months

DESCRIPTION   Nurse; early 20s; single

CONCLUSION   Released in September due to pregnancy

NAME	**Ediborah Yap**	CAPTIVITY	1 year, 5 days
DESCRIPTION	Head nurse; mother of four
CONCLUSION	Killed by gunshot June 7, 2002

NAME	**Joel**	CAPTIVITY	4½ months
DESCRIPTION	Hospital orderly; early 20s; single
CONCLUSION	Escaped during firefight October 14, 2001

Surnames of surviving Filipino hostages are withheld out of respect for their privacy.

All dates in this chart, and throughout the book, are local time. Central time zone in the United States (e.g., Kansas, Arkansas) is 13 hours behind Philippine time in the summer, 14 hours behind in the winter. (The Philippines, being close to the equator, has no need for a daylight saving time arrangement.)

FOREIGN TERMS

Abu Sayyaf: "father of the swordsman"

Al-Harakatul Islamia: the Islamic movement

alimatok: leeches

"Allah akbar!": "Allah is the greatest!"

apam: Muslim version of a pancake

banana-cue: ripe banana pieces rolled in brown sugar and fried

banca: a small boat

bianbons: roasted banana mush

bolo: knife; Filipino equivalent of a machete

CAFGU: civilian deputized to help the Philippine troops

carabao: water buffalo

Cebuano: Filipino language

CR: "comfort room" (Filipino abbreviation for bathroom)

hajj: pilgrimage to Mecca prescribed as a religious duty to Muslims

halo-halo: crushed ice with sweetened condensed milk and mixed-in fruit

Ilocano: Filipino language

kalaw: duckbills—beautiful, big birds with bright red bills

langaw: from Tagalog for housefly—obligation to share something with others if they want it and ask for it

malong: wraparound skirt made of batik material

mujaheed (pl., mujahideen): fighter in Islamic holy war

pantos: pants (like pajama bottoms)

Sabaya: "booty of war"

*sabaya*ed: when a captive is "wedded" to a captor

"Salam!": "Peace!"

"Salam alaikom!": "Peace to you!"; standard greeting among Abu Sayyaf

sindol: hot coconut milk that can be mixed with fruit

sundalo: soldiers

Tagalog: Filipino language

terong: head covering, head shawl

tolda: multistriped plastic awning thrown over a rope between two trees for shade

tsinelas: flip-flops

viand: anything that goes on top of rice, such as a sauce

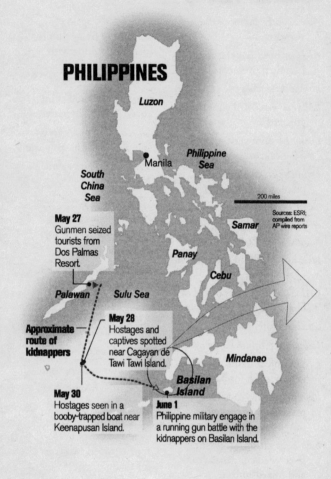

PHILIPPINES

Luzon

Philippine Sea

● Manila

South China Sea

Samar

200 miles

Sources: ESRI; compiled from AP wire reports

May 27
Gunmen seized tourists from Dos Palmas Resort.

Panay

Cebu

Palawan

Sulu Sea

Approximate route of kidnappers

May 28
Hostages and captives spotted near Cagayan de Tawi Tawi Island.

Mindanao

May 30
Hostages seen in a booby-trapped boat near Keenapusan Island.

Basilan Island

June 1
Philippine military engage in a running gun battle with the kidnappers on Basilan Island.

Paul Soutar/The Wichita Eagle

Labason

Gutalac

Mindanao

Baliguian

Ipil

Friday's gun battle
between Philippine
soldiers and Abu Sayyaf
leaves Martin and Filipino
nurse dead, Gracia freed.

Siraway

Tungawan

Sulu Sea

Sibuco

Gracia taken to
hospital with
gunshot wound
to her leg.

PHILIPPINES

200 miles

KANSAS

25 miles

Zamboanga City

Basilan
Island

Basilan Strait

Malamawi
Island

Linungan
Island

Baluc-
Baluc
Island

Isabela

Lamitan

Santa
Clara

Maluso

Basilan
Island

Bohelebung

Kaulungan
Island

Tamuk
Island

Amaloy

Mangal

Paul Soutar/The Wichita Eagle

Introduction

This is my story, but it's not my whole story. The whole story would take too long to write and would be too cumbersome to read. My coauthor, Dean Merrill, and I wrote and revised the manuscript and made cuts and more cuts. Unfortunately some of those cuts involved people who are near and dear to my heart, who worked incredibly hard to support me during and after my ordeal in the jungle. To these people I say, you were not left out because you aren't important. I hope you know what a special place you hold in my heart.

My goal in writing this has been to tell Martin's story. I hope we've done it well.

CHAPTER 1

SEIZED AT DAWN

(May 27–28, 2001)

Bang, bang, bang!

Martin and I woke with a start. It was still dark outside and we couldn't see a thing. We could only hear the pounding on the wooden door of the beach cabin where we were celebrating our eighteenth wedding anniversary.

Bang, bang, bang, bang, bang!

Ugh—they want us to move to the next cabin, I thought. During dinner the night before, a member of the resort staff had said something vague about wanting us to change rooms but then had dropped the subject. I yelled to the person pounding on the door, "It's too early to move!"

Bang, bang, bang!

Martin yelled this time: "What?"

"It's a guard," came the reply.

I'll bet he's drunk, I thought, thinking that maybe the guard had been drinking during his overnight shift and was now out raising a ruckus. Once again, the banging resumed.

"Martin, I think the guard is drunk."

"No, I think something's wrong," he replied. He got up and started to head for the door.

"Honey, wait—you need to put some pants on first!"

Martin grabbed some knee-length khaki shorts, the kind with baggy cargo pockets, from beside the bed. Meanwhile, I sat up and began to gather my clothes as well—a pair of shorts and a gray T-shirt I had worn the night before.

Just as Martin reached the door, it burst open. Three guys holding M16s charged into the room. All were short, and one was very young—probably in his teens. Another was perhaps twenty-three or twenty-four, with long black hair. I could tell the third man was somewhat older. All wore long-sleeved black shirts; two had camouflage pants. But there were no uniforms, no masks or sunglasses; we could see their faces.

Immediately, they swept Martin out the door, while the older man began yelling at me, "Go, go, go!"

"No, no, no!" I replied, clutching the sheet up around me. "I'm not dressed." I didn't know how much English he knew, but I was not about to obey him in my present state regardless. Shaking, I began pulling on my shorts.

"Okay, okay," he answered. I continued dressing.

One man had taken Martin outside, while the third one began to rifle through our belongings. He found our camera and our cell phone.

"Move, move, move!" came the order again. As I was hurried out the door, I grabbed our thong *tsinelas,* the common flip-flops that everyone wears in the Philippines. There wasn't time for me to grab my purse or anything else.

The young guy who followed me out wanted me to walk faster, even run. I knew from previous training that in the first few moments of a kidnapping, you're supposed to comply with orders in every way you can, until everybody's adrenaline calms down. But I was just so mad at this kid—I was *not* going to run!

"Faster, faster!" he said, jabbing me in the back with the barrel of his weapon.

With a calm voice I replied through clenched teeth, "I'm walking fast enough." I kept my pace. He jabbed me again, and it did hurt, but I was determined to exercise my will.

Once I got to the dock, a speedboat maybe thirty-five feet long with three massive outboard engines—the kind of boat used for drug running—was waiting. Four or five frightened hostages were already sitting on the floor of the boat. Martin, still shirtless, let out a sigh of relief to see me, having been forced to leave me in the room not fully clothed. "Oh, I'm so glad to see you," he said. "Did anybody hurt you?"

"No, no—I just had to get dressed."

Naturally, he was without his contact lenses, which made his vision a blur. Fortunately for me, he had encouraged me a couple of years earlier to have laser surgery on my eyes in Manila. So I was in good shape to see distances, even if he was not.

As I sat next to Martin in the boat, we watched as others began to arrive from the various cabins. Dawn was just starting to paint the eastern sky.

Some of the people started showing up with suitcases! One rather chic-looking couple came not only with suitcases but also with a big cooler of water. *My goodness,* I thought to myself, *I really didn't have to run out of the room so fast. I could have dragged my feet a little more and gotten some stuff together.*

I stood up and announced, "I'm going to go get Martin a shirt!"

"Sit down," barked one of the captors. "We'll get him a shirt."

I promptly obeyed. But I took notice of the fact that his English was quite good. *At least we can communicate with this one,* I thought. We later learned his name was Solaiman.

"I have our *tsinelas* here," I said to Martin, holding them up. I was really proud of myself.

"Yeah," he said. We didn't put them on our feet, however; we just held them. Martin was quiet as he looked around the boat, first at the men with guns and then at the other hostages. I could tell that he was trying to size up the situation, trying to figure it all out. This wasn't easy, however, since nearly everyone else on the boat was speaking languages we didn't understand. Occasionally, someone would throw an English word into the conversation and we'd be able to piece together some meaning. For the most part, however, we simply had to watch faces and listen to a person's tone of voice to figure out what he was saying.

I glanced down and the shine of my wedding ring caught my eye. *These guys are* not *going to get my ring!* I vowed. I pulled it off, along with a turquoise ring I was wearing on the other hand, and slipped them into my shorts pocket when no one was looking.

"Don't you think you should give me your wedding ring?" I asked Martin.

"Oh, no, we'll be fine," he answered, ever the optimist.

"Are you sure?"

"Yeah, it'll be okay."

::::

This whole romantic getaway at Dos Palmas Resort had been my idea, a fact that weighed heavily on my mind as I sat there shivering in the boat. It came about after Martin was offered a promotion with New Tribes Mission, the group with whom we had served in mission aviation for more than fifteen years. The agency wanted him to become chief pilot for the entire organization, which would mean moving back to Arizona and overseeing all flight programs worldwide.

Although he was flattered by the offer, Martin really didn't want the position. "I just want to be what I've always been: a line pilot," he told me. Martin was never happier than when he was flying the mission's little red-and-white Cessna into jungle airstrips, bringing groceries and medicine to our missionary colleagues, or help-ing ferry tribal people out to medical appointments.

Nevertheless, Martin's extraordinary piloting and ability to work with people kept moving him higher and higher up the organization's chain of management. In fact, he had turned down this promotion several times because our three kids were still young and he didn't want to do all the required traveling.

I kept telling him, "You know, I don't want to move back to the States any more than you do. But the truth is, you're the right man for this position. You really are!" I loved the Philippines, but to be honest, I didn't care where we were or what we were doing, as long as we were together. Martin would just smile and shake his head at me.

About May 10, Martin left for a two-week trip to the United States so he could meet with the senior New Tribes leadership team. While he was away, the mission pilot on the western island of Palawan was called home due to a death in the family, leaving the island un-manned. Through e-mail, Martin and I concluded that as soon as he returned, Martin should go to Palawan to fill in; after all, the missionaries in the tribes needed flight service. Plus, a translator was already scheduled to come and do some tribal work on those particular days. He'd need a pilot.

As I went over Martin's schedule in my mind, I knew he would be returning to the Philippines tired and jet-lagged—and would immediately take off for a week's duty on Palawan. I also knew that he would put in long days on the island and that he'd have to cook for himself. It didn't seem right. I knew he needed help.

My schedule was packed as well, with visitors com-ing through—but then, oddly enough, a couple of things canceled. *I can go along with him and help him out,*

I thought. Plus, with our wedding anniversary coming up on the twenty-eighth, if I went along I could at least be with him on that day. *Maybe we can even do something special while we're there. We've never had time to really enjoy the sights of Palawan.*

I called one of our coworkers on the island and asked her, "Where's a good place for Martin and me to celebrate our anniversary? He'll just be back from the States."

"Ooooh, you should go to Dos Palmas," my friend said. "It's a wonderful resort on an island all its own; you can only get there by boat. The food is terrific, and they have two kinds of rooms—garden cottages on land and cottages on stilts over the water."

"What would you recommend?"

In the background I heard her husband call out, "Over the water! Those are the nice ones."

"Okay, why don't you go ahead and book one for us for Saturday night the twenty-sixth?" I said. After that, I arranged for our neighbors, Bob and Val Petro, to take care of the kids. I began cooking ahead and freezing some meals for them to eat while we were away.

When the Dos Palmas reservation came through, I looked at the price—10,000 pesos for the two of us ($200)—and got cold feet. Yes, it covered lodging, activities, and all meals, but still . . . that was an awful lot of money for our budget. Would Martin be upset with this extravagance? What would our donors think if they knew? *Maybe I should just call my friend back and ask if there's a nice place in town instead,* I thought.

If only I had. . . .

::::

I looked around and counted: there were seventeen hostages in all packed onto the floor of the speedboat. Up on the deck, ahead of the pilot wheel, a group of our captors stood, while a few others stood back by the motors. Conversation flowed, in both English and one or more other languages I didn't recognize.

The whole loading process had taken maybe twenty-five minutes—all the hostages had been taken from the cabins over the water, none from the garden cabins. At the last minute, somebody said, "Wait! We need a cook." Quickly, one of the kidnappers jumped out of the boat and ran up to the top of the hill to abduct the resort's cook; his name was Sonny. Two security guards were nabbed as well. Obviously, they were no match for the raiders.

With Sonny and the guards, our hostage count rose to twenty.

The engines powered up, we pulled away from the pier—and suddenly one mystery was solved. The entire group of fifteen or so captors began to pump their fists in the air as they chorused in unison, *"Allah akbar! Allah akbar!* [Allah is the greatest! Allah is the greatest!]" Instantly, we knew who we were dealing with: the dreaded Abu Sayyaf. They were the only ones with the audacity to do something like this.

I didn't know a lot about the Abu Sayyaf, other than that they were terrorists. Throughout the southern Philippines, people were afraid of them. We learned later the meaning of their name, which set the tone accurately: *Abu* ("father of") *Sayyaf* ("the swordsman").

This was the same group that had taken Jeffrey Schilling, an African-American Muslim who had come to the Philippines to marry a Muslim girl the year before. Upon hearing about the Abu Sayyaf, he thought he could go to them, as a fellow Muslim, and explain that their tactics violated the Koran. His attempts at reeducation backfired immediately; they said he was a CIA agent, turned him into a hostage, and demanded one million dollars in ransom. Jeffrey was held for seven and a half months. We had heard he finally escaped by slipping out of his handcuffs, made possible by his weight loss.

I turned to Martin with a heaviness starting to press down upon my shoulders. "We are in big trouble," I said.

"Yeah, we are," he quietly agreed.

I watched as the white cabins of Dos Palmas grew tiny on the receding horizon, and soon I couldn't see any land at all. We roared out into the Sulu Sea, heading who knew where? The ride across the open water grew rough, and we found ourselves bouncing into the air and slamming down onto the floor again and again. The boat was seriously overloaded with thirty-five bodies aboard. We bumped ahead regardless.

I wasn't crying or shaky yet; all that would come later. I was steeling myself to stay calm, trying to stay focused as each event unfolded. I was also working to recall a class I had taken back in the late 1980s, when New Tribes Mission had sent their contingency planner, Guy Sier, to prepare the missionary team for hostage situations.

"The first few moments, when everyone is being rounded up," he had said, "is when the captors are the most trigger-happy. So do what you're told. But soon after that, begin to make eye contact with your kidnappers. Start to become a real person to them, not just an item. Go ahead and let them know what your needs are. That helps establish your individuality in their minds."

What else had he said? I hadn't really been paying full attention that day, and neither had Martin. Kidnapping was something that happened to other people, not to us.

I decided to put into practice the part I remembered. When the driver throttled back just a bit, I caught Solaiman's eye and announced with a firm voice, "We need a CR [the Philippine abbreviation for 'comfort room,' or bathroom]." After all, we'd all been pulled out of our beds and hustled straight onto the boat. "Where can we go?"

"Yeah, yeah," the other hostages agreed, nodding.

"There's no CR here," Solaiman declared.

That wasn't good enough for me. "Well, we need to go to the bathroom, so we're gonna go," I retorted. I got up and headed for the stern of the boat.

One of the other hostages volunteered to hold up a *malong* (the big Philippine wraparound skirt made of batik material) to give us women a bit of privacy as we squatted, one after another, right on the floor. When this process was complete, the engines powered up again, and we were off.

As we sped through the sea, the spray of salt water came flying over us from time to time, leaving us drenched and chilled. An older man began to visibly shake with cold, and someone passed him a shirt to wear.

A young woman sitting near me was almost hysterical. I began talking with her and learned that her name was Divine. She looked at me with terror in her eyes and said, "Our family has no money for ransom! We don't have anything!"

I put my hand on her shoulder and said, "You know, it doesn't matter if you have money or not. Money won't do any good right now anyway. The Lord's the only one we can trust. Try to calm down, and let's just think about getting through today."

She clung to my hand and seemed to settle down a little.

About an hour into the trip, one of the older Abu Sayyaf leaders, Mang Ben, a bearded man in his thirties, leaned over toward Martin. Looking down at Martin's hand, he announced with a stately air, "I want that ring!"

Martin could do nothing but hand it over.

I looked at my husband and whispered, "What did

I tell you?" I couldn't help remembering the day when I had bought that simple gold band. I'd paid fifty dollars for it at Service Merchandise in Raytown, Missouri, outside Kansas City. Now it had been stolen in broad daylight. I tried to remind myself that we could get another ring. *It's just a gold ring,* I told myself. *A ring can be replaced.* I gripped Martin's hand even more tightly.

Occasionally, another boat would come into view on the horizon. Whenever this happened, the captors herded us together so they could cover us with a tarpaulin in order not to be noticed. During one of these times, we heard the engines throttle back, and another boat came alongside. A conversation ensued in a language I couldn't understand. Apparently it had to do with getting food, because the other crew tossed the Abu Sayyaf some kind of packet.

Once the boat left, the food was passed under the tarp to us. It was cassava, something I'd never eaten before, although I knew it was grown by some Philippine farmers. I later learned that cassava is poisonous if eaten raw, but it can be peeled, boiled, and then drained for eating. Or it can be pounded, mixed with water, and put into banana leaves for steaming. It comes out like a hard paste.

My first bite was very vinegary. "Is this okay to eat?" I asked.

"Oh, yes," one of the other hostages replied. "In fact, once it's fixed like this, it can last for days and days."

I hadn't realized how hungry and thirsty I was until we began to share the cassava. The couple who had brought the big water jug passed it around so the rest of us could have a drink. That helped a little—but I couldn't help but think about the delicious peanut M&M's I'd left in the room, and I mourned the loss.

As the day progressed, the sun grew hot and the tarp was rigged up to provide some shade. The captors said nothing about where we were headed. We studied them, trying to figure out their names and who were the bosses. One of the men quickly stood out for his colorful personality and ability to turn a phrase. Sabaya was short and stocky. While everyone else wore army fatigues or baggy pants, Sabaya wore tight red stretch pants, looking oddly out of place.

We found out later that his name, and most of the others', were not their given ones but rather their "jihad names," chosen to evoke their new personas for battle. Sabaya, for example, meant "booty of war." Other names had equally vivid meanings, of which they were very proud.

Around two or three in the afternoon, Solaiman came to the group of hostages with a Big Chief pad of yellow paper to start interviewing us. He began by saying, "We're the Abu Sayyaf. Some people call us terrorists. We want you to know, we're not terrorists. We are simply people whom the Philippine government has robbed of our homeland, and we just want it back. No one in the government will listen to us, and so we have to do things like this to gain notice."

He asked us our names and what our jobs were. One by one, he wrote down the information:

- Francis, an older gentleman and banker, and his wife, Tess
- Chito, a sales representative with a cell-phone company, and his coworker Janice
- Reggie, who was well connected to the power circles of Manila, and his girlfriend, Rizza. This was the couple who had brought the suitcases and the water jug.
- Buddy, a publisher of a travel-guide magazine (for which he had been scouting an article on

Dos Palmas), his wife, Divine, and their eight-year-old son, R. J.
- Angie, Divine's sister, a young woman who appeared to be in her early thirties
- Guillermo Sobero, an American contractor, and Fe, his young fiancée
- Letty, a Chinese businesswoman, and her daughter, Kim, who was perhaps thirteen or fourteen, plus Letty's niece, Lalaine, also a young teenager. Lalaine had been staying in the garden cottages with her own family but had gone down to the water to spend Saturday night with her aunt and cousin.
- Sonny, the Dos Palmas cook
- Eldren and Armando, the two Dos Palmas guards
- Martin and me

Except for Guillermo, Martin, and me, all were Philippine citizens and well-off enough to afford a place like Dos Palmas.

When Solaiman got to us, Martin replied, "We're American missionaries with a group called New Tribes Mission. We try to help the tribal people. We live up on Luzon."

A cloud of disappointment came across Solaiman's face. He had hoped that we would be European—or at least American—business types, whose company would readily pay to get us back. Mission groups, on the other hand, were *(a)* poor and *(b)* on record with standing policies against ever paying ransom.

May 27
2:00 A.M., Rose Hill, Kansas: The phone rings in Martin's parents' bedroom with news that their son and daughter-in-law have been kidnapped.

"Missionaries? Did you know Charles Walton?" he asked. We did. Charles was an SIL (Wycliffe Bible) translator who had been taken hostage on the island of Mindanao some ten years earlier. He eventually got out alive, but not before spending weeks in a cramped cage up off the ground.

"Yes, we know him," Martin replied. "He's a friend; he works for an organization much like ours."

"Well, some of us were there," Solaiman answered, with a touch of mystery.

Then he returned to our case with this ominous announcement: "Yours will be a political ransom. We will make demands, and we will deal with you last."

Uh-oh, I thought to myself. *We're going to be in this a long time.* I immediately thought of the promise I had made to the kids: "Dad and I will be on Palawan for just a week, and then we'll be back home again." I felt sick at heart, trying to imagine how they would feel when they learned what had happened to us. I leaned toward Martin and murmured, "How long did they hold those Sipadan people?" referring to a group of twenty-one tourists captured the year before from a resort in Malaysia.

"I can't remember. Three, four months?"

I tried to guess in my mind what "a long time" would actually be. Six weeks? I tentatively set my hopes on two months at the very outside. *Worst-case scenario, we'll spend the summer with these guys and be out by the time the kids go back to school,* I told myself.

Meanwhile, the other hostages were already busy figuring out how much money they could raise. It seemed that everybody knew this was the name of the game. Muslim advancement may have been the announced overall goal, but cash was the necessary fuel. The bargaining was in full swing.

"Maybe my family could come up with one million [pesos, or $20,000]," said one person.

A more middle-class fellow said, "We might be able to raise 250,000 [$5,000]."

Solaiman kept writing down the amounts. (We learned later that this was the first time he had been allowed to handle these negotiations, and Sabaya was not happy with how it had gone. "You don't let them set the amounts," he told Solaiman, "you just look at them, size them up, and tell them how much to pay. If they have a Chinese last name, that means they're wealthy, so—10 million pesos [$200,000], end of discussion.")

After Solaiman worked through the list, the conversation ended. The engine roared, and we moved on.

At one point that afternoon, Solaiman said to Martin, "You know, people think we're a third-rate, primitive group out here. Actually, we're very modern, high-tech. See our satellite phone? See our GPS? We know what we're doing!"

(I couldn't help smiling, however, at the fact that somehow the Global Positioning System device hadn't helped them very much in finding our resort. We had pieced together their conversations enough to know that on their trip to Dos Palmas, they had gotten lost and had had to ask a fisherman for directions. Obviously they didn't know how to use their GPS!)

I kept scanning the horizon for land. None appeared. Everywhere I looked, I saw open sea. I now know that the nearest islands of any size were more than

May 27
Paul and Oreta Burnham ask New Tribes Mission personnel in Manila to evacuate the children to their home in Rose Hill, per Martin and Gracia's standing instruction.

three hundred miles to the southeast. It was probably better for me not to know that at the time.

After a full day of bouncing across the water, we were terribly sore. At sundown, we came up to a larger fishing boat. Here, another ten to twenty Abu Sayyaf, plus the fishing crew, were waiting. We joined them. We were relieved to get off the speedboat. At least we would be able to stand up without being jarred onto the floor. We hoped this move would be more comfortable for us.

A bamboo "lead" no more than five inches wide was laid down from the speedboat up to the fishing boat, and I realized I was going to have to walk across maybe eight feet of open water to get there. It scared me to death. *I can't do this!* I thought.

The water below swelled gently as I stared at the bamboo. When it was my turn, I admitted I had no choice. I began to crawl across the void on my hands and knees, praying that I would not fall.

Martin came right behind me, and by the time we all piled aboard, there were close to sixty people—again, a far greater load than this seventy-five-foot craft was ever meant to carry.

The boat had an inboard engine and outriggers—bamboo poles lashed together to make extensions off the sides. The pilot wheel was inside a small cabin in the middle of the deck. Down in the hold were large tunas packed in ice, fish the crew had caught before being hijacked by the Abu Sayyaf a few moments earlier.

We sat down on the deck while the captors quickly began their evening prayers. As the chants washed over the boat, I felt my mind slipping into a fog. *I can't believe this is happening.* When they finished with their prayers, we ate some rice and tuna, which helped a bit. But again, there was no place for the women to go to the bathroom. Again, we were forced to use a corner. Angie,

Fe, and some of the other women were distraught and crying.

"Do you think people know yet that we've been captured?" I asked Martin as the darkness grew around us.

"It's hard to tell," he said. "But don't worry, Gracia. We're gonna be okay." His optimism was contagious.

A song I'd heard the previous week began to run through my head. "Martin, I heard this song while you were away. Try to sleep and I'll sing it to you." I began to quietly repeat the melody:

> Be strong, be strong, be strong in the Lord,
> And be of good courage for he is your guide.
> Be strong, be strong, be strong in the Lord,
> And rejoice for the victory is yours.*

"Mmmm, that's a good song," Martin murmured when I finished. "Thank you, honey."

Nobody really stretched out to sleep that first night; we all just sat up and dozed, leaning on one another from time to time. It turned cold, as ocean breezes began to replace the heat of the day. Solaiman's earlier promise to get Martin a shirt had produced nothing, so Francis gave him a sleeveless one to wear. We huddled together for warmth.

Sleep was fitful. I remember waking once to find that my head had fallen down to the deck, and somebody's foot was on my hair. I jerked it loose.

::::

The next morning was Monday—Memorial Day in the States, but hardly a holiday for us. When the sun came up, we explored the boat to see what we had missed in the twilight before. Someone made a "CR" for us—a platform out on the bamboo outrigger with a tarp curtain around it. Getting out there was still tricky, but there was a rope to hold, and at least we could go in the ocean rather than on the boat's floor.

People got busy on the satellite phone, calling their relatives in Manila and elsewhere to arrange ransom payments. Impassioned discussions ensued. Reggie showed his connections right away, getting a government official to call Sabaya back and say, "I know this guy, and he's a good guy. Let him out, since you owe me a favor, remember?" They agreed on an amount of money to be transferred, and Reggie's release was promised.

By this time, Guillermo was definitely showing signs of stress. He was on a lot of medication due to a recent nervous breakdown, he explained, adding something about being overwhelmed by a messy divorce that wasn't yet finalized. Now we could see him going through withdrawal. His body quivered from time to time, and his voice was shaky.

This boat was certainly slower than the speedboat had been. "Where are we headed?" one of the hostages asked.

The answer from the Abu Sayyaf was vague: "We'll just see. . . ."

I was painfully aware that I wasn't dressed properly for the Muslim standard. Of course, they hadn't given me time back in the room to do anything better. Other women were still in their pajamas. I sat there feeling embarrassed that, in their minds, I was just another typical "loose" American woman in my shorts and T-shirt. I began asking the Lord to protect me.

Sometime that morning Fe gave me a long piece of lace for a *terong* (head covering), and someone else threw me a *malong*. Although my bare arms were still showing, I was at least somewhat more presentable to Muslim eyes.

Solaiman wanted us to know that we were in an

atmosphere of high morals. "Would we ever lie to you? No. Would we ever steal from you? No. Would we ever touch the women? Never. The Koran forbids these things." He began to rhapsodize about how great it is when Allah is the ruler and the Koran is the guidebook—as in Afghanistan, their cherished model. "Afghanistan will show the world how great the truly Islamic state can be. You know, in Islam, if you're a thief, they cut off your hand. That's how things ought to be."

I thought to myself, *Wait a minute—didn't you guys just steal Martin's wedding ring?!*

"In Islam, all the women are dressed properly, with nothing showing but their eyes. If a lady's eyes are causing a scandal, even they will be covered. There are no enticements to sin, no Western movies, no drinking, no smoking, no drugs."

Our captors' greatest goal, it seemed, was to get to Afghanistan. What a utopia that would be, they said. But if that didn't work out, they would settle for their second choice: to go to America and get a good job!

At some point that day, Sabaya asked Martin to get on the sat-phone and make a statement to Radyo Agong in Mindanao. This radio station, we eventually learned, was friendly to Abu Sayyaf interests and willing to air their messages when asked.

So Martin prepared to speak; the voice would be his, but the script came from Sabaya, of course:

> I, Martin Burnham, along with my wife, Gracia, who have lived in the Philippines for fifteen years, mem-

May 27
Lynn Burggraff, New Tribes missionary and close family friend, is assigned to break the bad news to the Burnham children, Jeff, Mindy, and Zach.

bers of New Tribes Mission, have been taken hostage
by the Abu Sayyaf, the Janjalani group. . . .

Actually, Sabaya wanted him to say *Al-Harakatul
Islamia,* which means "the Islamic Movement," but
Martin was afraid he would blow the pronunciation.

"Okay, then just call us 'the Osama bin Laden
group,'" Sabaya said.

Here in late May 2001, a full three months before
September 11, that name meant nothing to me. Martin
told me later that he had heard it once or twice.

"Can I just say 'the Janjalani group,' because I know
that term, and I won't get tripped up?" Martin asked, referring to the group's founder, who had died in battle a
couple of years before. Approval was granted. His speech
continued:

> We appeal to the American and Philippine govern-
> ments to work to bring this situation to a peaceful
> end very soon.

As usual, Martin kept his cool, talking very calmly
without notes. When he finished, he came over to me.

"You did a good job, honey," I said. "You always do."

Near the end of the day, Chito, who was full of life
and spunk, decided to organize a "getting to know you"
exercise for his fellow hostages. We all crowded into the
wheelhouse and sat around on the floor or whatever else
we could find. Going around the circle, each person gave
his or her name and the person's name to the left. Soon we
all had one another's names nailed down. We talked and
even laughed together a bit, trying to make the best of the
situation. We talked about our interests and other personal things.

Guillermo told us he'd been born in Peru but had

immigrated as a teenager to the Los Angeles area, where he now had a small construction business. He had come to Dos Palmas on vacation the year before, which is when he had met Fe working in the gift shop. They had been in touch by e-mail ever since, and now they were engaged.

As we learned bits and pieces about each of the other hostages, we became more of a team, more willing to encourage one another and try to keep our spirits up.

By that evening, the "ecumenical" nature of the boat was in full evidence. The Muslims, of course, conducted their ritual of bowing down and praying as they faced west, toward Mecca. The Catholics got out their rosary beads. Finally, one of the hostages asked Martin to pray aloud for the benefit of the group.

"Lord, all of this doesn't surprise you," he began in a calming voice as we all bowed our heads. "You know where we are, even though we don't. We know that people are worried about us. But you hold us in your hands. Give us the grace to go through this trial. We're depending on you. Amen."

A peace settled into my heart as I listened to my husband's words. The same seemed to happen for the others. "Wow, you can really pray good!" they said. Martin laughed. For him, prayer was just his way of talking to God, sharing the thoughts of his heart.

By that night, we had generally figured out where

May 28
Philippine president Gloria Arroyo appears on national television to declare "all-out war" on the Abu Sayyaf, telling them she will "finish what you have started."

May 28
Martin's sister, Cheryl Spicer, and her husband, Walt, drive seven hours north from Manila to Aritao to stay with the Burnham children.

---

we'd all like to sleep. The younger members of the Abu Sayyaf had already staked out the roof of the wheelhouse as theirs. Near the bow were places to hang hammocks, which were claimed by their comrades. A few others rigged up hammocks near the back. The fishing crew claimed their turf.

As for the hostages, we mostly stacked ourselves along the narrow sides of the deck, heads inward and feet hanging out over the ocean. A few others settled into a central well space in front of the wheelhouse. All together, we covered every inch of available space.

There was one luxury about these circumstances, I noticed: No mosquitoes! They had nowhere to breed here in the midst of salt water. We could lie out here and stare at the stars above without being bitten. There was a gentle breeze, and the sound of the water lapping against the boat sounded peaceful.

Francis and Tess, as it turned out, were fans of the old Beatles music, and in fact, they sang quite well together. As we stretched out under the open sky, they began to sing the mellow songs: "Yesterday," "Ticket to Ride," "Let It Be," "The Long and Winding Road." The rest of us joined in when we could. Even the Abu Sayyaf sang a little, though such music was technically forbidden by their faith.

Then we came to the song "Imagine," John Lennon's ballad about a different world. When we got to the line "Imagine all the people, living life in peace" I finally lost it. For the first time since we'd been kidnapped, tears began to stream down my face. It was so poignant—all these hostages singing about a world so near and yet so unbelievably beyond our grasp. As we lay there in that moment, a bond began to form, connecting us with one another, even our captors. Looking up at the sky, I found myself drifting into ragged sleep.

CHAPTER 2

BRIGHT BEGINNINGS
(1959–81)

Learning to get along in crowded conditions was a skill I had acquired early, as the fifth child of six in the Norvin and Betty Jo Jones household. In fact, I was born just as my parents were recovering from the tragic loss of my oldest sister, Terry Lynn. Only nine years old, she had been cut down by a reckless motorist who had, on June 10, 1958, ignored a bus's flashing lights and arm signal and pulled around it anyway.

I was in the womb at the time. My mother told me later that being pregnant forced her to keep going from day to day, to eat properly, and not to sink into abject despair. I arrived at St. Mary's Hospital in Cairo, Illinois, on January 17, 1959.

They named me Gracia (pronounced *"gray*-sha"). We moved a year later so my father could pastor a church in Ripley, Tennessee. Then in 1962, he was asked to help start a Bible college in Woodstock, Ontario, which is where my memories begin. My baby sister, Mary, was born there. I went to school in Woodstock, and of course I learned to ice-skate there. In my little pink-and-gray leggings outfit, I would fall time and time again, but no matter how many times I hit the ice, I always got up again.

It was a wonderful childhood in so many ways. In addition to Mary, I had two other sisters, Becky and Nancy, and one brother, Paul. We always seemed to get along well, thanks to our parents' wise guidance. They put the Lord and his Word at the center of our lives. I could sing hymns from memory even before I could read, although not always with full comprehension. I puzzled for quite a while over the song "Bringing in the 'Cheese'" (instead of "Sheaves"), until someone finally enlightened me.

Our family was in church every time the doors were open: Sunday school, morning services, evening services, midweek prayer services, plus the assorted dinners and special events that always seemed to come up.

When I was seven or eight, I had a wonderful Sunday school teacher who explained to me the importance of committing my life to Christ. Not long after that, I remember begging for the opportunity to be baptized.

When I was a little older, the Bible college moved northwest to Sault Ste. Marie, where it was really cold. All four of us girls had to share one bedroom, using two sets of bunk beds. Somehow we stayed warm through the long, dark winter that year. A year later, my father accepted a pastorate in southeastern Illinois, at Congregational Christian Church in Olney. I started fifth grade in Olney and built many friendships that I've maintained to this day.

Somewhere around the house I picked up a book about Amy Carmichael, the young Irish woman who went to India around the turn of the twentieth century to work with children. She found out that little girls were being forced into prostitution in the Hindu temples, and she set up a refuge to shelter them. Her writings over the next fifty years of her life were profound and inspiring.

Even more vivid in my imagination was the Scottish missionary Mary Slessor, who was the subject of another book I must have read half a dozen times. Mary worked in Africa—specifically, Nigeria—a little before the time of Amy Carmichael. There she battled witchcraft, cannibalism, alcoholism, and the particularly gruesome practice of killing newborn twins because they were supposedly a bad omen. What I liked about Mary Slessor was that she was gutsy; she'd stand up to tribal chiefs and tell them exactly what she thought! They didn't quite know what to do with her.

At this point I had no conscious thought of ever becoming a missionary myself. But I found these biographies inspiring.

Our family moved once more when I was fifteen and Dad became a professor of Bible and theology at Calvary Bible College in Kansas City. My sister Mary and I attended a private academy called Tri-City Christian School, from which I graduated in 1977. This gave me the chance to expand not only my love of music but also my first and best talent: socializing. I really liked planning and organizing parties and events, both at church and at school. I loved being around people and always wanted to make sure everyone was having a good time. My friend Diane Jaeger and I would often arrive at class to comments of "We heard you coming!"

When I wasn't doing homework, I managed to sing, play basketball and soccer, help with fund-raisers, meet yearbook deadlines, and be a cheerleader—such wonderful days.

I applied to and was accepted by several colleges, but the thing that hooked me on Calvary Bible College was its music program. Peter Friesen, the greatest choir director I'd ever met, gave me voice lessons even before I enrolled as a freshman. I fell in love with his instruction, and soon I was enveloped in the busy swirl of college life.

My first roommate was Marcia Miller. We were both poor, and the cafeteria didn't operate on weekends. So we'd scrape our money together and walk to Wendy's to order a single Frosty. At the condiment rack where you pick up your spoon, we'd also pick up some crackers that were supposed to go with chili . . . only we would sit and dip them in our Frosty in order to make a meal. (That's probably not what the Wendy's corporation had in mind.)

I learned a lot from watching Marcia's spiritual walk with God. She inspired me to live a simple, genuine faith. She taught me to look for God's hand in even the smallest daily events.

Believe it or not, I did love to study. But even more than that, I loved the social life. I got involved in about everything there was: singing alto in choir as well as a small ensemble that traveled on weekends, teaching fourth-grade Sunday school at Tri-City Baptist Church, visiting a detention center once a week to counsel kids who had gotten in trouble with the law. Eventually I became the yearbook editor, student council secretary, a resident assistant on the freshman girls' floor—and in between, I worked in the snack shop to pay my school bill. It was crazy, but I loved every minute of it.

Even when my parents moved away to northeast Arkansas to take a pastorate and be near my grandmother, I knew I wanted to stay at Calvary. At that time, Calvary was located in a former nunnery with a beautiful chapel. My friend Margie and I would go in there at odd moments and sit where the acoustics were just right, then sing every song we knew.

Another friend, Kathy Stech, had a car, which gave the rest of us some mobility. By my senior year, I had yet another close friend, Elizabeth Redden, who was dating a really cute guy named Doug Burnham. I didn't know much about him, except that he was sort of quiet and an "MK" (missionary kid) from the Philippines. Even though Doug was quiet, everyone on campus seemed to know who he was. Soon after returning from Christmas break my senior year, Elizabeth said to me, "Hey, did you know that Doug's older brother is transferring here for the second semester? His name is Martin, and I guess he's already had some pilot training, because they're going to let him teach in the flight program as well as go to classes himself. He'll be a junior. Do you want to meet him?"

Sure, why not? I thought. *If he's as cute as Doug, this could be a worthwhile conversation.* She guided me over to a lunch table where the two brothers were eating. Martin was a handsome guy with hair a little darker than Doug's, more reddish than blond. "Hi, guys!" said Elizabeth. "How's the spaghetti today?"

She introduced me and we made some small talk. Our conversation didn't last long. As we walked away to head for our afternoon schedules, I remember thinking that Martin seemed just as nice as his brother.

As the semester rolled along, I was busy, of course, getting ready to graduate. Even though we didn't know each other well, Martin and I always seemed to be in the same place. He seemed really nice, and he ran with a crowd of guys I enjoyed—fun-loving, casual guys in their jeans and flannel shirts, not out to impress anybody. Martin even wore cowboy boots. Whereas a lot of the other male students seemed fascinated with designer clothes and ties, wanting to look like they were headed somewhere important in the world, Martin and his friends would rather be wearing "kick-back clothes." Some of them were pilots in training, some were farm boys, and all were down-to-earth. I liked that.

Graduation day, when I received my bachelor's degree with a major in Christian education, was special, of course. My older sister Nancy surprised me by coming along with my parents. After the ceremony, my sister-in-law, Beth, hosted a lovely luncheon for the whole family.

The college had already offered me a job as secretary to the student-services group—the dean of students, the dean of men, the dean of women, and the chaplain. I was glad for this chance, not only because it would pay the bills but also because I'd get to stay at Calvary, a place I loved. Kathy Stech and I rented a small, roach-infested apartment nearby, and we enjoyed being on our own; even the bugs didn't daunt us. By August I was settled into my desk at one end of the administration building, juggling the needs of four busy people as they organized their programs for the fall semester.

As the semester began, it became apparent that one of the men's dorms housed a number of especially rowdy guys. Its resident assistant, whose job was to keep a lid on things, was Martin. Time and again he would show up at my desk with one of his charges in tow, summoned to face the dean and explain the latest antics. This gave Martin and me chances to sit and talk while waiting for the ominous door to open.

He talked about his classes and about his folks far away in the Philippines, serving a tribe called the Ibaloi. He told me he was the oldest of five children; besides Doug, there were Cheryl and Brian, who were both in high school in Manila. And then there was his little sister, Felicia, still a preschooler. He said one day, "Did you know I had to help my mom sew up my leg one day after I cut it with a machete?" (All boys in the Philippine rain forest carry a machete.) That's when I learned that his mother was a nurse.

Understandably, he was very involved with the Missionary Prayer Fellowship (MPF), a student organization that focused on world outreach. He and his friend Clay Bowlin planned weekly meetings to focus on various populations overseas and their spiritual needs. They prayed for missionaries—many of them Calvary alumni—serving all around the globe.

When it came time for the annual MPF chapel service, Martin and Clay put together a drama highlighting various mission pioneers through the centuries.

Martin played William Carey of England, the first

modern-era missionary. Dressed in full Georgian costume, complete with knickers, he began in his rich, baritone voice:

> As a young child I learned the importance of putting my best effort into all that I did, and completing each task that I started—a discipline that was to pay off in my later years on the mission field. . . .
>
> From the beginning God gave me the desire to know exactly what his Word said. . . . As I continued my study and meditation on his Word, I could not help but be impressed with the fact that we, as believers, were simply not doing all that God had commanded.
>
> When his Word says, "Go ye," he means *Go ye!* And when he says, "into all the world," he means into *all* the world. To "preach the gospel to every creature" means exactly that. God means exactly what he says.
>
> He has commanded us to "go and make disciples of all nations." The promise that follows is "lo, I am with you always." Do any of us have the right to play leapfrog with the command and [only] hug to the promise?

I didn't know it at the time, but Martin could have been describing his own upbringing, his study of the Scriptures, and his personal passion as well as William Carey's. The bigger perspective had already taken root in his soul.

On another occasion, MPF staged *Through Gates of Splendor,* the tragic story of the five missionaries massacred in 1956 by warriors of an indigenous tribe in Ecuador. We all knew the story, of course, since it had gotten so much press. But even so, we sat there riveted as the five men waited on the sandbar of the river beside their little mission plane, expecting the Aucas to return for another friendly conversation like the day before.

One of the actors jumped up and pointed toward the imaginary jungle. "Oh, good!" he cried. "Here they come again!"

And then his face froze. "But look—they've got their blowguns with them. . . ."

The play ended abruptly. The actors didn't need to show what happened next; we all knew.

I stood up to leave the chapel that day, unable to say a word. *Will the Lord ever require me to do what those men did? to go through what they went through?* I was stunned. I slowly headed out the door, tears streaming down my face.

CHAPTER 3

THE NICEST GUY
(1981–83)

My dating life that fall was not going well. I had been in a relationship with someone whom I deeply cared about, but it was becoming clear to me that a long-term commitment was not in our future. After much anguish and discussion with my friends, I finally mustered the courage to break it off.

I was devastated. As I approached my twenty-third birthday, my future was nothing but a haze. One afternoon, Martin stopped in the office. After some small talk, he smiled and said, "The fall concert is coming up, and I wonder if you'd like to go with me."

I was standing by the typewriter, and my face went white. (At least that's what he claimed later.) I slowly sat down and said, "Oh . . . are you asking me for a date?"

"Yeah."

All kinds of thoughts swirled through my head. *Do I want to get into all this again? What if it ends up like the last time? I don't want to be hurt again.*

Finally, I got out the words "Can I let you know?"

What I had no way of knowing was that Martin had heard that same line from other girls so often, in fact, that he was tired of it. He had convinced himself that the line was simply a way for them to put him off until they could decline his offer later, either in a note or through a friend.

So he had decided that if he heard "Can I let you know?" one more time, he would call the girl's bluff and retract his invitation.

When I said the dreaded line, Martin steeled himself to say, "No, you can't. Never mind."

But for some inexplicable reason it came out, "Yeah.

You can let me know"! With that, he turned and headed off to class.

The instant he left the building, I dashed into the office of my friends Kay and Joyce.

"Hey, guess who just asked me out?" I bubbled to Joyce. "Martin Burnham!"

"Oh, really!" they responded with big grins. *Everyone* liked Martin. He was just such a nice guy.

"Should I do this?"

"Of course! Of course!" They encouraged me to go for it.

I returned to my desk and quickly pulled out a notecard embossed with roses that I had on hand. I wrote:

> *Thank you for asking me [out] for Saturday night. It really encouraged me. I would love to go with you. Stop back by and we'll talk about the time.*

I sent it over to the flight department with the very next person headed that way.

That weekend, I went out and bought a new dress for the occasion, even though I rarely spent money on clothes for myself. I chose a beautiful yellow dress that had spaghetti straps and a lacy jacket.

On Saturday evening, we double-dated with another couple. During the concert, I looked down and saw that despite his suit, Martin had on cowboy boots. I got this big smile on my face.

Martin caught my expression and said, "What?"

"Oh, nothing," I replied. I didn't want him to think I was criticizing his outfit. It wasn't that I thought it was funny, actually. It just confirmed to me that he was his own person—that he wasn't going to let the laws of social etiquette dictate to me. I liked that.

After the concert, he took us flying to see the lights of Kansas City at night. As a resident assistant, he needed to be back at the dorm by a certain time, but we used every minute before Martin delivered me home.

We started dating more after that, and I quickly came to appreciate Martin's unassuming ways. If he wanted to be the life of the party, he could. But if someone else was playing that role, he could just as easily be one of the guys. There was nothing egotistical about him. He was very confident in his talents, but he didn't have to tell you about them. Instead, he was just quietly competent, and he was always kind to everybody in the process.

He had a cool car—a green Chevelle. He would let me drive it, which was quite a step up from my little Datsun B210 that needed to be overhauled. Bless his heart—when I told him about my car, he took it into the school shop and overhauled it himself, with some help from a friend.

::::

The more we got to know one another, the more I learned of his interesting past. When he was a little guy, his family had attended Wichita Bible Church, a strong mission-minded congregation that held a one-week missions conference every October. The year Martin was seven, a guest speaker from New Tribes Mission made a deep impression on his parents, Paul and Oreta Burnham. Paul worked for a chemical plant and Oreta was a nurse. They already had four young children, but they began to wonder if maybe God had different ideas for them other than staying in central Kansas the rest of their lives.

The following spring, they attended a five-day New Tribes conference in Wisconsin for missionary prospects. Paul's dad paid for the two plane tickets, while

Oreta's parents baby-sat. They came home more challenged than ever to venture toward overseas ministry—enough that they put their house on the market. It sold quickly, providing the funds for a year of training.

Some people said they were crazy to attempt this, given the size of their family and the fact that they were already in their thirties. But off they went to Wisconsin in their six-year-old Chevrolet packed with kids and clothes and lots of home-canned green beans. To young Martin and his siblings, it was all a great adventure. He understood what it meant to give your life to the Lord's work, having made his own personal commitment to Christ back in a first-grade Sunday school class.

After a year of training in Wisconsin, the family headed to Camdenton, Missouri, for another year of language school. By the end of their training, the house-sale proceeds were running out. The Burnhams moved back to the family roots in the small town of Rose Hill, Kansas, just east of Wichita, where Paul took odd jobs to put bread on the table while he talked to churches about supporting their missions dream. And so it happened that in the summer of 1970, they boarded a freighter called the *Philippine Corregidor* in San Francisco's harbor for the monthlong voyage across the wide Pacific. Martin was now ten years old.

Martin played hide-and-seek with his brothers between stacks of zinc ingots on the deck of the ship. The boys had fun flying kites off the stern and watching the flying fish alongside the railing as they soared for amazing distances.

When the family finally docked in Manila Bay, they were immediately struck by the hot and steamy climate. They were also surprised at how much English they heard. The American presence in the country for fifty years had made a difference. While Filipinos do speak

Tagalog and Cebuano and Ilocano, English is the language that seems to tie them all together.

Since there appeared to be no practical way for Martin to attend school in the tribal area where his parents were working (homeschooling had not yet flowered into the option that it is today), he was sent to boarding school. He didn't want to be away from his family, but the fact that he could fly home occasionally on a mission plane made dormitory life easier to take. It was on these flights home that Martin first found his fascination with airplanes and flying.

Mission aviation was not a luxury but rather a necessity in rural areas of the Philippines, where roads were few and rough, and waterways constantly blocked travel. New Tribes Mission, which specializes in working with indigenous people groups, was extremely dependent on the pilots who ferried groceries, medicines, mail, equipment, and people from town to short jungle airstrips. Paul and Oreta Burnham, for example, were a two-and-a-half-hour climb from the nearest road.

Martin made model airplanes out of split bamboo to thrust off the peak of his parents' roof and see how far they'd soar. He eventually even built one with a tiny engine. As the years went by, he got himself into aviation ground school while he was still a high school student at Faith Academy in Manila. By the time he graduated in 1977, his goal was firm: to go home to America, buy a car, become a pilot, and make lots of money.

But then his dad said, "Wait a minute, Martin. We want you to do at least one year of Bible school." Martin wasn't happy about that at all, thinking it would just delay him from what he really wanted to do: fly.

A spirited debate raged, but in the end, he submitted to his parents' wishes and trekked to New Tribes Bible Institute in Jackson, Michigan. He did his classwork, even though he says he was "cold all the time!" He'd grown up in the tropics where you wear shorts and a T-shirt, or maybe a pair of jeans at the most. Even shoes were optional in much of the Philippines. Martin refused to dress warmly at school, and he said the Michigan winter just about froze him to death.

Nevertheless, it was during that year that the first small spark of a future in missions was kindled for Martin. As he studied the Scriptures, he thought back to the mission pilots he'd known in the Philippines and mulled the possibility of joining their ranks after all.

The next summer, he moved (with his parents' blessing) back to Wichita, the "air capital of the world." In Wichita, Martin got his flight training and his Airframe and Powerplant certificate, a license that allowed him to work on aircraft. His uncle Ron Eyres got him a job at Coleman, the camping-equipment manufacturer, and helped him find an apartment in an elderly lady's basement.

It wasn't long before his night-school air mechanics instructor saw Martin's potential and recommended him for a job on the flight line at Cessna Aircraft. That allowed him to join the Cessna Flying Club, which opened up all kinds of opportunities to fly.

One day, Martin received the news that a New Tribes Mission pilot he knew well in the Philippines had crashed his plane and been killed. Martin could well envision the gap in service that would leave. Who would step in to fill it? Maybe the Lord wanted him to complete his Bible studies after all.

Rose Hill Bible Church, which his family had helped start, was without a pastor at that point, and a professor from Calvary Bible College was filling in. Martin volunteered to fly up to Kansas City each Saturday and pick him up, then return him the following evening. That gave him a lot of time to talk to the man about the college's program and the whole idea of Christian service.

One thing led to another, and soon Calvary's missionary aviation program contacted him to say, "If you'll come as a student, you can teach a course or two in our flight department." And that's how this wonderful young man showed up in my life.

::::

One day in the summer of 1982 Martin told me, "My sister just graduated from Faith Academy, and my mom is bringing her back to the States to get ready for college. They're flying in here; would you like to come with Doug and me to the airport?"

"Sure," I said, excited to learn more about what this family was like.

When they came out of the jetway, we saw that there were three of them: Cheryl, Martin's mother, and little Felicia. I could tell that Martin's mother was not entirely happy with him for bringing me along—after all, I wasn't even a family member and I was taking up space that could have been used for luggage! We wound up holding suitcases on our laps.

But as the minutes ticked by, we all got along fine. We stopped at a pancake house to eat, and I sat there amused and amazed as I listened to this very practical family make plans. It was almost like a business meeting: "Okay, we are going to do this, and then this and this, and do you need anything for this . . . ?" I was watching a family that was used to living apart from one another, so they just dived right in to the necessary logistics, while Felicia played contentedly with the little coffee creamers, drinking them down one by one.

In a few weeks, Oreta and Felicia returned to the Philippines. I still wasn't sure where I stood with Martin's mom. When I asked him, however, he said, "You did just fine. She thinks you're really nice."

As Martin and I continued to date, I became more and more convinced that this was indeed a very special man. I was definitely falling in love—no question about it. And I could tell that he loved me, too.

I had planned to go home to visit my parents over spring break in 1983, and Martin decided to go with me. "Let's take off early and meet about noon," he suggested. "We can be all ready to start driving then, and that way we won't arrive in Arkansas at an unearthly hour."

I left work early, but when I arrived at the appointed place, Martin wasn't ready yet. I thought, *This is kind of odd. He told me to be ready, and he's not.* It was out of character for him.

Finally he showed up, a bit breathless. He apologized for being late, and we headed out of the city. By late afternoon we had traveled as far as Springfield, Missouri, where we stopped to eat at the Battlefield Mall McDonald's. As we sat together in the booth, we had so much fun goofing around and laughing. I was talking very animatedly when the ketchup in my hand squirted all over my shirt. We laughed and laughed. I just kind of wiped it off with a napkin, and soon it was time to go.

"Aren't you going to clean up your shirt?" Martin asked.

"Well, no, I hadn't really planned on it. We'll be home in a few hours, and I'll change then."

He got an odd look on his face and said, "You know, I really feel like you ought to wash your shirt."

I didn't say anything, but I was a little irritated. *You were the one who was late—and now you're telling me to go waste more time washing off my shirt?* I thought.

I went into the rest room, squirted soap from the dispenser onto the red stain, scrubbed it off, and stood under the blow-dryer for a few minutes. I went back out. "Is this better?" I asked him.

"Yeah, I think it's really good that you did that."

We drove another hour or so, until we saw a sign ahead that pointed right: "Burnham 2 miles."

Martin slowed down and looked at the sign. "Have you ever been to Burnham, Missouri?" he asked me.

"Well, to tell you the truth, yes—one time I was on my way home and pulled off to see it. There's nothing there."

"Well, I think I want to see it," he said. He turned up the gravel road toward the few buildings that still remained: an old, dilapidated filling station that had gone out of business, a Burnham Baptist Church, and maybe one or two houses.

"Hey, let's get out and check the service times at this church," he said brightly.

Oh brother, I thought. *Now we're really wasting time. I thought the whole point was to get to Arkansas at a decent hour!*

But I didn't say anything. We got out and walked over to the steep-roofed building with brown siding. And then . . . he pulled a tiny ring box from his pocket.

"Gracia . . . would you marry me?"

I gasped. So that was what this detour had been all about! I looked up into his face in shock and said, "Are you sure?!"

"Yeah, I'm sure!" Martin said with a grin.

"Are you *sure* you're sure?"

"I'm sure."

I was getting up the courage to say yes, but in that moment, a flock of worries crowded into my mind. I wondered if I should wait to talk to my folks about such a big decision. But I knew I had absolutely no doubts about marrying Martin. And I knew my parents approved of this relationship. In fact, Martin was already popular with my dad, who had flown in World War II in Italy. When he had heard I was dating a pilot, he was enthusiastic. The fact that Martin was an MK made it even better.

"I've already talked to your dad, and he says it's fine," Martin's voice broke into my thoughts. I quickly snapped back to reality.

"Yes, I'll marry you!" I cried. We fell into a long hug right there on the front lawn of the Burnham Baptist Church.

He ran back to the car to get his camera. Now everything started making sense—why he wanted me to deal with the ketchup on my shirt, and why he had been late that morning. He'd been running around the campus making sure he had everything ready to make this day perfect.

We talked and laughed the rest of the trip. He told me he had already had a "she's the one!" phone conversation with his parents back in the Philippines, and they had assured him they would come for a wedding that summer even though it wasn't time for their next furlough.

When we arrived at my parents' home around seven o'clock, supper was waiting in the Crock-Pot. What a special celebration we enjoyed together as my family gazed at my ring and congratulated us.

::::

We were married in Kansas City on May 28, 1983, just a few short months after we had gotten engaged. The ceremony and reception were simple but meaningful as we celebrated our happiness with friends and family.

We spent our honeymoon in Branson, Missouri, long before it was the famous tourist destination it is today. We had so much fun and made so many wonderful memories, I just knew my life was going to be wonderful as long as Martin was by my side.

All too soon, it was time to leave. At the end of that week, we were due in the far southwestern corner of Nebraska, where Martin had landed a summer job as a crop duster with Stegg's Flying Service. We made quick stops in Arkansas and then in Rose Hill to say good-bye to Martin's parents, who were soon returning to the Philippines.

In the farm town of Imperial, Nebraska, we settled into a little apartment and quickly began to make friends. We attended Imperial Bible Church, and everyone was so kind to us; newlyweds sort of bring out the hospitality in people, I suppose. We were often invited places for a meal or a dessert, and I got involved in a women's Bible study. I took a class on refinishing furniture so we could redo some antique chairs my mom and dad had given us. It was a wonderful summer.

Before long, Martin was offered a permanent job by one of the farmers there. We talked about it at length. "You know, it would be so easy to settle down in this community and make a good living, wouldn't it?" Martin said one evening, staring out at the big Western sky. The money was indeed attractive. "But that's not what we're called to do."

He was right. Even though we really loved it there, we both felt that God had other plans for us. So we decided that we'd better leave Imperial before we got too rooted. We headed back to Calvary Bible College that fall so Martin could teach again in the aviation department until the next New Tribes Mission orientation cycle came around.

CHAPTER 4

ROOKIES
(1984–87)

New Tribes called it "boot camp"—a year of primitive living and demanding study so they could determine if you were cut out for foreign service or if you just thought you were. Martin and I landed in the small Southern town of Durant, Mississippi, one January day in 1984 and moved into a one-room apartment in a converted Civil War hospital. Our apartment had a stove and a refrigerator, but the common bathroom was down the hall. We had to carry our water from the bathroom back into our apartment in order to do the dishes and then carry our slop water up the hill and pour it into a pit when we were finished.

We were required to haul our garbage to another special pit up the hill. Everything in this compound was meant to imitate the way we might be called upon to live overseas. The mission wanted everyone to have both eyes open about the realities of tribal ministry.

Our boot-camp group included three families with kids, two other couples, and two single women. The living conditions were pretty rough, and it was no wonder that we bonded very closely with the others in our group. We also made some really good friends at the First Presbyterian Church in nearby Kosciusko. Those people welcomed us warmly.

Our weekday classes during boot camp covered everything from ecclesiology to sociology. We spent a lot of time studying what a New Testament church really is—not necessarily an American church, but the essentials of the church God wants to be established regardless of context. We did cross-cultural work, taking up an extended case study of the Yurok Indians in northern California, their traditions, their values, and their god, *Wapakumu*. We pretended we were Yuroks, and each person in the group had to attempt to teach a lesson that would make sense, with fitting illustrations. For example, if portraying Jesus as "the Lamb of God" would only mystify the Yuroks, we needed to come up with a way to solve the dilemma. It was an excellent education.

As far as finances were concerned, once again, things were pretty simple. New Tribes Mission is not a cushy operation. All missionaries and would-be missionaries are required to raise their own funds. The head office in Sanford, Florida, serves as a collection point for receipting purposes but makes no guarantees and provides no safety net. Whatever dollars come in are forwarded to the missionaries—no processing fees deducted, but no extra grants added either. If their account plunges in a particular month, the problem is theirs alone.

After several months, Martin's parents began to send about fifty dollars a month, even though they had their own missionary budget to worry about. Several of our college friends began sending a little as well, and soon our monthly total came to somewhere near one hundred dollars. We mainly lived off our savings from the summer of crop dusting in Imperial. Needless to say, we watched every penny.

I can't say that Martin and I loved boot camp. After all, we both had college degrees and felt like we knew a few things. Here, we were simply a couple of rookies; it was kind of a blow to our pride. But it was a necessary experience.

We learned to get along with people who weren't like us, we learned to live in close quarters, and we learned to obey leadership, even when we didn't agree with their decisions. We figured out ways to be hospitable on a shoestring budget, because even if we didn't have a lot of money or food, we were still put on the rotation schedule to host visitors when they came through. It was great training for what happens all the time on the mission field.

Our training included "jungle camp," a period of time when we were dispatched to go live in the woods. We had to build a house from only what we could carry to the site. When our time for jungle camp arrived, Martin constructed a quite respectable A-frame in the middle of the woods—the first home we ever owned! Then several days later, he returned for me. We packed up everything we would need for six weeks and rafted across the lake to our spot.

We carried all our food, because we knew we weren't allowed to go out for anything. If we had forgotten something important, we would just have had to live without it. After a hard morning of lugging the gear and supplies up the hill, Martin set up the half barrel he had cut to make a stove so I could cook over a wood fire. It even had an oven that worked very well.

Although jungle camp was pretty rough, it truly was a special time for Martin and me, as well as those training with us. I have special memories of the guys kneading bread and baking it over hot coals. We celebrated our first anniversary there and enjoyed the top tier of our wedding cake. (When you're young and in love, you remember to bring along those important items!)

We made our own fun. Many a night we played Dutch Blitz and Trivial Pursuit long into the night.

Near the end of that six weeks, Martin had to leave for pilot evaluation at the mission's flight base in Arizona. That didn't win me any reprieve from jungle camp; I was expected to fend for myself. I was thrilled when my parents made a special trip to visit me in my little jungle home. I even managed to fix them a halfway decent meal.

I was doing okay all alone—until suddenly the announcement came one morning: "Today you're all moving back home. Pack up." This was part of the training strategy, to throw us curveballs and see how we adjusted.

"But I have no husband to help me pack up," I protested.

"Yes, you're right. But that may happen to you on the mission field someday," our leader replied.

I had no choice but to get our stuff together and carry it all down the hill to the lake, where a teenager helped me raft it across. I loaded it onto the tractor-trailer for the return to the compound, grumbling under my breath the entire time about what a dirty deal this was.

When I finally finished hauling our belongings back up the two flights of stairs to our little apartment, I was dripping wet with sweat. I decided to head for the backyard swimming pool. *I deserve a pity party!* I told myself.

At the pool I met a woman whose family was passing through on furlough. I began complaining to her about how upset I was at having to move home from jungle camp without my husband to help.

She listened quietly, then said, "Would you like to hear what just happened to me?" She went on to explain that her husband had just had a heart attack in the jungle overseas. He had been flown out of their village and then immediately evacuated to the States for medical care. This woman had been left alone to pack up her entire house all by herself and move out—with several young children.

I was duly rebuked. *So this is what boot camp is for,* I thought, *to find out if we can handle adversity and take what life sends our way.* I learned so much during those days. I learned that sometimes we need to go through a lot of unpleasantness in order to get the job done. That life isn't always wonderful. That happiness is not dependent on our circumstances but on our attitudes. Little did I know how important those lessons would be sixteen years later in the Philippine rain forest.

::::

When we left boot camp after a year, I was devastated. We had bonded with these eighteen people, and it tore my heart out to say good-bye. I cried and carried on until I realized, *Girl, your whole life is going to be a series of good-byes. You've got to get your act together if you're going to survive in the future.* I determined never again to let good-byes devastate me as they had this time.

We had been certified to move to the next level of missionary training, which took us to the flight base in Arizona. There Martin's work involved more intensive preparation for the technical side of mission work.

When discussions began about where we would actually serve, Martin went to the leadership and said, "Please send us anywhere except the Philippines." Not that he disliked the country—but he had grown up there and was worried about acceptance as an adult. Would the old-timers in the mission, who remembered him as a little kid, be willing to crawl into an airplane and entrust their lives to him now? Maybe it would be better to go somewhere else.

I personally didn't care where we went. Martin was so fun to live with and I was so in love with him that I knew I'd be happy anywhere as long as we were together.

The leaders understood Martin's concerns and began to talk about the needs in Paraguay. This went on for a while, and we were feeling pretty positive about this option. But then one day, we were called in for another meeting.

"You know, they really do need a replacement pilot in the Philippines," we were told. "Martin, you know the culture and you partly know the language. It's kind of ridiculous to send you somewhere else. Would you be willing to go back?"

Without hesitation, Martin nodded yes. He was just that kind of person. Wherever he was asked to serve, he would accept the call willingly.

Because of his prior language exposure, they waived our requirement of language prep school. The need on the field was urgent, they said, so we were given a quick target date for arrival: early 1986. We still didn't have any financial support to speak of, and our crop-duster savings were basically gone. Obviously, we would have to get busy on the fund-raising front.

This was tough for Martin. "Gracia, I just don't like the idea of begging for money from strangers," he told me. "We're not that kind of people."

"I know," I agreed. "What if we just talk to people who know us, the ones who have already shown interest in us? Would that be enough to take care of our needs?"

We didn't know but decided it was worth a try. We began by calling Jack Middleton, the pastor of Wichita Bible Church, where Martin had attended.

"We're headed for the mission field," Martin announced cheerfully that autumn day. "We are going to go early next year."

"Sure you are!" Jack said with a hearty laugh. "Don't you know how long it takes a missionary to raise support these days? Three years! And you're going to do it in less than three months?"

"Well, they really need us in the Philippines," Martin replied, unflustered. "If we get the cash for the tickets, we're going to go. We'll figure out the monthly support later." That was just how Martin thought. He had seen the Lord supply for his family time and again while growing up in the Philippines, so he didn't feel it was presumption on his part to make such a statement now. In his heart, he just knew. Martin's confidence and faith in God were so strong, they were contagious. I had no worries or concerns.

We didn't hear from Jack after that, so we made other contacts. Back in Mississippi, the young-couples Sunday school class that Martin had taught got inspired to help. "We are going to try to take care of your tickets to get to the field," they said when they called us. (Those tickets cost around two thousand dollars.) "You pray for us—we've never done anything like this before. But we're going to have some spaghetti suppers and garage sales, and see what we can do."

A week later, they called back with even more exuberance. "We not only have money for your tickets, but we have enough money for you to ship your stuff!"

Whoa—it was clear our pledge was being kicked into gear, ready or not. We thanked them profusely, and as soon as the money arrived, we took a deep breath and purchased our tickets for February.

When Pastor Middleton heard what was happening, he called an emergency meeting of his church's missions committee about a week before we left. He asked us to make a special appearance to explain our vision.

When we finished, they said, "Hey, we really want to support you. We just thought we had plenty of time to make our decision." By the end of the evening, they had put themselves on the line for a monthly sum. We thanked them and went back to packing.

We found that, generally, as soon as people knew we

had our tickets and were really going, our support picked up. When we got to the field, it picked up even more, and we always had what we needed. I'm not advocating this approach for anyone else. I'm sure there are other valid ways to fund missionary work. But this is the way God chose to work for us.

We were set to leave for the Philippines on the very day that President Ferdinand Marcos had to flee the country. The Filipino people decided they'd had enough of dictatorial rule and came out in droves to overthrow him. Because of the unrest, our travel agent called to say our flight had been canceled but rescheduled for two weeks later. Here we were, "all dressed up and no place to go."

We passed the two weeks enjoying more time with relatives, and soon enough, the day of departure arrived again. A small group gathered at the Wichita airport—my parents, various relatives, friends from local churches. I must say that I handled good-byes very well that day. In my mind I pretended that I'd see these folks again the following week, so I didn't need to indulge in tears or drama.

But when we got on the Philippine Airlines flight at Los Angeles International Airport, the greetings to the passengers began in Tagalog instead of English. Suddenly tears began streaming down my face. I was truly leaving home, and I didn't know when or if I would ever return. But then Martin held my hand, and I didn't cry long.

When we stepped off the plane in Manila, the humidity nearly took my breath away. Walking into the terminal reminded me of times I had spent in the jungle house at the Wichita zoo—it was humid and very warm. Steve Roberts, New Tribes Mission's chief mechanic, picked us up, and as we wove through traffic, there seemed to be no rules. The lines painted on the pavement meant nothing. I was thinking how brave this man was when, all of a sudden, a little kid walked out into five lanes of traffic and right in front of our car. I almost sucked my teeth down my throat. The little guy was just trying to sell newspapers!

After that drive, our New Tribes Mission guesthouse was a welcome haven. When we went to bed that night, I was totally wiped out. But about three-thirty in the morning, my eyes popped open—my first experience with jet lag.

As I lay there, I listened to the night noises in Manila. What was that I heard—roosters? *Why are there roosters in a city?* I wondered. Martin woke up soon afterward and explained to me that roosters are everywhere in the Philippines, not just on farms.

The next morning, it was time to get busy. We sat down with the business manager for some orientation. Charlie Breithaupt pulled out the agenda sheet and said something like, "Okay, mailboxes—well, Martin, you've been here before so you know how the mail system works. . . . Finances—you've been here before; you know how that works."

I sat there hoping Martin had a good memory, because I was clueless.

Martin said, "Well, actually, I left here when I was just out of high school. You'd better back up and treat us like any other new couple."

For the next couple of days we went through all the necessary orientation. They took us to get our Philippine driver's licenses; we also had to stop at Immigration to be fingerprinted. But soon we were on our way north into the interior of Luzon Island, a seven-hour bus ride to a mission compound with an airstrip at Aritao.

The compound was located in a beautiful area. Our home was built up off the ground on stilts. We even had a bathroom inside the house and running cold water. Out on the veranda was a porch swing, my absolute favorite thing about the house. I knew it would be a wonderful place to sit and enjoy the beauty of the mountains and to watch the farmers plowing with their water buffalo in the rice fields down in the valley.

Very few missionaries live in communities like the one at Aritao anymore. It's rare to find groups of houses all clustered together like that, but it was standard practice back in the 1950s when this one was built. Such a design can certainly be questioned for its "us-them" appearance. However, it does have some practical advantages. The missionary staff certainly communicates better since everyone's so close. They also avoid sickness better because they're living in a more controlled environment.

New Tribes Mission had three airplanes in the Philippines: a Super Cub, a Helio Courier, and a Cessna. The plane Martin began flying right away was a red-and-white Helio Courier. He was in the air almost immediately, tending to the needs of missionary families who worked with four different remote tribes on Luzon. He delivered everything from milk powder to eggs, meat, and fuel for refrigerators and stoves.

I had hardly had time to unpack in our little two-bedroom house before I took over the radio responsibilities. Twice a day—once at 7:00 A.M. and again at 3:30 P.M.—I went through roll call and talked with each tribal station. If anyone had "traffic," as we called it, meaning messages for anyone else, I made a list and then started matching up the parties like an old-time telephone operator. I also took grocery orders, medicine orders, requests for appointments, and flight needs.

I had never done anything like this before, but in a way it reminded me of my old days at Calvary Bible College, when I had had four bosses. I would be up to my ears in producing some document, and the president would walk by and say, "Oh, I have a chapel announce-ment—take this down . . ." and instantly I'd have to stop whatever I was doing and begin typing what he said. The phone would be ringing, and people would be coming in to see the chaplain or the dean—I was used to multitasking, I guess. I could tell already that's how this flight program was going to be.

The other part of radio work was to "flight-follow" Martin whenever he was in the air. He called me every ten minutes or so with a position report, which I re-corded in case of an emergency, so I'd know his last loca-tion. I also had to keep track of the weather by checking with the person at the destination. In other words, when-ever he was in the air, I sat by the radio and never left.

To be quite honest, I loved it all. I settled right into it. We were instantly busy, and that's what we wanted.

A friend of ours on the field once wrote a humorous letter to his financial supporters that we found gratify-ing. He said that if you ask a group of missionary kids, "What's the grossest thing you've ever had to eat?" you will get all kinds of different answers, depending on the country where they've grown up. An MK from the Phil-ippines will say one thing, somebody from Bolivia will say something else, somebody from the Congo some-thing else.

But if you follow up with the question "So how did you get it down the hatch?" the kids will all give you the same answer: ketchup!

And how do missionary kids and their families in re-mote areas stay well stocked on this vital substance called ketchup? Answer: the missionary pilot! Without his as-sistance, everyone would be in big trouble.

Martin's initial fears that his flying ability would not be given full credit in the Philippines proved somewhat true at first, but people quickly were won over by his exceptional abilities as time and time again he put the Cessna down safely on airstrips as short as three hundred meters with trees crowding in on both sides. His skill was little short of amazing. He could stop a fully loaded plane on a dime, and sometimes he needed to do just that. I admit I'm an admiring wife saying this, but it really was true. And after he hopped out of the cockpit, people quickly realized how big a heart he had for tribal people and for the frontline missionaries trying to serve them. He knew that people who hadn't talked to another English speaker in weeks just needed someone to hold a cup of coffee and listen.

Before long, Martin knew everything about every missionary. He knew who was struggling financially. He knew which husbands and wives weren't getting along. He knew who was discouraged with language study because they weren't catching on as fast as they had hoped. He saw the newborn babies. He got to congratulate MKs on their homeschool projects. He met villagers who had recently become believers.

Martin was the perfect person to hear it all. He just had a heart for everyone he came in contact with, and everyone who knew him loved him.

As for our own financial situation, we saw the Lord provide for us in amazing ways. Yes, there were times when we didn't eat very well; there were times when we walked instead of taking Martin's motorcycle. But we always had what we truly needed.

:::::

We had been at Aritao about six months when I gave Martin some very happy news one day: We were going to have a baby!

When I approached my due date in February 1987, Martin flew me to Manila, which had the closest hospital with a proper maternity department. We stayed at the mission guesthouse while we waited for the baby to arrive.

Martin was supposed to leave for a safety seminar in New Guinea, and the baby wasn't here yet. Obviously, he didn't want to be gone for the big event. My due date came and went.

A couple of days later, the Filipino doctor finally said, "You are starting to dilate. We'll go ahead and admit you, and we'll just induce labor and get this over with." But although they gave me the drugs to induce labor, the baby still didn't come and didn't come. It was a long and painful day and we were all starting to get a little nervous.

After many hours, the doctor came in again, looked at me, and said, "We are going to help you."

I didn't quite know what he meant, but I soon found out. I was wheeled into the delivery room, and before I realized what was happening, two interns stepped up on either side of me—and basically pushed Jeffrey into the world! I had never had any Lamaze classes, but I'd done some reading about giving birth, and I remember thinking to myself, *I don't think this is how you're supposed to do it!*

Thankfully, Jeffrey was fine and so was I. In fact, I felt so good we were ready to leave in less than twenty-four hours. Martin signed all the papers, paid our bill (I think it was around seventy-five dollars), and it was time to go.

"Where are my clothes to go home in?" I asked when he came to get me.

"Oops, I forgot them," Martin replied. "Can't you just wear what you have on?"

That wasn't exactly what I had in mind, especially in front of all the wealthy people who patronized this prominent hospital. But there wasn't much choice. I ended up being wheeled out the front door in my bath-robe.

Of course, we didn't have a vehicle in Manila, so we had to use a taxi. Martin went out to the street and waved down an old rickety taxi. The car had no air conditioner and was about to fall apart, but the driver was so proud on the thirty-minute drive to the guesthouse because he was taking an American home with his firstborn son! Martin gave him a big tip.

Oreta, Martin's mother, came to Manila for the arrival of her first grandchild. Martin had to leave for New Guinea, but Oreta stayed and continued to take care of me while he was gone. She and I bonded more closely than ever during those days in the guesthouse; she served me wonderfully and taught me what to do with a newborn.

It wasn't long, however, before we were back home in Aritao, a family of three. We could not have been happier.

CHAPTER 5

TODDLERS AND TRAFFIC
(1987–2000)

Jeff was still a tiny baby when a delegation of New Tribes missionaries from the southern island of Mindanao came to see us one day.

"We really, really need a flight program on our island," they said. "There are eight families altogether—more than you have here on Luzon. Would you consider coming down and putting something together?"

Martin flew down to check out the prospects. He found, as we had been told, a place of rich natural resources but less development on this, the second largest island of the Philippines. It was a long way from the bustle and advantages of Manila. It was also closer to the Muslim minority population, which for decades had resented living under "Christian" domination, as they viewed it.

But the needs for aviation support were obvious. We began working toward a move, lining up a replacement for our present post, and rebuilding an airplane, a Piper Super Cub, for this new post. I helped out every chance I got, usually when Jeff was sleeping. The Super Cub's surfaces are fabric rather than metal, and I enjoyed sewing the fabric onto the struts along with the other NTM missionaries. This kind of sewing is a two-person job, one on each side of the wing, so we had plenty of opportunity for talking and joking.

Soon we packed up and headed for Malaybalay ["m'*lye*-b'*lye*"], a small city in the mountains with several colleges. Martin found a home for his airplane almost sooner than he found a home for us; the municipal airport leased him space to build a hangar there, and con-

struction started right away. Meanwhile, we stayed at the
mission's guesthouse while we house hunted. There was
no mission compound here, which was fine with us; we
looked forward to living in a regular neighborhood and
making local friends.

One day a friend of ours saw an empty house while
jogging and took Martin over to see it. He came back to
me all excited. "You know, that house has real possibili-
ties!" he said with his typical enthusiasm. "And the rent
is only thirty dollars a month."

"Okay! Let's go for it!" I said without hesitation. I
probably should have waited to see it first. What I found
once I arrived was a place that was basically falling apart.
The roof had gaping holes. And the kitchen—oh, my.
Filipinos normally have what they call a "dirty kitchen"
at the back of the house where they cook over an open
fire. Well, in this house, the previous renters had used the
house itself as their dirty kitchen, leaving the ceiling covered with soot.

"Martin! When will we ever have time to fix up this
house?" I cried.

And Martin, true to form, said, "You know, I think
we can do this. Don't worry."

All our coworkers said we should look elsewhere.
But anything else we found was too expensive for our
budget. So we began to fix up that house in our spare
time. We didn't have many belongings anyway, so it's
not like we had much furniture to show off. We just
bought some beds and a baby bed for Jeff and moved in.

And you know, that house turned out really nice.
In the back was a field where a tenant was growing peanuts, corn, and cassava. The landlord had promised us
this space as soon as the current crops were harvested.
So in time, we had a decent backyard. We tallied all the
fruit trees one day: coconut, marang, papaya, guava,

calamansi (musk lime), banana, and even some coffee trees.

Malaybalay became our home for the next eight years, and we loved everything about it. We got to know our neighbors, and even though I didn't speak much Cebuano, I went outside every afternoon when everyone sat around talking. I loved to listen to the women chat, and eventually I made some very good friendships, even though my vocabulary was limited.

On Sundays we went to Bethel Baptist Church, which had been established way back in World War II. We grew to love the people there so much. The church had an English service in addition to one in Cebuano, which was very nice for us. There were several generations of believers in Malaybalay, and we really felt a connection with these folks. They were such a fun group of people and they seemed to really like having Martin and me at their parties. This is probably because we were always willing to do something silly—like sing along with the karaoke machine or perform a goofy skit.

In late 1989, our daughter, Melinda Joy, came along. I gave birth at the nice little Baptist hospital in town, very early in the morning on October 17. A surgeon was visiting that day—they didn't have a resident staff surgeon—and the room was needed for procedures. Since I was feeling so good after the delivery, I got out of their way and went home before noon. I wanted to go and Oreta had come from Luzon to be with me, so I knew I'd receive good care.

Just for fun, I did the radio "sked" (schedule) that afternoon as if nothing had happened. I sat down at the radio, pressed the microphone button, and gave my usual opening spiel: "Good afternoon, this is 4FE202 signing on for traffic. . . ."

Diane Thomas, one of my missionary friends who

knew I had just given birth, broke through on the other end. "Gracia Burnham, what are you doing on the radio?!" We had a good laugh. I hadn't missed a beat.

Mindy was a wonderful, healthy baby, but when she was only a few months old, I started not to feel well. I didn't say anything for a while, but my stomach was always upset. Finally one day I admitted to Martin, "I just don't feel good."

We thought it was probably a case of intestinal worms, a common malady in the Philippines. I took the standard worm treatment, three days' worth of Combantrin. It didn't help.

After a while, Martin said to me, "You know, Gracia, you're acting just like you did when you were pregnant with the other kids."

"Don't be ridiculous," I shot back. "I have a seven-month-old, and I'm still nursing!"

Eventually I went to the doctor for help. And would you believe it? I was pregnant again! Oh, my.

I headed out to the airport hangar to tell Martin. "It's not fair to Mindy!" I cried to him. "And it's not going to be fair to the new baby." Obviously, there wasn't anything to be done about it now, but I just had to vent. Later I consoled myself with the notion that I'd probably have another sweet little girl to play with Mindy. They could grow up together being best friends.

Well, delivery day arrived that December, a couple of weeks before Christmas—and here came Zachary, a boy with enough rambunctious energy for two babies! We took him home and loved him just as much as the first two. And even though he was unexpected, I have to say he's added a wonderful dimension to our family. The year in the jungle that I was forced to spend without him, I thought of him so often and realized just how much I would be missing if he hadn't come along to join our family.

:::::

In 1991, we finally headed home for a furlough. We had left the United States with no children. A little more than five years later, we got off the plane with three kids aged four and under. Someone gave us an old station wagon to use while we were home, and we drove all over the country visiting our list of about ten supporting churches and twenty individuals. We thanked them not only for sending checks but also for praying for us.

Our time in the States was short. In less than a year, we were back in Malaybalay, serving the eight New Tribes missionary families scattered across the island. We loved our life there. It was a wonderful time; new churches were being planted among the tribal people, and Bible translations were moving ahead at full tilt. Since these new churches were hidden up in the mountains where there were no roads, Martin stayed very busy.

I was at the radio all day, it seemed. Martin arrived at the hangar by six in the morning to load up for a flight; he preferred to fly then, when the sky tended to be clearer, before the afternoon thunderstorms built up. Meanwhile, I fed him weather information and handled anything else he needed. The flights were usually thirty to forty minutes each, plus all the miscellaneous ground time, and on some days he managed to make two round-trips instead of just one.

Things got even busier for us when the two other New Tribes pilots left the Philippine field at the same time. The Nordicks had been working on the island of Palawan but had recently lost a thirteen-month-old daughter to a mysterious, fast-moving illness. By the time they realized how seriously sick she was, she was gone. Then Sheri Nordick was diagnosed with diabetes, and right on the heels of that, their son Jake began crying day after day that his leg hurt. The Filipino doctor admitted that he didn't know what was wrong with him. "This little boy may have cancer or something," he told them. That did it—they headed almost straight for the airport to catch the next plane out for a furlough.

The other pilot and his wife had sons graduating from high school and felt they needed to be back in America with their boys. So they left as well. Suddenly Martin and I were trying to service three programs simultaneously. For a while, he went to one island and stayed two weeks, then to another island and stayed two weeks, then came back to Mindanao—this meant he was away from home for nearly a month at a time. We quickly saw that this wasn't going to work.

We asked another mission organization, Wycliffe Bible Translators, to take over for us on Luzon, while we tried to juggle the remaining two islands. Once a month Martin made the long overwater flight to Palawan and stayed there ten days or more. Mostly he went alone, but sometimes I went along and brought the kids. The trips were tiring either way.

Palawan ["pa-*laow*-an"] is the 275-mile-long, thin island that, on a map, appears to poke out from the rest of the Philippines like a javelin thrown toward the southwest. It's a naturalist's wonderland—a concoction of mahogany forests, stunning beaches, coral reefs, and all kinds of animals, from hornbill birds to six-foot-long monitor lizards. Near Puerto Princesa, the provincial capital, is a subterranean river you can paddle for five miles if you don't mind the bats hanging overhead. Palawan has been called "the last unspoiled frontier," although migration, logging, tourism, and poverty are today starting to take their toll.

For a New Tribes missionary pilot and his family,

Palawan was a lonely assignment. They lived neither on a compound, like Aritao, nor in a city with other missionaries nearby, as we did in Malaybalay. They were all by themselves in a house beside the grass airstrip. They did everything, from buying supplies to keeping the books to maintaining the airplane to battling back the ever advancing foliage. Because the climate was even more tropical than the rest of the Philippines, they had to think more about malaria and dengue fever. We found that every time we went to Palawan, we came home exhausted.

It helped a great deal that Martin really believed in the value of family vacations. Even though we didn't have a lot of money, he was always willing to spring for some wonderful getaways. Every year we went to Camiguin, a delightful little island that had been formed by a cluster of seven volcanoes. The only way to get there was by ferry. We'd spend a week just exploring and sitting on the white sand beach. It was so refreshing.

I always returned ready to get back to work—especially when I began to homeschool Jeff. I arranged a little desk for him right near my radio desk, so I could do both things at once if necessary. I ordered curriculum from Calvert, a well-known home-education supplier out of Maryland, and I also got some material from the missions co-op resource center on the island. As people's kids moved from grade to grade, they passed along their books and other materials to those of us with younger ones.

If a textbook didn't have a teacher's manual or a workbook, I just made up my own; after all, I'd been an education major back at Calvary. And of course, I read aloud to the kids all the time.

During Jeff's third-grade year, we took a break from homeschooling. Several of us mission families—New

Tribes and Southern Baptists—got together and rented a jeepney to transport our kids each morning and afternoon to an SIL-Wycliffe school about thirty minutes away. Jeepneys are these brightly painted, colorful Philippine contraptions that look like military jeeps in the front but have benches on an extended flatbed in the back, with a metal roof overhead. They're the local version of a minivan, only they're open to the air and thus a lot more noisy.

::::

Early one morning, Martin was flying an American businessman and another mission colleague to the city of Davao. As usual, I was at the radio; Jeff had just gotten up and was having a bowl of cereal on the other side of a row of bookshelves we used as a partition.

Martin's voice crackled through the speaker. "Uh, Gracia, we have a problem here. . . ." Then the radio went silent.

I waited for the next word, but nothing came.

"Three-zero-nine, are you going to tell me what your problem is?" I anxiously radioed back.

"I'm losing engine power. There was a puff of smoke—I'm not sure what it was. I'm over the mountains right now and into the clouds; I'm trying to climb while I've still got power to get as much altitude as possible to work with. . . ." And then it was quiet again.

My palms began to sweat, and I prayed with all my heart. *Oh, God, help him know what to do!*

At just that moment, a Filipino friend stopped by to return a book she had borrowed. I burst out, "On your way to work, pray for Martin! Something's wrong!" She said she would.

I kept waiting for Martin's voice. Still nothing. I yelled over the partition, "Jeffrey! Are you there?"

"Yeah."

"Pray for Daddy! He's in trouble in the airplane!"

"Okay, Mom."

A few moments later I called again. "Jeff, Jeff—please pray for Daddy! He's in trouble!"

My six-year-old called back with a touch of sternness in his little voice: "Mom! I prayed already!"

The little guy had faith that he had talked to God once—and that was adequate. He had gone on eating his breakfast.

A peace seemed to settle down upon me. *Okay, God—you're going to take care of Martin, aren't you?* Some ten minutes later, Martin called again. He had gotten out of cloud cover and could see the valley in front of him. By then the engine had seized up completely and the propeller had stopped, so he was gliding with no power.

"Gracia, I'm going to head for this Wycliffe base I see, the one at Nasuli. I think I might make it."

Another four minutes of silence. I sat frozen to my chair.

Then: "Okay, I'm switching to Nasuli frequency to warn them that I'm coming. We'll be out of contact for a little bit."

Again, I held my breath.

"Gracia, we're on the ground; I made a dead-stick landing," he radioed. "There's a whole 'hallelujah meeting' going on here! Everybody is out on the runway rejoicing." He had cleared the last fence with a mere fifty feet of altitude left. The engine had pumped out all its oil through a hole in one of the lines—but my husband was safe.

I slumped down in my chair and just sat quietly for several minutes, thanking God for sparing his life.

A coworker drove to Nasuli to pick Martin up. Later

as Martin walked in the gate, he glanced at his watch and said nonchalantly, "I told you I'd be back around ten, didn't I?" We just looked at each other and laughed.

:::::

Like the first one, this term of service ran longer than the standard four years, because there was no one to take Martin's place in the cockpit. Finally, in 1997 we got pilots for each island and went home again. We stayed in the States fifteen months because a plane needed to be rebuilt at the Arizona base and readied to go to the Philippines. Jeff was old enough to help in the hangar this time.

The kids were at just the right age to really enjoy traveling as we renewed contact with our supporting churches and individuals. Jeff was in sixth grade, Mindy was in third, and Zach was in second. We didn't homeschool that year; we "carschooled." Each child had a personal box of books and a little lap desk, and we did our work rolling across the highways of America. Since all three of them were together, I even figured out some joint assignments for them.

The one subject they could not work on in a bumpy car, of course, was handwriting. We had to wait for that until we stopped at a rest area or got to someone's house. But they got an education regardless. They had a little atlas in which they tracked each state we went through, putting a sticker on it. They learned a lot about the country of their roots, even though they had never really lived in the States.

For six months of that furlough we settled down in Arkansas next to my parents, and the kids went to public school. We wanted the kids to know what it was like to live in America, not just to live in a car. So we made a point of establishing a routine. Meanwhile, Martin traveled alone to see some constituents and also made a short trip to the Philippines to take care of things.

Then the furlough was over, and the whole family returned again, this time back to our original post on Luzon at Aritao. Although the kids had made lots of friends in Arkansas, they were just as excited as we were to head "home" to the Philippines.

With other pilots in place on all three islands, Martin was named chief pilot for the Philippines. This meant he did a lot of instruction, safety management, and general oversight. He also became the substitute whenever one of the pilots had a medical problem or a family needed to go back home.

We continued to enjoy our family vacations while serving in Aritao. If we weren't at the beach, we often traveled to Baguio, the summer capital of the Philippines. Baguio is up in the mountains, so the climate is cool. We liked to rent a place there that had a kitchen, and then we'd buy our food in the local open market, where there was always a wonderful variety. We would cook vegetables I couldn't get elsewhere. Between trips to town, we'd go horseback riding or sightseeing. In the evenings, we'd enjoy a cozy fire.

By now, of course, we had a pretty good understanding of how to get along in Philippine society. For most Filipinos, bribes were just a way of life. The police stopped people for no reason at all and took their licenses on a pretense, when what they really wanted was a payoff. We always tried to tell them how wrong this was—but after all, Martin needed his driver's license, and so in the end we'd give them the money.

We had more than one ethical debate with ourselves about whether this was wrong for us to do. As the years went on, we decided the wrong was on *their* part, in stooping to extortion, rather than on our part for doing the necessary thing in response. I suppose some people would disagree with me on that, but we had clear consciences.

Our kids got an education in Philippine culture the time someone stole Zachary's bicycle. Everybody in the barrio knew who had it; in fact, we did too, because we saw the person riding it around. "Dad, that kid took my bike!" Zachary cried one day. Martin proceeded to do the logical thing—at least so far as we understood Philippine ways. He sent a go-between to talk with the parents, politely asking for our bike back.

They immediately got very upset and embarrassed, because that's not how it's done in their culture. Our go-between returned to explain that a person doesn't accuse the other person of wrongdoing. Instead, the person offers a ransom for the property, and then everyone can be happy again.

Martin said, "How about if we send you back with a homemade cake and some cookies?" We really hated to give them cash.

This was done—and they quickly returned Zachary's bike. In their view, we had established a relationship with them; we were their friends now, and they were our friends. Everyone in the barrio was pleased that we had handled this in the proper way. No one had to be ashamed or embarrassed.

The next time I had reason to think seriously about the word *ransom,* of course, a lot more than a bicycle was on the line.

CHAPTER 6

THE PERILS OF PALAWAN

(November 2000; May 29–30, 2001)

If you asked my kids today to name a favorite memory of life in the Philippines, they'd probably say Thanksgiving Day 2000. It was one of those special occasions when we all piled into the airplane and got to fly with Martin to a tribal station.

We were on Palawan covering for the pilot who was away, and we got this great idea to surprise our missionaries there, Norm and Jacqui Rice, with a full-fledged American Thanksgiving meal. They were living in a village all alone, struggling to learn the language, and we knew this would lift their spirits.

On one of his runs into Puerto Princesa, Martin found an imported turkey. It wasn't cheap, but he brought it home anyway. We excitedly radioed Norm and Jacqui that we'd come the next day and "bring dinner."

I basically stayed up all night cooking. Besides the turkey, I made pumpkin pies and vegetables; I baked bread; I even brought along a can of cranberry sauce I'd managed to find back in Manila, which was more rare than turkey in this part of the world.

By the next morning, I had it all ready and boxed up to fly.

The approach to this particular jungle runway was about as exciting as the best roller-coaster ride at Disney World. Martin followed the tree-lined river, edging lower and lower. We all gasped as he suddenly spun off into a sharp curve at the last minute to drop onto the grass. But as always, his technique was flawless.

The Rices were in a huddle with a group of villagers at the edge of the runway. After the propeller stopped spinning, we crawled out of the plane.

"Hi, everybody! We're here! Happy Thanksgiving!"

The look on Norm's and Jacqui's faces as we started unloading our meal was unforgettable. I had a table-cloth, china, candles, and little doilies. We just kept pulling things out of boxes until we had set a beautiful table.

All the while, Norm kept teasing the kids. "So, didja bring a turkey?"

"Yeah, we did."

"Oh, you did not—you just brought a big chicken," he'd say. (That is the usual substitute for Americans in the Philippines at holiday time.)

Finally, with a great flourish, we unveiled the golden bird.

"No way, you guys! This is incredible!" They absolutely freaked out. "Where did you find this?" We told them the story as we all squealed with delight.

I'd even managed to find some Dream Whip for the dessert that day. And so, there in that little tribal hut in a Palawano village, we had a complete Thanksgiving dinner.

Afterward, we all went to the river with their dog to play in the water. Martin took the airplane back up for more landing practice. He was trying to see if, with some additional tree cutting, the approach could be less hair-raising. Late that afternoon, we flew out again. What a special memory we made that day.

:::::

It was only six months later that we were back on Palawan, this time without our children. A busy schedule of flying awaited us, so we were grateful for a chance to relax at Dos Palmas for a day.

The resort staff were right there to meet us at the commercial airport with big smiles and warm welcomes as we got off the plane. Martin and I were among thirty or so other guests who had come to Dos Palmas for a tropical getaway. Traveling on a small hotel yacht, we arrived on the island about lunchtime and had a wonderful buffet. The weather was perfect.

Two giant palm trees rose in the middle of everything—hence the name of the resort. There was a walking path around the island's perimeter for strolls or rides on rented bicycles. Other activities at the resort included diving, snorkeling, and fishing. A lovely gift shop beckoned.

Our cabin was air-conditioned and had a refrigerator. The floor was tile (this being the tropics), but the room had a nice decor. Beyond a set of drapes was the outside deck maybe three feet wide and about six feet long. I thought to myself, *This is such a perfect spot! Tomorrow morning, while Martin sleeps off his jet lag, I'll come out here and do my nails. Then maybe I'll even write some letters.* I was really looking forward to this break, even though it was to be less than twenty-four hours.

We took a nap that afternoon. I'd brought along some snacks: some pop, mozzarella sticks, and peanut M&M's for the room. We opened mail, and Martin talked nonstop about his time in the States.

Soon it was time for the evening buffet. As we were leaving the room, I said to Martin, "You know, this door doesn't look very secure."

He glanced at it and then quickly said, "No, they never do. But don't worry—I'm sure our things will be fine." After all, the resort had its own security staff patrolling the grounds.

We returned to the circular building with the thatched roof for a sumptuous spread of roast beef, fried fish, and sweet-and-sour pork. There was also a fresh salad bar—everything we could want. The open-air eating area was pleasant and breezy; dress was, of course, casual.

At the table next to us was a somewhat tall, brown-skinned man with a big smile and an attractive, young Filipina woman. Little did I anticipate that I would soon know them much better: it was Guillermo and Fe. We could tell by his accent that he was an American. When their food came, I overheard the woman say something about returning thanks for their meal. He demurred but said, "You go right ahead."

That evening, on the way back to our cabin, we noticed the videoke place. Videoke is a popular thing for Filipinos to do. Someone with a great voice was performing, and we almost stopped in to listen. But instead, we decided to keep walking and enjoy the evening air.

We stopped to overlook the pool for a while, and then we turned back toward our room. The sky was clear, the water totally still. We talked and talked late into the night, and then we went to sleep, without a care in the world.

::::

Six hours later—and for the next year—there was neither bed nor hot water nor electricity nor Bible, not even the most basic things of a woman's life. I woke up each day with nothing to accomplish—nothing at all, except to stay alive. What a strange feeling this was, compared to my previous life as a busy missionary wife, mother of three growing children, homeschooling teacher, family bookkeeper, letter writer, household organizer, flight supporter at the radio, hostess to a never-ending stream of houseguests—my "to do" list had constantly overflowed. Now, the page was entirely blank.

The first days aboard the fishing boat, I didn't even have to belabor what to wear. There was no choice: it would be the same gray short-sleeved shirt I had worn round the clock since the abduction.

Sonny, the Dos Palmas cook, at least had a little dirty kitchen with a woodstove to use in preparing meals for us all. He used fish brought up from the hold below; there was also a stash of rice. One night they gave us something hot to drink—coffee, we assumed. It actually tasted quite good. The truth was it had been prepared from rice that had been burned all the way to a charcoal state, then mixed with water.

Guillermo volunteered to become our "water boy," perching on the edge of the boat with a pail to bring up water for washing. (Not that I could get very clean with salt water—I learned that soap won't lather up at all— but at least it was better than nothing.) This task sounds easy, except that with the boat moving along at a good speed, Guillermo had to be very careful not to get pulled overboard.

Our freshwater came from two large plastic barrels, perhaps fifty gallons each in capacity. The longer we traveled, however, the more we were warned to conserve. Rizza, however, seemed not to get the picture; more than once I noticed her washing out her clothes, probably in order to keep looking her best for Reggie. "Oh, Rizza, please don't use up our water!" I begged. My pleas didn't do much good.

Rizza didn't seem to get the whole idea of Muslim modesty, either. The Abu Sayyaf admonished her at least to wear a long-sleeved shirt, which she did—but then promptly unbuttoned the front down low.

Eventually, we could tell that the freshwater was running low, as "floaties" started to appear. Soon it was completely gone and we were forced to resort to drinking melted ice brought up from the fish hold below. Yes, the smell and taste were less than appetizing.

Guillermo was another one who never quite bought into the modesty idea. Muslim men are supposed to be covered at all times from the navel to below the knees. Somehow that didn't stop Guillermo from stripping down to his Skivvies in order to take a saltwater bath (or more precisely, to pour water from a dipper over his head). Everybody else on the boat was just dying with embarrassment, especially the Abu Sayyaf.

"Martin, come on!" he called out. "Join me for a bath."

"No, no, that's all right. You go ahead."

All of this did not endear Guillermo to the captors. They had pretty well tagged him as a "bad guy." Martin, on the other hand, was viewed as a "good man" (even though he was a Christian missionary) because he didn't drink, didn't smoke, didn't swear, and he had a wife and children.

Our captors raised their eyebrows, though, when they went through Martin's wallet and came across a picture of Felicia, Martin's sister in her midtwenties, who is beautiful, with long blonde hair. "Who is this?!" they demanded, assuming she was Martin's girlfriend.

"Oh, that's my little sister," he replied. This seemed to settle their concerns.

Several of the younger Abu Sayyaf began to figure out that Martin was handy with mechanical things. Soon they had him fixing their transistor radios and showing them how to set the watches they had stolen. They had been randomly pushing buttons and getting nowhere up to that point. He also gave lessons on how to use their newly acquired cameras.

They began sorting out the ID materials they had swept out of our rooms, and in fact, returned much of it.

They never gave back Martin's pilot licenses, though. He had worked his way through layers of Philippine bureaucracy to get those little slips of paper, and now they were gone. (At a later point, we happened to notice a bag in the wheelhouse, and when we peeked inside, it was the leftover documents. We promptly snuck these out, keeping some things, including a 2001 pocket calendar, and shredding others into the ocean.)

::::

A sober, moon-faced captor named Musab established himself as the Abu Sayyaf's spiritual leader and began conducting Koran studies up in the bow of the boat. Those who attended were soon bored to death with his lengthy orations.

They had Korans, but only two in the whole group had read the book all the way through. One day, after listening to them read in a distinctly nasal, singsong tone, Martin asked one of the guys, "What did that say?"

"Oh, we don't know," he responded. "We just learned how to pronounce the words in Arabic, but we don't know what they mean."

"Really?"

"Of course not. We don't know Arabic."

I asked, "Why don't you translate the Koran into Tagalog, then, so you know what you're reading?"

"Oh, no, no—then it would be corrupted. The only true Koran is in Arabic."

Our captors, however, seemed eager to show us the similarities between Christianity and Islam. In fact, we do share a number of the same personages, such as Adam, Abraham, Moses, and David—they termed them all "prophets." When they found out that our youngest son was named Zachary, their faces lit up: "Oh yes, Zacarias!" they said, and congratulated us for naming our child for one of their prophets. They even began call-ing Martin by the name "Abu Zacarias" (father of Zachary).

One of the captors was named Zacarias as well—the short, stocky one who had ransacked our room. He had a unique personality and really liked to make people laugh, especially with his fractured English. Sometimes he excitedly combined phrases into fanciful sayings, like, when it started to rain, "The rain is coming and the peo-ple are running!" Everybody just stared at him and then cracked up.

On Tuesday afternoon, our third day in captivity, the sat-phone batteries went dead. This greatly upset Sabaya and the others. How would they keep making their pronouncements to the outside world? Soon Mar-tin and Chito came to their rescue by showing them how to line up six D-cell batteries and pack them together se-curely enough to recharge the sat-phone battery.

"You know, you guys really ought to think about getting a solar panel," Martin suggested. "That way you wouldn't be so dependent on these batteries that run down." They thought that was a great idea and promptly called one of their buddies on land to order one.

Watching all this, I said to Martin, "Maybe you ought to keep your bright ideas to yourself, you know? You're going to become so indispensable to this group they'll never let us go!" On the other hand, it was to our advantage for them to continue communicating. So maybe Martin's advice served our purposes after all.

Somewhere along the line—perhaps in apprecia-tion?—they finally got Martin a white T-shirt with sleeves, so he wouldn't be so cold at night. I tried to help out by sharing part of my *malong* with him.

One other provision came along: a few toothbrushes for the group. Martin and I were glad to get one to share between us. It was our only possession besides the clothes on our backs. No toothpaste, however.

Letty, the Chinese-Filipino businesswoman, was a middle-aged person of means. I could tell she was very worried for the safety of her young daughter and niece; she almost never took her eyes off them.

She moved over by me one afternoon with a second concern. "I've started my monthly period," she whispered, self-consciousness written all over her face. "What am I going to do?!"

I looked around the boat in vain. "Uh . . . I don't know what to tell you," I replied, hopelessly. I walked around a bit, trying to think what I would do if it were me.

Then I came up with an idea—a bad one, to be sure. But at this point, I was scavenging for any option. "Over there on the floor of the engine room, there's some cardboard. Maybe we could soften it up somehow if we cut it up in pieces and played with it awhile. . . ."

"Oh, no, no, that won't work," she said, and went off to search the boat.

Not too many minutes later she came back with cardboard in her hand and began to rip it up quietly. The rest of us ladies silently joined in the effort, kneading it with our hands to smooth out the rough edges.

(I don't know why I didn't think to mention Rizza's stash of extra clothes! That would have been a much better answer.)

Pretty soon a little knot of girls began to laugh uproariously at something. What in the world could be funny? I went over to check them out, and they were dreaming up commercials for this new kind of feminine hygiene product—ideas on how to package it, how to advertise, sales slogans to use—it was hilarious. As I watched these girls giggling, I thought to myself, *Isn't it amazing how the human mind can find humor in even the darkest situations?*

Sssssst! Sssssst! Sssssst! The Abu Sayyaf began to hiss at us, using the typical Philippine sound that means "Cut it out! Shut up!" Too much humor was not appropriate in a climate of jihad. But our funny bones were all thoroughly tickled by then and we couldn't calm down regardless of their scolding. Eventually, we asked Solaiman if we could start making a list of things we needed, not just Letty, but all the women. He agreed and gave us a piece of paper.

Now most people in this situation would probably stick to the basics: soap, shampoo, etc. But oh no—our list looked like we were headed to some kind of mall: Sunsilk for oily hair, Rejoice shampoo with conditioner, Secret solid deodorant, Colgate toothpaste, Close-Up minty fresh toothpaste, Dial soap, various pieces of underwear by size—it was crazy! I sat there chuckling to myself and thinking, *Shouldn't we be just a little more realistic here?*

Finally someone turned to me and said, "What do you want?"

"Any kind of soap would be good," I replied, "and I think we ought to have a box of amoxicillin." With sixty of us on this boat built for only ten fishermen, I knew it was just a matter of time before someone got sick.

They then took this long list, which included everything from cologne to bras, to Sabaya. He gave it one glance and handed it back, saying, "Well, figure up how much all this is going to cost."

Janice took charge of the accounting effort. The estimate came to some 14,000 pesos ($280).

Back to Sabaya again. "Well, you don't have that much," he announced. "Of the money we took from your rooms, you get 10 percent, which is only 2,000 pesos. Go back and cut it down." Faces fell all around as we headed back to try to write a more down-to-earth shopping list.

When that effort was finished, a messenger was sent on a speedboat to head for shore and bring back supplies. He left but never returned. We heard later on the radio that he was spotted in town by the authorities and arrested. We also wondered if perhaps he had defected. Anyway, we got nothing from our list!

:::::

The hardest part of those early days on the boat, of course, was every time my thoughts turned to Jeff and Mindy and Zach. We knew that the mission policy was to evacuate our kids out of the country so as not to leave opportunity for further mischief. But we kept wondering who had told them about our capture, and if they'd flown off to the States yet.

Everything in our lives had been snatched away from us in one swift moment. No one cared that Martin was an excellent pilot, or that I could make a great pizza. We were no longer defined by our ministry or careers; we were just two human beings in the middle of the Sulu Sea with no idea of what would happen next, and no way to influence it.

I sat there and watched the Abu Sayyaf talking to Martin, ordering him around, and thought to myself, *You guys don't even realize what a neat person he is. You've got this great guy sitting among you, and you don't even care.*

The boat's engine conked out from time to time, and guys went below deck to fiddle with it. Sometimes only after they let it cool off did it start again. One night during low tide, we ran aground on a sandbar. It took a lot of work to free us, and I worried about getting stuck there indefinitely. Another night it rained hard for a short time, so all twenty of us hostages retreated to the engine room.

One afternoon, the hostage group amused itself with more singing. "Somebody think of a Disney musical. . . . *Mary Poppins*? Okay, what are all the individual songs?" And then we'd sing "A Spoonful of Sugar," "Let's Go Fly a Kite," and anything else we could remember.

Chito, who came from a similar church environment as Martin and me, joined us in singing hymns: "Praise Ye the Lord, the Almighty," among others. The Abu Sayyaf tolerated our singing, for the moment anyway; they assumed it meant we were happy and content, whereas they hated to see us cry.

Sometime that day, dolphins began to follow the boat, jumping gracefully into the air. The blue of the water was exquisite, almost metallic. It was such a beautiful sight. We oohed and aahed with each leap. I couldn't help thinking that under different circumstances, this would be a wonderful cruise. The only problem was that Martin, without his glasses, couldn't see the marvelous show of nature at all.

At last on Wednesday evening, we found ourselves drawing close to land. The lights of a big city loomed on the horizon of one island. We hostages still had no idea where we were.

We began trolling up and down the coastline, looking for a flashlight signal from the shore that would indicate to the Abu Sayyaf a safe place to disembark. But the signal never came. So far as we could tell, we were truly alone.

CHAPTER 7

HOSPITAL OF HORROR

(May 31–June 3, 2001)

The Abu Sayyaf seemed convinced that they were in the right area, and so they maneuvered among some small islands to wait out the daylight hours of Thursday. Getting off the water after five days and four nights would indeed be a relief for us all. But what would we find once we stepped onto firm soil? Would conditions be better or worse?

During the afternoon, some Abu Sayyaf support people came out in a small boat. They found out what we needed, went back to shore, and then showed up again with cookies and Coke. Later that evening, we went back along the coast to search again for a flashlight signal. This time it came—two lights, in fact.

The shoreline at that place was rocky, and the fishing vessel couldn't get all the way in. So we all unloaded into water that was about chest-deep, like marines hitting the beaches of Normandy or something. Only we didn't feel nearly as brave.

More Abu Sayyaf were there on land to greet the comrades. Once again the cry of *"Allah akbar!"* went up, accompanied by the traditional double-kiss greeting, one to each cheek. *"Salam! Salam!* [Peace! Peace!]" echoed through the air. There was a lot of laughing and talking in languages I couldn't comprehend.

Then they started us up the hill in the dark. Not a house, not a campfire—nothing pierced the darkness at all. For some reason, Martin had lost his *tsinelas* in the boat; he was now barefoot. It was just as well, because I found that the steep trail was too rough for my *tsinelas* anyway. They kept sliding around to the top of my feet, so I finally took them off. Most others did the same.

At the top, we came to a little shelter built for coconut husks, elevated about a foot off the ground. These structures are made so that a fire can be built underneath, in a pit, and the husks can be cooked into a form of charcoal. Meanwhile, the coconut meat inside the shelter is smoked, which preserves it for transporting to market.

This one was maybe twelve feet square. We climbed inside and lay down to sleep for the night on the split-bamboo floor. It had just a little give to it—a small improvement over the rigid deck of the ship. However, now that we were back on land, the mosquitoes were back with a vengeance.

We were all grimy, and when the morning light broke, we were thrilled to hear that we would be taken to the river, a few at a time, for baths. Letty, Kim, and Lalaine were the first to go, while the rest of us waited in the forest.

I need to stop here and clarify what the word *bath* means in this context. Put out of your mind all images of hot water, bubbles, or privacy. What I mean instead is stepping into a cold river fully clothed (so as not to be indecent before the watching guards), washing yourself under your clothing as best you can, coming out looking like a drowned rat, pulling a *malong* up around yourself to the point that you can hold one edge in your teeth, then fumbling around underneath trying to shed the wet clothes and put on dry ones—assuming that you have any. Otherwise, you just dry off gradually in the sun.

Letty and the girls had just started bathing when suddenly, without warning, gunfire erupted. The Armed Forces of the Philippines (AFP) had found us within just a few hours of landing onshore. I heard someone scream,

"Drop!" and we all hit the jungle floor. I began to crawl on my stomach, using my forearms for traction, back toward the coconut shelter. The Abu Sayyaf immediately began to return fire, running into the forest to press the battle.

"Run, run, run!" came another command, and I stood up and began to run with my head down. I was petrified, my heart thumping through my chest. Several times we were interrupted with the order to drop; then we got up and ran again. Back in the shelter, we flopped down to catch our breath. Soon Letty and the girls stumbled in, absolutely panicked.

As the shots continued to ring out, Sabaya came into the shelter, looking specifically for Tess. "Come with us," he said. "We want you to call the radio station and give a message to President Arroyo. You tell her to call off the troops on Basilan and stop the indiscriminate shooting of the Abu Sayyaf, because they're going to injure innocent hostages."

Basilan—so that's where we were. For the first time in five days, Martin and I knew our location, although the name didn't ring a bell. Basilan, we learned later, is a small island only about forty miles across, just off the tip of Mindanao's Zamboanga Peninsula. Heavily wooded, it's a poor island to start with, made all the worse since the Abu Sayyaf sprang up in the early 1990s and established their stronghold here. Fear and chaos have since become the daily reality.

Tess did as instructed, using the sat-phone. Whether her message was immediately heard by decision makers or not, we don't know. But after some ten minutes, the shooting stopped. Amazingly, no one in our group was injured.

We sat in the coconut shelter trying to calm our nerves for a while. I had obviously never been shot at in my life, and neither had most of the other hostages. What a jolt to be going along in my day and suddenly find myself in mortal danger!

If someone had told me that this was the first of seventeen eventual firefights over the next months, I think I would have died on the spot.

As our nerves began to settle, one of the captors cooked a big pot of rice and passed it down the line of hostages. Each of us reached in and grabbed a handful. I was still so tense I really didn't feel hungry, but I took some anyway. I knew I'd better seize the opportunity to gain nutrition while it was available. The pot was passed back and forth several times. The outside of the pot was blackened from having been placed over an open fire, so our hands were soon covered with black soot. There was no place to clean up, however; instead, we were quickly herded out the door and down the trail to another site, since the AFP knew we were here.

Less than an hour later, we stopped. Angie, Fe, and I really needed to use the bathroom. We weren't sure what to do, with so many men around us, so we just went off into some tall grass. Meanwhile, the Abu Sayyaf began rigging up their hammocks to some trees.

But then, for some reason or another, they decided this wasn't a good spot after all, and we were put back on the trail. As we hiked farther into the jungle, the terrain became much rougher and heavily forested. When we sat down for a rest again, we were attacked by a nasty swarm of bees. People jumped up and began to run and scream, even though the captors tried to get us to calm down. Several hostages got stung and began to cry.

The whole morale of the group plunged in that moment, as we realized that everywhere we turned, things were only getting worse. Fear wrapped itself around me. *How is this ever going to end?* I wondered. Darkness fell, and as we continued walking, they roped our wrists together like a chain gang. Martin was in front of me, Chito behind. We plodded on single file for another couple of hours and finally came to another coconut hut. This one, unlike the first, was full of husks; we had no choice but to sit on top of them, which was very uncomfortable.

A few civilians were around, and we could sense the tension in the air—something was going to happen. From the few pieces of English thrown into the conversations around us, we knew they were talking about a jeepney. Close to eleven o'clock, one rumbled up, and we were all herded onto it in the pitch-blackness—except for Sonny, Eldren, and Armando, the three Dos Palmas employees, for whom there simply wasn't space.

"Just keep them here," a guard directed.

The Abu Sayyaf piled onto the roof and we headed out. As we pulled away, one of the hostages said, "I wonder what's going to happen to Sonny. . . ." We learned much later that he and Armando were both beheaded within hours. Eldren was subjected to the same attempt, but it was botched. He escaped with his life, and a major neck scar.

The first driver was obviously inexperienced and went barreling down the bumpy trail at way too fast a speed, jostling all of us inside and perilously bouncing the guards above. One even fell off, as I recall. Sabaya soon took over the wheel, although he had trouble shifting the gears as well.

After an hour or so, we began to see houses and lights. We were coming to a town. Suddenly, we screeched to a stop under some lights. "Move, move, move!" came the order from a guard, who wanted us to get out of the jeepney as quickly as possible.

There was only one problem: We were still all tied together by the rope. The first person tried to step down, but the cord was all tangled, and our exit turned into a big pileup on the ground. The guards continued to scream at us, "Move! Move! Move!" obviously upset that we were wasting precious time. Eventually, we stumbled out onto the ground and were directed toward a small, one-story, U-shaped hospital. Later we learned the name of the town: Lamitan.

My heart sank. *This is the last thing this place needs!* I thought. *Patients are already sick and trying to get well—and here in the middle of the night comes a bunch of terrorists with their captives. Now even more lives are going to be endangered.*

Three of our captors—Hurayra, Bro, and Zacarias—began bashing out the jalousie windows with their gun butts. I think they were just trying to intimidate the staff with the noise of the shattering glass. They ushered us hostages from the courtyard into a one-bed patient room that happened to be unoccupied.

"Start taking baths," we were told, since this place finally afforded soap and freshwater—well, at least cold water. Someone suggested we should go alphabetically. Of course, we Burnhams loved that idea!

But by the time Martin and I got into the washing area, gunfire had erupted outside again. The hospital was getting blasted. This was a surprise to the Abu Sayyaf; they really didn't think the government troops would have the nerve to fire on a hospital. Their plan had been to stage this confrontation and thus force negotiations. I think they figured that after some talking and compromising, they would get concessions from Manila, the hostages would be released, and we would all go on our way.

But clearly, things weren't going according to plan. The AFP didn't care that this was a hospital and did not hold off as expected.

Martin and I dumped water over ourselves very quickly and got out. As for clothes, we had no choice but to put our dirty sets back on. We sat down in a corner to wait, choosing a spot on the floor far away from the door, just in case hostile forces came bursting in. As the gunfire ebbed and surged, one of the other hostages pointed to the windows just over our heads and told Martin and me we'd better move to a safer spot in the room. We did, now watching the door and windows closely. In the midst of this chaos, believe it or not, one of the captors poked his head in the room and handed us some Cokes and "biscuits" (cookies). We ate quickly, but with gratitude.

Imam, an elderly man with a goatee, stood guard at our door. His eyes crinkled when he smiled, and I thought he looked like somebody's nice grandpa. However, he was Abu Sayyaf nonetheless, and several of his family members belonged to the group as well.

I studied him as he stood by the door, gun in hand. *Why is he sitting here?* I wondered. *He's too old for heavy fighting. Maybe his job is just to wait and watch . . . and if things go badly tonight, he'll be the one to shoot us all?*

I nudged Martin and pointed to Imam. "Do you think he's been given the order to shoot us if things go wrong tonight?" I whispered.

True to his nature, my husband saw things differently. "Oh, no," he assured me. "I don't think anyone's planning to kill us. What they want from us is money."

::::

As the wee hours of the night wore on, the fighting intensified, and we were moved into another room, this one with two patients lying in their beds. I'm embarrassed to admit what happened next. The other hostages promptly began to loot the room, taking everything from baby powder to soap to the patients' clothing. We had suddenly become as unscrupulous as our captors. The law of "I need this, so I'm taking it right now, whether it's mine or not" held sway.

What's the difference between us and the Abu Sayyaf? I said to myself. *We're all stealing.* Someone held out a toiletry item to me. "I'm not taking that," I answered. "It's not mine. We're stealing from these people!" The other hostages continued to get cleaned up in this patient room, while the rest of us sat outside on the floor along the hallway. As I sat there, I pondered what I had just witnessed. Up to this point, I had assumed we hostages were "the good guys." Now I had to admit that when you're thinking only of yourself and your own needs, you'll do just about anything.

What I would have hotly denied that night in Lamitan, of course, was the prospect that before the year was out, I would behave in much the same way.

In time, nurses moved the two patients out to other rooms in order to give us their space entirely. They also brought us some hospital scrubs to wear, which we gladly accepted. Martin finally got to change his shirt.

The gun battle continued throughout the rest of the night. The sun came up that Saturday morning, and we were exhausted from no sleep. Yet the firing continued. Some kind of aircraft arrived overhead and began to fire mortars at the hospital; one of them hit the operating room. A canister of oxygen exploded, starting a fire. Several of the Abu Sayyaf went running to fight the fire, while their comrades continued shooting.

Some time later, we were moved again back into the hallway, perhaps because it was more interior. Imam continued to sit and watch us, cradling his M16. Bro, a big, muscular warrior type with long and unusually wavy hair, came running back through the hall to rejoin the battle after fighting the fire. As he tiptoed between people's legs and bodies, he kept saying, "Excuse me . . . excuse me . . . excuse me." Martin and I looked at each other and couldn't help but chuckle at the display of politeness amid the carnage. It was so typical of Filipino courtesy.

By now the AFP had cut off the hospital's electricity and phone service. This infuriated the Abu Sayyaf, of course, who had hoped to use the phones to call the press and set up interviews.

Martin was summoned to the courtyard to make another communication on the sat-phone; signals were clearer out there. It made me nervous to have him leave my side, and especially to venture outside. But there was no choice.

"Call your mission in Manila," said Sabaya. "Tell them to call the American embassy, and have *them* call President Arroyo." The message was to be in the same vein as before: Stop firing on the hospital; you're endangering not only hostages but patients as well.

As Martin stood outside with the phone pressed to his ear, he soon heard the familiar voice of our friend Bob Meisel, NTM office chief in Manila. Bob didn't recognize Martin's voice at first, and it took a while to convince him that it was really Martin on the phone. Meanwhile, gunfire echoed in the background. There was no chance for honest talk, of course. Martin could only deliver his message as ordered.

"Martin, is Gracia with you?" Bob wanted to know.

"Yes, she is."

"Can I talk to her?"

"Well, she's not right here beside me. She's inside the hospital."

In the background, Sabaya kept saying to Martin, "Remind them that the Geneva Convention prohibits hostilities against hospitals!" Martin did as instructed. But it was all he could do to keep a straight face. It seemed so ironic—here was Sabaya, a radical terrorist, lecturing official governments on the rules of engagement as spelled out in the Geneva Convention!

By this point, the phone battery was dying, and the conversation ended abruptly.

Somehow in the middle of all this confusion, the Abu Sayyaf got word that Reggie and Rizza's ransom money had arrived. Since we were in such a public place, it would be easy to recruit a civilian to take them out of the hospital.

The captors decided that Divine's little boy, R. J., should be released as well. They had said on more than one occasion that R. J. was an "innocent" and should never have been kidnapped in the first place. When he learned that he was going to have to leave his mother, R. J. was terrified and began to cry. But Divine encouraged him, telling him it was for the best and that she would join him soon.

She struggled to stay calm—we all did—as we watched him leave the hospital with Reggie and Rizza. These events motivated the other hostages to get back on the sat-phone and try to make their own arrangements for release.

The day wore on, and the shooting raged without abatement. We ached for quiet so we could finally sleep, but that was not to be. My nervousness began to show itself in diarrhea, but a trip to the bathroom meant crossing the main corridor that opened to the front entrance—an open-fire zone. I took the chance a few times but then grew afraid to risk it.

"Is there another bathroom I can use?" I asked one of the nurses.

There was, inside an unoccupied patient room. As I

entered the room, who should I see sleeping comfortably on the bed but an Abu Sayyaf member! Now I had a new worry: *What happens if he wakes up while I'm in the bathroom?*

I ducked back out to tell Martin. "I'm going to go ahead and use the bathroom in there," I told him. "But if I don't come back within a couple of minutes, you need to come looking for me, okay?" He promised he would.

Despite the gunfire all around, the nursing staff tried to manage the situation as best they could, even though I know they were scared themselves. They provided blankets for us to cover ourselves with when glass shards began to fly from the shooting. That was a good thing— except that under the blankets it was absolutely sweltering. It was about this time that someone named Sniper, a guide who knew Lamitan well and served the Abu Sayyaf, got shot directly in the eye. He was brought in from outside and laid in the hallway where we were all sitting. Blood poured from his face, and he moaned pitifully.

Nurses came over and began to bandage his eye. His breathing grew heavy and labored. Suddenly, his head turned to one side and he began to vomit blood onto the floor. As if in reply, the artillery from the sky grew all the louder. We watched in horror and sadness as Sniper writhed in agony.

A hospital staffer came into the hallway carrying T-shirts from the local school, which other hostages quickly grabbed. He also had a number of half-kilo bags of brown sugar. I didn't take one because I wasn't sure what I would do with brown sugar all by itself. (I hadn't yet learned to hoard any food I could grab at any time.)

The staffer dropped the sugar bags onto the floor. A couple of them burst open, and I watched as the brown granules mixed with the vomit. Suddenly the roar of the shelling ratcheted up, and someone cried, "Drop!" We all hit the deck. For the next thirty minutes, I lay on the floor, my face pointed directly into Sniper's sugar-soaked, bloody mess. It was almost more than I could bear.

Is this what it's like to watch someone die? I asked myself. I felt my mind starting to cloud over; I could no longer think straight. I was slipping into shock.

Glass began to fly through the air, and someone threw a blanket over me. I huddled there and knew I had to try to pull myself together. I gasped a prayer. *Oh, God, help me! Calm me down, please. Keep us safe, and keep me sane.*

The heat and the smells were unbearable. I got to the point I couldn't stand it anymore, and I threw off the blanket.

"What's wrong?" Martin asked.

"If I die, I die—but that blanket is going to suffocate me. It makes me feel claustrophobic under there," I told him.

:::::

By now it was late afternoon. Our emotions were drained. Even the Abu Sayyaf were pulling out their prayer beads to recite their pleas. I watched them as they silently prayed, their fingers working through the colored beads. Each rosary (the Muslims also called their beads a rosary) was made up of three sections of thirty-three beads each, plus one special addition on the end, making one hundred in all.

I couldn't help but feel as if this hospital was going to be our tomb. I looked at Martin and said, "They're just going to gun us all down. We're all going to die here."

Again, Martin reassured me. "I'm not so sure of that," he said. "It's got to end soon." Just then, out of nowhere, a new jeep pulled right up into the courtyard.

Out jumped six or seven Abu Sayyaf reinforcements with guns and new ammunition! Immediately, the whole tone changed.

"How did you guys get through the roadblocks?" one of our captors asked incredulously.

"We just told them we were the governor's bodyguards." The governor of Basilan was, in fact, a former Abu Sayyaf who had hatched the kidnap-for-ransom strategy back in the beginning of the movement. He had since turned to politics, so he was no longer appreciated by his former comrades. But he still remembered how to organize his own personal army, his own jail, and so forth. At any rate, the mention of his name was enough to get this jeep through the AFP checkpoint.

Within half an hour came a new order: "Everybody start packing up! We're leaving!" I picked up a nearby sheet and formed a makeshift knapsack for Martin's extra shirt, our toothbrush, and a few pieces of leftover food. Some of the other hostages were eating a bit of rice, but I was too emotionally distraught to eat.

Before we left, the Abu Sayyaf began to divide up the group, picking out certain people to be released to work on ransom arrangements on behalf of their partners. For example, Janice was selected while Chito was told he'd be staying. Letty was chosen, but not her daughter and niece. Tess was picked, but not Francis. As they prepared to leave, Janice, Letty, and Tess were given instructions on how to send money to a contact point in Zamboanga City. They were told that if they did so, their loved ones would be freed.

After another emotional parting, the three left in one direction, while the remaining eleven of us were re-tied with rope in groups of three or so, then herded out the back, accompanied by Abu Sayyaf. I was amazed to see Sniper get to his feet and walk out with the rest of us.

Meanwhile, four new hostages were added to our group: three nurses named Ediborah, Reina, and Sheila, and an orderly named Joel.

In the courtyard, a breeze brushed across my face, and I found myself thinking, *Thank you, Lord—at least I'm going to die outside where it's a little cooler.*

I didn't have much time to reflect, however, as the shooting started up again. "Drop! Drop!" came the signal. Then "Run!" Then "Drop!" again.

We dropped near one house that had a little store attached to it. Bro bashed in the door with his foot and, with gunfire raging on all sides, coolly went inside to scoop up candy from the little jugs. He stuffed his pockets, then came back out and moved along the line of us on the ground, dropping a few pieces in front of each of us.

How weird is this! I thought to myself. *We're in the middle of a firefight, and he's thinking about candy.* We ran again and then were commanded to drop. I found myself lying between Martin and Guillermo. I looked up and saw the flash of a grenade over my shoulder, accompanied by a sudden burst of heat. Guillermo cried out, "I'm hit! I'm hit!"

Martin was very quiet. I turned to him and asked, "Did you get hit, too?"

"Yeah, in my back. But I can't tell if it's bad or not."

In the distance, I could hear Divine and Buddy calling out the same distress. "We've been hit!" they cried. "Just leave us, just leave us," Buddy told the captors. "We're wounded very badly."

One of the Abu Sayyaf said to another, "Just leave 'em."

It would have been nice if they had simply left us all behind at that moment. However, we were not so fortunate. One of the captors came over, looked at Martin's back, and quickly announced, "You're fine." Next he looked at Guillermo's wounded foot and again declared, "It's not serious. Let's go!"

We had no choice but to jump up and run again.

As we got to the edge of town, we slowed to a walking pace and began our second straight night of travel. Guillermo hobbled in pain. Martin's shrapnel wound proved not to be serious and eventually scabbed over. (Later on during our captivity, we heard on the news that Buddy and Divine had escaped from the jungle and had recovered from their wounds after a couple of months in the hospital.) Every hour or hour and a half, we stopped for a rest. Each time I was so exhausted I just sank down on the ground and instantly fell asleep. They woke us when it was time to march on again.

Oddly, the AFP didn't pursue us. As time went on, we noticed that they never pursued us. A battle was one thing, but pressing on for capture didn't seem to be on their agenda. This was one of the continuing mysteries of our ordeal.

We got to a hill beside a farmhouse, and as we looked far across the valley, we could see a firefight underway. Tracers were exploding in the sky.

"What is that?" we asked Sabaya.

"It's a gun battle our guys started over there to draw the AFP away from us," he explained.

We lay down under a tree, the first of many nights we slept on the cold ground. By this time, Angie was hysterical without her sister Divine. She was in such bad shape that I said to Martin, "Maybe I ought to sleep beside her tonight, just to help her through." He nodded.

I brought the sheet I had picked up at the hospital and spread it out for Angie and me. I found two stones to serve as pillows, almost like Jacob of the Old Testament had done. "Everything's going to be okay," I murmured to her as I tried to comfort her. "I'll stay with you tonight. I know you'll miss Divine and Buddy, but it's better that they aren't with us. They're free, Angie. . . ." I kept my arm around her through the rest of the night.

The next morning, however, Martin admitted that he had just about frozen during the night alone. He needed me, and I wasn't there for him. I cried and cried as I thought about my husband lying all alone, shivering in the cold. *From this moment on,* I vowed, *I will never leave his side when it is time to sleep, no matter what the circumstances.* I kept that pledge all the way to the end.

CHAPTER 8

THE THREAT

(June 3–7, 2001)

The Abu Sayyaf leaders had spent the night inside the farmhouse, while the other captors had strung their hammocks between the piers that supported it, up off the ground. That morning they killed a goat and boiled it to go along with our usual rice for breakfast.

While we were grateful for the nutrition, the meat proved to be extremely tough. We chewed and chewed and chewed, then finally just swallowed it whole.

Outside the farmhouse, Sabaya found a pair of old, holey boots made of bright blue vinyl—what some people call gum boots or rain boots. They had slits in the back, and the soles were starting to separate from the top. "Do you want these?" he asked me, holding them up.

They looked as if they were falling apart, so I declined them in favor of my *tsinelas.* He moved on to offer the boots to others, but nobody else wanted them either.

Soon he came back around to me. "Sure you don't want these?" he asked.

I thought I might be able to find a use for them later, so I told Sabaya I'd take them.

By this time, somebody in the group had given Martin a pair of Boston polo slippers, a type of fairly substantial rubber sandal. We left the farmhouse and began walking again that day. While we were fording a brook, the current swept away one of my *tsinelas* and I promptly switched to the new boots. I breathed a silent prayer of thanks to God for giving me a second chance at taking them. I actually ended up wearing them for the next eleven months. I may have looked like a milkmaid just coming out of the barn, but at least I wasn't barefoot.

About a week later, my guard lost one of his *tsinelas* in the water as well. I gave him my extra one so he'd have a "matching" set.

As we hiked through the jungle trails, we saw *alimatok* (leeches) everywhere. These thin little inch-long things look like worms and sit on leaves waving around, looking for something to grab. When they fasten onto your skin, they begin to suck blood, swelling up in the process.

At every rest along the trail, I'd pull off my boots to inspect for *alimatok*. I got to the point that whenever I felt a slight itch on some part of my foot or leg, I knew right away it was probably an *alimatok*.

There's a certain kind of *alimatok* that goes straight for your eyes. If not quickly removed, it can cause blindness. We learned to be especially vigilant against these.

::::

Meanwhile, guns and weapons were everywhere. More than once I found myself with a captor sitting across from me, his M16 casually pointed straight in my direction. I would gently reach out and nudge the barrel to one side or the other.

One fellow saw that this was bothering me, so he was nice enough to reach down and place his finger over the end of the barrel! *That's really good!* I thought to myself. *First his finger will get shot off—and THEN I'll die!* Finally I just gave up and accepted that having guns pointed at me was going to be a never-ending hazard.

At night, we began to see a spy plane patrolling the

⊕ ───────────────────────────────

Early June
U.S. State Department and FBI advise politicians inquiring into the kidnapping to say little in public, so as not to raise the Burnhams' "market value" in the Abu Sayyaf's eyes.

sky above us, apparently looking for campfires. We didn't know whether it was Philippine or a loaner from the U.S. military. Martin thought it sounded like an un-manned craft, and his knowledge of airplanes was con-siderable. Back and forth the plane searched. Every time we heard the plane approaching, we'd stop walking and stand perfectly still, so as not to draw attention. Once the plane passed, we'd continue on.

The Abu Sayyaf didn't want to be recognized by the armed forces, of course. And neither did we. Why? Be-cause we knew by now that a frontal attack to rescue us would probably turn out badly. The AFP wanted to help us hostages, but pulling off an operation that sensitive was simply beyond their training. At this point, we knew that our only real hope of getting out alive lay instead in negotiation. And for the Abu Sayyaf, negotiation meant only one thing: ransom money.

We saw few if any civilians along the way; they mainly fled whenever fighting broke out. As a result, we passed through one deserted village after another. It was eerily quiet.

At a certain time every night, a commercial airliner would pass overhead, its wing lights blinking in the starry sky. Where it was headed, we could only wonder. Australia, perhaps? Lying there on the ground, we would gaze up, and I would say wistfully to Martin, "I wish I was on that plane. . . ."

"I wish I was, too," he'd quietly reply.

::::

As the days passed, I was gradually learning the many uses of the *malong*. This piece of batik material is some forty inches wide and probably twice as long, with the two ends sewn together to form a large tube. You can step into it and roll it up around your waist to form a long skirt. You can pull it over yourself on cold nights for a blanket. You can use it as a towel or even a tissue when necessary. Whenever it's time to move, you can spread it out to become a knapsack for any belongings you're carrying. If someone is injured, you can turn it into a stretcher if you cut down a couple of tree saplings for poles.

When I stepped inside and pulled it up high to the point where I could grab the top edge with my teeth, I had a privacy curtain for changing clothes, with both my hands free. When it came to bathroom activity, I could also squat inside my *malong*. However, I wound up soiling mine more than a few times as I was learning. That meant trips to the river to wash it out.

One of the most difficult adjustments in the jungle was forcing myself to get along without toilet paper. The others seemed not to mind, but I really struggled. To clean up after a bowel movement with only cold water and my hand was almost more than I could take. And occasionally, there wasn't even any water to use.

The next mealtime, when I had to eat with only my hands, I almost gagged.

Whenever we went through a stream, the guys refilled the water jugs. For some reason, I found that I especially needed a lot of water when we were "mobiling," the Abu Sayyaf term for hiking. Otherwise, my face would get really red and my breathing would intensify, scaring the others.

I found that if I asked for a drink at certain times of the day, the Abu Sayyaf got very irritated with me. Sometimes they said a flat no. It took me a while to figure out

June 4
About half a dozen men begin meeting at Rose Hill Bible Church from 6:00 to 6:30 A.M. to pray for the Burnhams' release. They continue six days a week for more than a year.

that they were saving the water for the ritual washing that preceded their three prayer times each day—dawn, 12:30 P.M., and sundown.

Those on jihad are excused from two of the five daily prayer times normally required of Muslims. However, an additional prayer time is expected of them at 1 or 2 A.M. Our guys never did it; they were too tired after long days of mobiling. Once when the group was feeling a lot of pressure from the military, there was a discussion about whether the lack of this prayer was the reason. They tried to get up in the middle of the night a few times to pray but soon lapsed.

Before they could recite their prayers, the captors went through the washing ritual. Every day, three times a day, they did this. The ritual consisted of:

1. Washing their right hand and arm up to their elbow—*twice*
2. Washing their left hand and arm up to their elbow—*twice*
3. Washing their face—*twice*
4. Washing their ears
5. Washing their mouth by taking in a swallow of water and then spitting it out
6. Sniffing water up their nose and then blowing it out
7. Patting water onto their hair
8. Washing their feet

(I must confess that the constant spitting and blowing of mucus was not exactly my favorite thing.)

All of this activity consumed a fair amount of water, naturally, and the captors took it very seriously. One evening, we were getting ready to eat and Angie accidentally brushed up against one of the guys after he had washed for prayer. "Why did you touch me?!" he erupted. "Now I'm unclean, and I have to go start my washing all over again!" This meant waiting in a long line at the mountain spring we were using in that place in order to refill his jug. He was thoroughly frustrated as he stomped away.

::::

A couple of days after we escaped from the hospital in Lamitan we came to another abandoned house. Several of the Abu Sayyaf, along with some of the male hostages, moved into the living room, giving us women a smaller room off to the side.

Just as we were settling in, I heard someone yelling, "*Sundalo! Sundalo!* [Soldiers! Soldiers!]" The army was coming once again. We hadn't spent even one night in this place. We scurried to collect our stuff for another dash into the woods.

But as we gathered to get ready to go, I noticed that Martin's shoes were missing. I got upset. Who would have stolen them?

"Don't worry about it," he said. "I'm sure they'll turn up."

"What do you mean?" I retorted. "We're going to have to go into the forest again, and you don't have anything to wear on your feet."

I approached Musab, who seemed to be the leader of our particular cluster. "Martin needs his shoes," I announced, with little attempt to restrain my anger.

Always slightly aloof, Musab looked around casually and then just shrugged.

Now I was really ticked off. "Martin can't walk through the forest in bare feet!" I lectured. "You've got to get him some shoes. This is ridiculous. He's going to get injured, and you have to do something about it. Do you understand me?"

All of a sudden, it dawned on me: No, he *didn't* understand me, because he knew very little English.

His face grew stern at being reprimanded by a mere woman. He turned and walked away. (I later found out Musab was the second in command of all the Abu Sayyaf!)

Solaiman came over and said, "Gracia, you need to calm down. This will all work out."

At just that moment, Musab's brother came walking up the hill from where we had been taking baths—and he was wearing Martin's Boston polos! I was fit to be tied. The guy had even broken them in one place. With a big smile on his face, he calmly handed them back to Martin without a word of explanation.

I was really angry, but gradually I settled down. I realized that if I wanted to get out alive and see my kids again, I'd better get a grip on my temper.

We walked all afternoon and toward evening stopped at another coconut hut to sleep. But just before sundown, *sundalo* were spotted again. So we took refuge on top of a ridge. When gunfire erupted at the bottom of the hill, several Abu Sayyaf ran down to engage the enemy.

They returned later, exulting in their achievement. We learned that they had beheaded three AFP soldiers and ransacked their belongings. One of the victims had been a medic. They brought back his medical bag for our future use.

Another had the company radio. Along with the radio, they found detailed paperwork that outlined the AFP's full strategic plan for seeking the Abu Sayyaf, complete with detailed maps. The goals were enumerated and included a list of all the battalions deployed in this effort.

Chito stared at the list and exclaimed, "Look at all the people looking for us!" We'd had no idea the deployment was this large. Obviously, we were in the crosshairs of a major military operation. Unfortunately, that thought was not comforting at all.

In this particular skirmish, several Abu Sayyaf members had been wounded and one was killed. His comrades cut down small trees to make poles, and by using *malongs*, they put together stretchers for the casualties. When we passed through a Muslim village during the night, they left both the dead and the wounded. The rest of us walked onward all night long once again.

The next morning, we stopped to rest. The nurses who had joined us at Lamitan tended to those with smaller injuries.

We continued this trek for several days. Along the way, Martin and I finally learned who the real Abu Sayyaf leader was. He had been part of our group from the time we landed on Basilan, but we didn't suspect, from his quiet way and his baby face, that Khadafi Janjalani was the man in charge. He also used the name Moktar.

Janjalani's older brother, Abdurajik Abubakar Janjalani, had founded the group more than a decade earlier, after returning from the Afghan jihad that evicted the Soviets back in 1989. Inspired by his Islamic professor there, whose name was Abdul Rasul (Abu) Sayyaf, the older Janjalani had settled in his hometown on Basilan to start up a similar effort. The AFP had finally gunned him down in December 1998, and now his younger brother had inherited the mantle.

Our group kept getting bigger and bigger. One day around noon, we came upon a school. Although classes weren't in session, there were a few teachers around, and for some reason they weren't afraid of us. We all looked a mess by this time, and we could tell they felt sorry for us. They graciously had someone in the community kill a cow, which they prepared for us. Boiled eggs, Maggi brand noodles, rice, and hot sweet milk were all added to the menu—a feast! It was the first real meal we had enjoyed in a week, since leaving the boat.

The ladies also gave me a change of clothes: some pants, a long-sleeved shirt, a bra, more underwear—and even an expensive green Penshoppe hand towel! The other women hostages received similar outlays. We were overwhelmed with their kindness. I tucked everything into my sheet knapsack, which I always carried either in my hand or over my shoulder.

We stayed long enough at the school to eat and catch a few minutes' rest before heading back into the jungle. Not long after that, we arrived at a place I dubbed "House 125," which is what the leftover census sticker on the front wall of the house said. A two-room hovel with a thatched roof, it had no electricity, no plumbing, and no glass or even screen in the window openings. It was elevated on stilts some five feet off the ground, like most rural houses in the tropics, and it was accessible by a wooden ladder. The space underneath the house was designed as a place to keep pigs and chickens—although now, with no animals around, some of the terrorists used it for their hammocks, slinging them from the supporting poles. Others tied up to nearby trees.

To the Abu Sayyaf, this was a safe haven: remote enough to avoid the armed forces that prowled in search of them, yet close to villages and farms with food supplies and a river only a few minutes' walk away. Here they could use their sat-phones to keep up the media pressure on the Manila government to accede to their demands.

June 5
Martin's brother Brian, his wife, Arlita, and their family arrive in Rose Hill from their mission post in Papua New Guinea to give support during the crisis.

As we settled into the house, we hostages had a big discussion about how we would sleep. Our Muslim captors had made it clear that Martin and I, as a married couple, should be in the middle to serve as a dividing line between the sexes—something about preserving decency. Next to Martin came Guillermo, since our captors were handcuffing the two of them together each night so as not to lose their prime bargaining chips. The rest of that side included Francis, Chito, and Joel, the young hospital orderly.

Meanwhile, on my side came the three nurses: Sheila, Reina, and Ediborah. Beyond them were Angie and Fe. The teenagers, Kim and Lalaine, huddled up against the wall. We were crunched together so tightly that every time I'd wake up and want to turn over, I couldn't get leverage. It reminded me of being nine months pregnant and trying vainly to get comfortable during the night.

"Hey, I have an idea," I said after the first miserable night. "What if some of you sleep over here at the foot of the row in the extra space? We're not using that. How about you, Lalaine and Kim? This would be a good spot for you two."

They looked at me as if I were crazy. "We *can't* sleep there! Don't you know it's bad luck to sleep facing a door?" Almost every Filipino apparently knows that you have to sleep at a right angle to a doorway, or something terrible might happen to you.

"Okay, then Martin and I will do it. That will give everybody more space."

"No, no, no!" they all protested in unison. "You've been assigned to sleep in the line with all the rest of us." I could see I wasn't going to win this debate.

I woke up one morning and I could hear the birds twittering in the jungle trees and the *thwack* of wood being chopped for the cooking fires. The clanking of pots made me think there might be coffee this morning. At the same time, the mournful prayers of our captors droned on. They began the day with at least twenty minutes of this ritual.

I tried to smooth out my pair of brown *pantos,* which are like pajama bottoms, that someone had given me. I arranged my *terong,* or head shawl, so as to ward off the disapproving stares of our captors. I still didn't have a pair of socks.

Necessity being the mother of invention, however, I had come up with a substitute to protect my feet. A day or two before, Lalaine had said to me along the trail, "Would you like an extra shirt I found?"

"Oh, thank you!" I was thrilled at her thoughtfulness.

She tossed a garment my way—and it turned out to be a little girl's Brownie uniform, about the right size for an eight-year-old. I was disappointed. But after looking at it, I realized that if I tore off the two sleeves, I could pull them onto my feet, folding an end over each set of toes, and then I'd have some padding inside the old blue rubber boots.

Soon it was time for breakfast. A couple of the "boys"—young cadres still in their teens—brought in our food on a big banana leaf. The rice was piled high, with a can of sardines in tomato sauce dumped on top. There were no bowls or utensils for eating; we simply dug in with our hands—and quickly, I soon learned. We hostages were friends and allies of each other, except when it came to nutrition. If we didn't grab quickly, we went hungry.

June 6
An FBI team spends six hours in Rose Hill gathering information about the Burnhams for their case against the Abu Sayyaf.

Something about the frenzy just saddened me this particular morning. I couldn't force myself to get in there and fight for my food yet again. It made me feel like an animal. I sat over at the side of the room and watched the scramble, until Guillermo noticed.

"Come on, Gracia—time to eat! You've got to keep your strength up."

"I just don't want to grab," I replied.

Francis overheard me, and after the banana leaf was wiped clean, he came over to sit beside me, a pensive look on his face. "You know, my dogs at home eat better than this," he volunteered in a low voice.

"Well," I replied, "to be quite honest, this is exactly what we *do* feed our dogs—rice with a bit of sardines and tomato sauce."

Neither of us was really complaining. We were just reflecting on what was becoming of us here in the jungle, pawns in the dark drama of a desperate face-off. We knew the government in Manila viewed the Abu Sayyaf as nothing more than greedy thugs to be squashed. The fact that they held innocent bystanders as hostages was a complicating factor, to be sure. But the battle must go on.

The only trouble was, the Abu Sayyaf knew every valley and ridge of this rain-forested island far better than the AFP, and they were not about to be caught in the open.

The morning heat grew as the hours slowly passed. We were not allowed to leave the room; this had become our quarters twenty-four hours a day, unless we needed to go outside "for the call of nature," as Solaiman en-

June 6
Jeff, Mindy, and Zach arrive in Rose Hill, escorted by their aunt and uncle, Cheryl and Walt Spicer. Everyone moves in with Paul and Oreta Burnham.

joyed phrasing it. He had learned the euphemism from an American acquaintance somewhere. He could be gracious toward us when he wanted to, although he harbored a smoldering resentment of the West—the fountain of all vice, self-indulgence, immorality, and coarseness, in his view. He did appreciate his Levi's, however.

Chatter drifted up through the floor from the leaders' council that was meeting underneath the house. There was something about negotiations, which sounded hopeful. As I listened more closely, I realized that Sabaya—the flamboyant spokesman for the group to the outside world—was talking with someone on the sat-phone. But it was clear the discussion was not going well.

"No, we don't want Castillo to negotiate with us!" Sabaya snapped. "Who is he, anyway? We don't know him, and we don't trust him. We want Malaysia to come in and mediate this problem. That worked fine last time, with the people from Sipadan. You need to appoint someone from there."

(William Castillo, we learned later, was an appointee of President Arroyo; he had already offended Sabaya by being abrasive the first time they talked. So things started off on the wrong foot.)

I listened quietly, thinking to myself, *If President Arroyo is smart, she'll get a new negotiator. The personal chemistry has to be good if there's going to be any hope of compromise.* Another hour or so passed. I wondered, as I had done every day multiple times, what was happening with our three children. Had the mission flown them out of the country and back to the States yet? Who had told them in the beginning that Dad and Mom had been captured? Did they handle it sensitively? Were Jeff and Mindy and Zach falling apart by now? Jeff, fourteen, would try to be the strong older brother. But Mindy was only eleven, and Zach just ten. This was so awful. . . .

My thoughts were interrupted by the sound of Sabaya on the sat-phone again—this time with the president herself. "Madam President, it does not seem that you are getting the picture. We have three Americans. We need a million dollars for Martin. If we get that, we'll let him go free, and his companion, too."

Whatever she said in reply unleashed a forceful rebuttal. Before long, Sabaya was almost shouting. "You want our unconditional surrender—what are you, crazy? If your generals think they can follow us into the mountains and finish us off, they are out of their minds!"

Then in the heat of it all, Sabaya stormed, "If you don't let Malaysia in here to mediate within seventy-two hours, we're going to kill one of the whites!"

Martin and I looked at each other in shock. Was this a death sentence for one of us? Was he really serious? The only "whites"—according to Sabaya's definition—were the two of us and Guillermo. (He had, in fact, been naturalized as a full American citizen only twelve days before his capture. But as far as the Abu Sayyaf was concerned, he was Yankee all the way.)

I looked over at Francis, who by now was sitting in a corner. I raised my eyebrows as if to ask, *Did I hear correctly?* He looked back at me but didn't nod.

When the phone call ended, I moved over beside Francis.

"Did I hear them say they're going to kill one of the whites?" I whispered.

Francis nodded slowly and confirmed, "Yes, that's what you heard," turning then to stare at the floor. There wasn't anything left to say. We both knew that when the Abu Sayyaf used the word "kill," they weren't just talking about a bullet to the chest. They were talking about their trademark procedure, of which they were very proud: beheading with a *bolo* knife, the Philippine equivalent of a machete.

I rehearsed what I might say if they came and started to take Martin away. I would tell them, "Take me, not Martin. My kids need a father. I'm a mere woman—the family can do without me." I knew that my captors didn't value me as highly as they did Martin, so I thought I might be able to convince them to take me in his place. On the other hand, the pragmatic side of my brain jumped in to say, *Calm down, Gracia. Surely Sabaya is bluffing. Think about it: His whole strategy depends on keeping you alive. You're too valuable to sacrifice.*

Martin seemed to agree with this thought. "They need us to bargain with," he said quietly. "If they kill us, what will they have left?"

It was this idea that led us not to say anything to Guillermo, who hadn't heard the conversation below and therefore had missed the threat. We figured there was no need to raise undue alarm. But Martin and I both looked down at our watches to calculate the time when the seventy-two hours would expire: 3:15 on Sunday afternoon. That evening we quietly prayed together that God would somehow keep us safe and set us free.

CHAPTER 9

LEFT BEHIND

(Rest of June 2001)

Friday and Saturday came and went without incident. We did very little other than sit in that hot little hut, talking and sharing stories. To relieve the boredom, Chito came up with brainteasers for us. One was about a river with three missionaries on one side and three head-hunters on the other. A small boat was available, but it would carry only two people at a time. The goal was to get all of the missionaries across the river without their ever being outnumbered and thus put at risk.

We worked at the puzzle for hours, using little stones and a piece of wood as markers. I think we eventually even came up with a solution, although I can't remember what it is now. We told stories about ourselves, our families, our jobs. We summarized books we had read. When it was my turn, I told parts of the life of Christ. Then Martin went on and related the story of a missionary like us whose name was Paul. He talked about the places Paul went, the people he met, and the things he accomplished. We told "hostage stories" from the Bible, such as the account of the little servant girl from Israel who introduced the Syrian general Naaman to the one true God. We told the Queen Esther story—another person who didn't choose to be in the situation in which she found herself.

Others talked about what they hoped to do if they ever got released. Joel wanted to be a fireman, maybe even in the United States. Fe wanted to go to college and learn about computers. Angie and I talked about the entertainment sites of Branson, Missouri. I told her Martin and I had honeymooned there and promised that when she came to visit me in the States, we'd take a trip to Silver Dollar City! We tried to comprehend the motivations of the Abu Sayyaf, and various opinions flowed back and forth.

At other times, my mind was pretty much consumed with the immediate trial of daily living. I struggled just to keep myself together. *Okay, I have to go to the bathroom, but I don't want to go out there in front of eighty men. Maybe I can wait a while longer. . . .*

Martin spent a lot of time with Guillermo those two days. He had already let us know he wasn't religious—"I really don't 'practice'" was his way of putting it. He was more preoccupied with wrapping up his divorce back home so he could marry Fe. But under the conditions, he had grown close to Martin and respected him as a friend.

"You know, Guillermo, we need to be ready for whatever comes," Martin said to him. He explained that all of us have done things that are wrong and that God, who is holy, considers these things to be sin. He told Guillermo that we can't save ourselves and that without God's mercy, we all face eternal death. This was one of several conversations Martin had had with him about the need for Christ's forgiveness and freedom from the captivity of sin.

Guillermo listened quietly. When darkness came, after the two of them had been handcuffed together once again, Guillermo said to Martin, "Thank you for all the things you've been telling me. You've really helped me a lot."

Sunday finally arrived. Sabaya's deadline passed without incident, amid a flurry of sat-phone conversations. Apparently, the government had agreed to some of the Abu Sayyaf's negotiation details. We didn't know the specifics, but we all breathed a little easier.

The next morning, which was Monday, some of the "boys" returned with a delivery of food. I looked down from our room toward the ground outside and was excited to see a pumpkin! We hadn't had vegetables for so long. There was also a goat or two tied up that would be cooked. My mouth began to water and I could almost taste the deliciousness to come.

Cooking fires were lit, and the preparation began. Just as they were getting ready to begin cooking the meat, gunfire erupted, as it had the previous weekend. This house wasn't a safe place after all. For the fourth time in less than two weeks, we'd been found by the AFP.

The Abu Sayyaf immediately began blasting back with their M16s, spraying bullets in every direction. Meanwhile, we hostages scrambled down the rickety ladder, clutching hastily gathered belongings in our hands. We huddled together under the house, wondering if these would be our final minutes on earth.

"Run!" came the order. We dashed up the hill, trying to get away from the advancing troops. I gasped for breath but could not stop; I had to keep going as fast as I could. As I ran through the jungle, I heard an unfamiliar sound. First there was a *thump!* Then a few seconds later, we heard a *shwoo woo woo* overhead. A short while later, I heard the same *thump!* But this time, the sound was followed by an explosion very close to where we were running. As we ducked down to avoid the blast, I realized what we were hearing: incoming artillery. Martin and I looked at each other in disbelief. "What in the world?" he exclaimed. "They're shooting artillery at us! They

June 10
An all-family prayer meeting is held at Paul and Oreta Burnham's home.

have to know the hostages are here—what's all this heavy firepower about?"

If this was the AFP's method for rescuing hostages, we were in deeper trouble than we had thought. The Abu Sayyaf had always wanted us to stay out of sight whenever soldiers were near, and now we quickly came to agree with them.

Martin turned to me and said, somewhat sarcastically, "These must be the most accurate artillerymen in the world; they think they can fire from ten miles away and kill Abu Sayyaf but avoid us?"

Once we got far enough away from the gunfire, we were finally able to slow to a walk. But we still needed to keep moving since we had no idea if the AFP was following us or not. Our hike that day was neither short nor easy; we had to make our own trails through the thick underbrush, uphill and downhill, until we were exhausted. We didn't stop until evening. It was dark when we finally got to a high place that the captors felt was safe. There we settled down for the night.

The Abu Sayyaf were clearly upset. Their threat hadn't worked. They'd hoped to get an acceptable negotiator on the scene—and instead, they were on the receiving end of bullets. The leaders huddled in agitated discussion.

Now what would they do? we wondered. As we looked around for a level place on the ground to sleep, a captor named Haija moved Martin over to a small tree. He didn't speak much English, but he made it clear that Martin should sit down on the ground and extend his arms around the tree, so that he could then snap on the handcuffs. "You'll sleep here," he announced. With his arms wrapped around the tree, Martin obviously couldn't lie down.

Once again, I spoke before I could stop myself. I

turned to Mang Ben and said, "It's going to be very hard for him to sleep this way."

Mang Ben looked me straight in the eye. *"I—don't—care,"* he spat. I bit my tongue as I turned to my husband and said, "I promise I'll be right here, Martin. I'm not going to leave you."

Guillermo, who had been cuffed to Martin every night up to this point, was given a new restraint as well. They tied his hands behind his back with a rope and then said, "You come with us. Someone wants to see you."

Guillermo had removed his shirt earlier that evening in order to cool off. Now, as he was being led away, he tossed the pink pullover to me. Kicking his backpack in my direction, he said, "Take care of my stuff till I get back, okay?"

Oh, my goodness, I thought as I picked up the backpack. *This definitely does not sound good. Are they going to . . . ?* I didn't want to finish the sentence.

I feverishly racked my brain for a less frightening explanation. *Maybe his ransom has come through, and they just want to talk to him about a release,* I thought to myself, trying to put the best face on what was occurring.

About five minutes later, we heard scuffling and shouts from down the hill.

"I wonder what that was," I said to Martin, straining to hear more.

"Hmmm, I'm not sure."

"Maybe a civilian found our camp or something," I ventured. It was a lame guess, to be sure, and we both fell into an uneasy silence. Martin figured out a way to recline, while I huddled up against him in the cold. We prayed together, and as always, our thoughts turned to our kids. We tried to think what they might be doing at that moment. Monday night in the Philippines would be Monday morning in the United States; they were probably sleeping in, since it was summertime.

As our conversation slowed, I began to doze off and on but kept jerking awake, looking for Guillermo to come walking back into camp to claim his stuff. I finally used his backpack as a makeshift pillow, and in time, Martin and I both fell asleep.

The next morning, Guillermo was nowhere to be seen. We didn't want to ask, but his fiancée, Fe, couldn't hide her concern. "Where is Guillermo?" she demanded of the captors.

"He went with a striking force during the night," one of the men told her. As we looked around, that made some sense; there were perhaps twenty Abu Sayyaf missing from the group as well, and it was not uncommon for these groups to raid villages and raise havoc during the night. Maybe they had forced Guillermo to join them.

Later that day, however, I was watching a group of the remaining captors as they horsed around with each other, just having fun. Somebody pushed a pleasant young man named Jaafar, who was probably no more than eighteen years old. In a slightly mocking tone, he retorted, "Oooh, oooh, don't kill me! I want to see my sons!"

What? It didn't make sense, at least in the present setting. But my intuition told me the sickening truth: *That was a quote right out of Guillermo's mouth.* I couldn't prove it, but somehow I knew I was right. I told Martin what I had just heard, and even though we hoped it wasn't so, we couldn't get the thought out of our minds that those may have been Guillermo's last words.

In the days to come, we heard that line repeated more than once; in fact, it became kind of an "in" joke among the captors. We gradually admitted to ourselves the awful truth: Guillermo's decapitated body was lying back there somewhere on a hillside, marked only by his head raised up on a bamboo pole like a trophy.

Sabaya had kept his word. The world had been shown that, indeed, this group was tough.

::::

A day or so after the murder, word arrived that Tess's work had been successful, and the money to release her husband, Francis, had come through. Young Kim's ransom had arrived as well.

This was not, in itself, a source of immediate joy, because the hazardous process of transfer was yet to be arranged. The Abu Sayyaf wanted to make sure the hostages did not fall into AFP hands. They kept working to find civilians they felt they could trust to spirit them across the seventeen-mile strait of water to Zamboanga, where they could make public statements.

Meanwhile, we hostages who remained wrote up a list of supplies for Francis to send back to us if he could: some more *malong*s, deodorant, toothpaste, chocolates, etc.

"Tell the people out there they really need to work to get us out of here," we added.

"Oh, yes, we'll get you out," he replied. "Filipino businessmen will give money; we can come up with the ransom for you, too."

Several days before, I had found an optician's discount card in the bag of abandoned IDs we had retrieved back on the boat and had penned a quick note to our

⊕

June 17, Father's Day
Following a family tradition, the three kids pose for photos that they hope will reach their dad. Paul Burnham intentionally positions them with the Rose Hill house showing in the background, so Martin and Gracia will know where they are.

children on the back of it. I had kept it upbeat, not wanting to upset them any more than they probably already were.

> *Hey Kids,*
>   *Wanted to say hello and let you know that we are fine. The Lord has given us special strength to hang in here when the going gets tough! We'll tell you all about it one day. Until then, we love you 3 w/ all our hearts. We have the best family!!*
>   *Love, Mom & Dad*

Francis took this note, too, and it made it to our kids. Jeff had it laminated and still carries it in his wallet.

We hiked several hours until we reached another farmhouse. Here, Francis and Kim were turned over to couriers, again with detailed instructions of what to say. Francis was to stop at Radyo Agong and repeat the familiar grievances: "We want our homeland back. We will keep causing trouble for the government until they agree to negotiate. More and more hostages will be taken."

Francis did as instructed; his words were heard on the radio the very next day.

Meanwhile, the Abu Sayyaf decided to split us into two groups. Ediborah, Sheila, Angie, and Fe were in one group. Our group included Chito, Joel, Reina, young Lalaine, Martin, and me. No reason was given for this split; perhaps it was just to complicate the AFP's task and not risk losing us all at once.

We didn't see each other for perhaps three weeks.

June 18
President Arroyo comes to Zamboanga City, meets with the hostages' relatives at a military base, and vows that no ransom will be paid.

During that time, we stayed by a really nice river, almost like a park. We rested and got a bath almost every day. We rigged up a *tolda,* a piece of multistriped plastic awning thrown over a rope between two trees and tied off at the corners to nearby bushes for shade.

Some logging was going on in that area, and we managed to scavenge some boards to lay down on the ground under our *tolda,* making a small platform for the five of us to sleep on and keep us out of the mud when it rained. (Joel had talked one of the Abu Sayyaf into giving him a hammock, which he strung nearby.)

A couple of the captors decided to hang their hammocks on the trees supporting our *tolda,* which perched them directly overhead, so low that we couldn't even sit up during the night. Talk about togetherness! But to the average Filipino, this wasn't unusual at all.

One day, Sabaya called each of us to meet with him for a reading from the Koran. Martin and I went together.

"I want to explain to you the meaning of my name, 'booty of war,'" he began. "You guys are our booty. We can make you slaves—but for now you're just our war booty. The Koran says we are allowed to do this. Here, you can read it for yourself." He handed an English translation to Martin.

My husband read the following passage: "So when you meet in battle those who disbelieve . . . when you have overcome them, then make prisoners, and afterwards either set them free as a favor or let them ransom [themselves]."

June 22
Gracia's sister-in-law, Beth Jones, and her boys come from Kansas City to visit the kids in Rose Hill. They go to the zoo and then the park; pictures taken on this day make it to their parents in the jungle.

Other passages Sabaya showed us said, "Those who repent before you, have them in your power" and "Say to the infidels: If they desist, what is now past shall be forgiven them; but if they return, they have already before them the doom of the ancients. Fight then against them till strife be at an end, and the religion be all of it Allah's."

Sabaya then explained his interpretation, as outlined by various Muslim scholars: "There are four options that can be pursued with people who are the booty of war: (1) kill them; (2) make them our slaves; (3) have them convert to Islam and live with us in peace; or (4) collect taxes from them while they continue to practice their religion in secret.

"All over the world, these are the four choices," Sabaya continued. "This applies to you, too."

We sat there wondering why he was telling us this. We waited for some big announcement, but there was none. We were then dismissed.

A little while later, Reina was brought over for the same speech. Perhaps twenty or twenty-one years old, she was pretty and spunky. We watched her reading the same passages and listening to the same discourse.

But when she came back, she was visibly troubled. The speech had ended a little differently in her case. "He told me I have to be *sabaya*ed to one of these guys," she said, her voice shaking. "I have to live with him and sleep with him and everything."

"Oh, Reina!" we cried. "That's terrible!" We already knew she had a boyfriend back home in Lamitan.

"I know. I told him I'd rather be dead. But he said I had no option. So then I said, 'What's next?'

"'Well, you get to choose which one you're going to go with,' he said."

What a predicament. We sat there staring into

space, trying to figure out what she should do next. Was there any way to avoid this atrocity? We racked our brains and came up with nothing.

I finally said, "Well, Reina, what about Daud [David]? He seems noticeably kinder than the rest." Daud had lost his wife in childbirth several years before. He was new to the group and had a softer demeanor, not like some of the tougher types.

Reina just shook her head in disbelief at the whole predicament.

That evening, if it hadn't been so sad, it would have been comical to watch all of the Abu Sayyaf come "courting" Reina's interests. They brought cookies and candy and coffee; it turned into a regular party. They introduced themselves and wanted her to know as much about them as possible.

The next day, Reina was called again to talk with Sabaya. But when she returned, the deal had changed. "I don't get to choose after all," she reported to us with a heavy voice. "I've been given to Janjalani." No amount of protest would change the matter.

"He's the head guy," Sabaya had said, trying to make her feel better. "He's educated, and you'll be treated better with him than anyone else."

So in the end, that is what transpired. Reina dejectedly picked up her stuff and moved over the hill to Janjalani's hammock.

CHAPTER 10

SURROUNDED

(Early July 2001)

With every passing night we spent in the open, my bones seemed to hurt more. I was becoming an old lady at a rapid pace. I awoke in pain every hour or so and had to sit up, sometimes even stand. This disturbed Martin's sleep, of course, since we were routinely handcuffed together (now that Guillermo was gone), and the handcuff was then chained to a tree.

I thought to myself at one point, *Has there been even one night's sleep in captivity that I could honestly term "good"? Not really.*

One night just about dusk, some of the captors who had been out to get food came running back to our camp to report, "Soldiers! We've been 'confirmed.' They're going to raid us in the morning."

We pretended to go to bed that night, then got up again after dark and packed. Walking along the river in the black of night, our group of forty or fifty came within just a few hundred meters of the soldiers' camp. We moved silently past them and into the darkness.

While mobiling, we each had our own guard who was assigned to watch us and make sure we didn't try to escape. My guard was Sakaki, a pleasant enough fellow who seemed like he would have been more comfortable in the city than fighting as a tough guerrilla. On this particular trek, I was having a lot of trouble seeing in the dark because of night-vision problems that have plagued me ever since I had laser eye surgery. I couldn't see where I was going, and we were now walking *through* a river on big rocks. Seeing my struggle to keep up, Hurayra was assigned to help me instead of Sakaki.

For some reason, Hurayra carried a sniper rifle instead of an M16 like everyone else. But he could be kind when he wanted to. All through the jungle are leaves that are fluorescent; they actually glow at night from a mold of some kind. Hurayra picked up a handful of these and hooked them onto his backpack so I could follow him. After he climbed over a rock, he extended his hand to help me up. This was rare; most of the others refused to touch a woman, especially an American woman. (Some, when required to help me, actually wrapped towels around their hands so as to avoid contact.)

Hurayra's kindness extended to Martin as well; he called him "sir." At one point he started showing up every morning between eight and nine with "a gift for Mr. Martin"—coffee or cookies or maybe hot milk. He would sit with a little notebook and ask us to help him learn English.

"What do you call such and such?" he would ask, and Martin would answer.

They would work together for at least an hour and sometimes longer. He would ask all about the United States. His real goal, he explained, was to get to Afghanistan and die in holy war so he could go straight to paradise.

One day Hurayra wanted to learn the English word for defecation.

"Well, in our culture we don't really get that specific," I replied. "We just say, 'I have to go to the bathroom,' or 'I have to go to the CR.' It's considered crude to go into detail about exactly what you're going to do there."

He looked at us for a long time and then said, "If you only tell me you're going to the CR, I have many questions!"

I broke up laughing as I said, "Hurayra, if you see

me heading out into the woods with my water jug and a *bolo* knife to dig a hole, you can figure it out, right? But I'm still only going to say, 'I'm going to the CR.'"

"Oh, okay . . . but I still have many questions!"

On another occasion while Martin and I were bathing at a little spring, Hurayra even volunteered to do our laundry for us. He seemed to understand that we were struggling to adjust to hostage life and needed to be helped along. He was just so polite and nice—for a terrorist!

Even though Reina was forced to spend most of her time with Janjalani now, we still tried to talk as often as we could. When we weren't mobiling, she and I had even more time together. She was understandably depressed about her new lot in life as Janjalani's mistress. But her natural spunk seemed to shine through, regardless.

Every once in a while, she would rise up and give Janjalani a piece of her mind. It was fun to listen. When he would say, "Look at all the support our movement has," she would fire back, "Well, sure the civilians support you—you've got money! You send them to town with 3,000 pesos [$60], and they bring you back one sack of rice and some dried fish—and they get to keep the rest. Wait till your money runs out."

Lalaine, on the other hand, seemed to be quite taken with Bro, who had been assigned as her bodyguard. This might have been a case of Stockholm Syndrome, a reaction common in kidnapping situations, in which a hostage becomes sympathetic to or even falls in love with his or her captor. In any case, I knew she was in danger. "Lalaine, you need to be careful," I told the young teenager. "Remember, this guy's a terrorist."

"What?" she replied. "They've never done anything bad to me. They just want their homeland back."

"Lalaine, think a minute!" I said, quickly turning into a scolding aunt. "They forcibly took you away from a resort where you were vacationing with your family. Right now your parents are possibly selling their house in order to raise 10 million pesos for your freedom. They're probably pleading with everyone they know, going into debt to ransom you out of here. And you say these guys have never done anything to you? Lalaine, you've got to keep clear in your mind who the bad guys are."

"Well, at least they're not like the armed forces, who are just out here for the pay," she tried to reason.

"A country has to have armed forces, or else it won't survive," I countered. "These bandits would be totally out of control otherwise."

I don't know that I totally convinced her. The Abu Sayyaf had fed her a lot of propaganda. Fortunately, her ransom came through along with Chito's not much later, and the two of them were allowed to leave. Before they left, we urged Chito to call our children. I especially hated to see Lalaine leave; I had really grown to love her.

I was tempted to send out my wedding ring, which was still safely hidden in my pocket after all these weeks. But I held back, thinking that we'd probably be released ourselves before too long. After all, others were getting to go; we would surely get our opening soon, wouldn't we?

Chito's last words to Martin and me were, "Give me two weeks—a month at the most—and I'll have you out of here." That was July 3, 2001.

::::

The motorbike that picked up Lalaine and Chito that night must have brought food, because after we walked for about an hour, we stopped in a deserted village to make a meal. The guys built a fire and we ate, even though it was two o'clock in the morning. By this time, we had learned to eat whenever food was available, regardless of what the clock said.

Actually, our food supply had been pretty good lately. We'd been eating about two meals each day, and even when we ran short, we could always resort to pacō, a dark green fern that grows in the jungle. We could snip off the curly tops and eat them raw. Since they're bright green, I assume they're quite healthy.

Sometimes the captors boiled the pacō. Other times they stir-fried it with a bit of onion. It was really very good.

Although they were still on a mission, the Abu Sayyaf didn't seem to be in an aggressive mode these days. They weren't pressing the battle against the AFP but were instead trying to avoid them, since they had to take care of us while waiting for their financial windfall.

This passivity was actually harder for these warriors than the gun battles were. They sometimes referred to their daily lot as "baby-sitting." Had it not been for us, they could have gone after the AFP with a vengeance.

At times, from up on a hill, we would spot an AFP camp. One of the guys would say to another, "Boy, if we didn't have these people, we'd go down there and raid them good!"

But the money was always thought to be "right around the corner," so we waited.

Somehow, the three of us—Joel, Martin, and I— ended up with a group of a dozen or so captors led by Mang Ben. We learned that as long as we were in Mang Ben's group, the goat meat would be extra spicy.

For some reason, he liked the idea of Hurayra learning English. He told the others in his group, "You need to do the same. You won't go far in this world without it."

Mang Ben organized his men into two-hour guard

shifts throughout the night, to make sure we didn't escape. One night when I was sitting up to work the kinks out of my joints, Mang Ben's stern voice came booming out of the darkness:

"Why you do that?!"

I couldn't see his face at all. "Do what?" I asked in return.

"You lay down!" he ordered from his hammock.

"I'm sore; I hurt, because I'm lying on the ground." I continued to sit there for a while, despite his command. Eventually, however, I did lie down again to try to rest.

Honestly, the Abu Sayyaf really didn't need to worry about our trying to escape. Martin and I talked about the possibility all the time, but every time, we came to the same conclusion: If we tried to escape and were caught, we would be shot, end of story.

I know that if I hadn't been there, Martin would have escaped. In fact, he often told me that if ever I had the chance to get away, I should take it. "If I know you're out, I'll get away, too. Don't worry about me," he said. But he knew it would be impossible for us to escape together. Whenever we talked about it, he'd ask me, "How far can you run? If we leave together, they'll be after us in no time. These guys can run all day. Can you do that?" I'd have to admit that no, I couldn't.

"Gracia, my gut feeling is this: We're going to get out of here sooner or later," he'd say. "Believe me, I don't plan to make a career of this hostage thing."

And so we waited for our ransom money to arrive.

::::

People in America often ask me if the Abu Sayyaf were cruel to me personally. Well, yes, of course—the whole kidnapping was cruel. But one incident stands out in my memory. I was suffering from diarrhea (a common condition for me). When Haija, an especially harsh captor, came one evening to chain Martin and me together, I knew I'd need to be up during the night. "I'm sick," I explained. "Would you please not chain me tonight?"

Without a word, he began securing us to each other and then to the tree.

"I'm going to have to go to the CR during the night," I said. "Please? I promise I'll be here in the morning. You know I won't leave Martin."

His handsome face remained a stone. He snapped the lock shut and handed the key to Sakaki, giving instructions in a language I didn't understand.

Guess I'll just have to bother Sakaki then, I thought to myself.

Not long into the night, I knew I needed to get up. "Sakaki! Sakaki!" I called. But I couldn't wake him.

Joel was sleeping nearby, and he heard my calls.

"Joel! Please go get the key from Sakaki!"

He sat up but didn't move farther. Instead, he started to rearrange and smooth the empty rice sacks on which we were sleeping.

"Joel—I have LBM [loose bowel movement]. I have to go into the woods!"

He still didn't answer but kept looking down at the rice sacks.

"What's wrong, Joel?"

Finally he spoke. "Haija said we're not allowed to let you free," he quietly admitted.

I started to panic. "Joel, what am I going to do?"

"I don't know."

Martin was still asleep. I looked around in growing desperation. I realized I had a plastic bag, left over from a bunch of bananas. So I gingerly slid over to one side, away from the others, squatted down, and used the bag as best I could there in the darkness. I felt utterly degraded. Any source of water for cleaning up was, of course, beyond my reach.

To me, that qualified as cruelty.

Early the next morning, as the sun was just coming up and before we were unchained, Joel was thoughtful enough to remove the bag into the woods. That day, we raised a healthy complaint about all this to Solaiman. We told him how awful it had been. He didn't apologize, but after that our treatment seemed to improve a bit.

Every so often, we'd make a wish list of things we needed. For example, on one such list, I put deodorant, two apples, two oranges, and peanut butter. We got the deodorant and peanut butter (a new food experience for the Abu Sayyaf). We also ended up with two big packages of Apple Dapple cookies (seventy-two in all) and two packages of orange crème cookies (again, a total of seventy-two)!

This was great for Martin and me, because Muslims refuse to eat anything that contains MSG or shortening. That meant we got the cookies all to ourselves.

My mosquito bites had gotten infected, and I didn't have enough self-control not to scratch them. One day I said to Martin, "If I could wish for anything right now, it would be a bottle of rubbing alcohol."

Not more than thirty minutes later, one of the guys walked by and tossed us a bottle of Green Cross rubbing alcohol. "From Solaiman," he said, and kept walking. Of all the random things!

One of the captors was the cutest seventeen-year-old named Ibno Sahid. He often perched his hammock directly over us. Whenever we said something to him, he got the biggest smile on his face.

Then I realized that he didn't speak a lick of English. He just knew when to smile and nod.

Eventually, he came to me, with Joel as his interpreter. "I want to learn to read," he said, explaining that he didn't know how to read any language at all.

"Well, you get a notebook like Hurayra's," I replied. "Get a pen, too, and I'll start teaching you English."

He found a little spiral notebook, and for our first lesson, I wrote his name on the opening page. I showed him an empty peanut butter jar and then wrote down the words "peanut butter." I also began teaching him what the different letters sounded like.

I figured it wouldn't hurt to be helpful to a young guy like this. And it gave me something to do with my mind other than worry about things outside my control.

::::

One day, some planes flew over in a pattern. "What are those?" the Abu Sayyaf asked Martin, knowing that he was informed about such things.

"Those planes are searching for us," Martin replied. We all grew a bit more nervous. Soon the order came to pack up again for moving out. But then we sat and waited for firm instructions while the leaders huddled together. They delayed so long that a couple of the guys put their hammocks back up again. I sat talking with Reina, and we began to relax.

All of a sudden, across an open field, we saw soldiers heading straight for us. The guns blazed, and we all dropped to the ground.

"Reina! Come with us!" I said.

"No, no—I have to go back to the emir," she answered, using the Arabic term for "leader." She headed one direction back toward Janjalani, while we headed the other way. We ran, then dropped, then ran, then dropped again.

As soon as we were able to regroup, we saw that Ibno had been wounded quite badly, along with two other captors. Reina had gotten some shrapnel in her face. The battle quieted down, and we walked about fifteen minutes down toward a river. Suddenly, gunfire opened up right ahead of us. We dropped and ran once again.

Joel landed right beside me at one point, and in his terror, I think he was praying every prayer he'd ever heard. First it was "Holy Mary, Mother of God, pray for us sinners both now and at the hour of our death." Soon, however, he switched to *"Allah akbar! Allah akbar! Allah akbar!"*

"Pray, Gracia, pray!" he urged.

"I'm praying, Joel, I'm praying!" I guess he thought because he didn't hear me verbally, I must not be doing my part.

A helicopter appeared overhead, searching for us. We huddled under trees in order to stay out of sight. In the midst of this danger, however, I looked up—and there was Bro using one of the stolen video cameras from Dos Palmas, filming the whole scene! *This man is absolutely fearless,* I thought.

The helicopter eventually flew away, and we tried to hike again—until we ran into yet another group of AFP soldiers. We realized we were trapped in the field. We had no choice but to sit down in the hot sun and wait.

There was a stream of water in that field, but it was full of leech eggs. We had to drink something in order to stay hydrated in the hot sun, so we closed our eyes and gulped it down.

Then out of nowhere, a bag of ripe lansones started going down the line of captors and hostages. Where they came from I have no idea. I absolutely love lansones— they're a fruit a little smaller than an apricot and sort of like a grape inside.

"Gracia, it's your favorite fruit!" Martin said.

"Yes, it is!"

"Can you believe it? Right here in the middle of this battle, the Lord managed to get you some lansones!" Martin said with a chuckle.

Around four that afternoon, I was off in the weeds when Sakaki began yelling, "Ma'am! ma'am! Come, come, come!" I got back to him just as the gunfire broke out again. This battle simply would not quit.

We crawled on our elbows until we got into a group again. While we were lying there, someone arrived with stunning news.

Mang Ben had been killed.

I stared off into space, thinking of his wife and three children back home—a boy, a girl, and then another boy—just like our family. I began to cry quietly. This man, our group's leader, was already at that moment plunging into an eternity he wasn't ready for.

I thought about the reason Martin and I had come to the Philippines in the first place: to help people like Mang Ben find forgiveness through Christ and get ready for the hereafter. The tears now came harder than ever.

The only way I was able to regain my composure was to remember that this is what Mang Ben had always said he wanted: to die in jihad. He had gotten his wish after all.

Suddenly, Hurayra bolted down toward the stream with bullets still whizzing by. As he ran, he screamed at the top of his lungs, "Fifty-seven! Fifty-seven!"

The AFP thought that an M-57—a bazooka that could do a lot of damage—was being loaded up to fire at them, and they scattered in retreat. This gave the Abu Sayyaf time to drag Mang Ben's body back to the group.

I stayed in the grass, lying facedown. It was so unbelievably hot, I began to hyperventilate. I looked over at the wounded Ibno, who was breathing heavily. It didn't seem as though his injuries were serious enough to be

fatal, but I still felt so badly for him. My mind began to
cloud over, the same sensation I'd felt back in the hospital corridor in Lamitan when we were being bombed.
My brain seemed to be shutting down. I fought to get
my breath.

"I'm just going to sleep," I murmured to Martin,
who was lying close to me.

"Okay," he answered.

I laid my head down and actually drifted off for a
few minutes.

My repose was broken, however, by a swirl of ani-
mated talk about what to do with Mang Ben's body. If
the AFP got their hands on it, they could turn it in for a
reward of several thousand pesos. The Abu Sayyaf were
determined not to let them have that satisfaction.

By then it was dark, and they carried the body to the
far end of the field. Someone used the sat-phone to call
Mang Ben's village and tell them to come get their fallen
brother.

That night, Mang Ben's gear was brought into camp
for dispersing. I ended up with a backpack—not Mang
Ben's, because it was too nice. But the person who got
that backpack gave his old one to someone else, and so
on down the line, until eventually I ended up with a
shabby one. At least it was a place for my things. I hap-
pily began loading up my sheet, deodorant, some sanitary napkins I'd been able to acquire, and the precious
Burnham toothbrush.

Amazingly, we were able to walk out of that area
under cover of darkness. I couldn't believe it. Just as at
the hospital, the government troops didn't seem interested in pursuing us. After all, it was night now; their
"shift" was over. Their commitment to the cause certainly had its limits—unlike that of the Muslim rebels,
who would fight to the death for the reward of instant

paradise (with its seventy-two dark-eyed perpetual virgins waiting).

We mobiled all night. Our three casualties were carried in *malong*s by the others. Then Ibno's older brother came along, leading a *carabao* (water buffalo). The water buffalo was pulling a rig with a huge woven basket, and we could use it to carry our wounded. Where he had commandeered it I could only guess.

Some new faces joined us, from where I didn't know; perhaps they were from Mang Ben's village. They followed at the end of the column as we moved along the trail.

Every hour or so, we stopped for a short rest. I usually used these stops to head out into the brush for another bathroom break.

At one such place, I left my backpack beside Martin, and when I returned, everyone was already standing up to walk again. I quickly fell in line behind Martin, who was tied to Sakaki ahead of him. I had an odd feeling of lightness. *I've just been through another gun battle, and we're not getting any sleep tonight—but I still feel so light, almost like I'm bouncing along here,* I thought.

Suddenly it hit me: I didn't have my backpack! No wonder.

I immediately turned around to retrace my steps the hundred yards or so and get it.

"No!" one of the new guys barked at me. "You go!"

"Oh, please, my backpack's there, with all my things!" I pleaded. "It's just a little way. Let me get it, please, and I'll catch up."

He cocked his gun at me as he repeated, "No—you go!"

I didn't know this fellow at all. If he had been one of the familiar captors, I would have ignored him and gone back up the trail anyway. But this one seemed so callous. Did I dare challenge him?

I turned around to run forward and catch Sakaki. I pleaded, "Sakaki, my backpack! I left it back there; help me!"

He tried to intercede on my behalf, but before he could get out half a sentence, the new guard cut him off. "No—you go! Hurry!"

My heart sank to the bottom of my toes. Everything we owned in this life was back there in that backpack. The sheet we pulled over us at night, my long-sleeved shirt, our toothbrush—it was all there. A horrible wave of guilt swept over me. *How stupid of me! I just lost it all.*

"Oh, Martin, I'm so sorry, I'm so sorry!" I cried between my sobs.

My husband did not reproach me. He just quietly answered, "You know, honey, we've got to save our energy for walking. I forgive you. And you need to forgive yourself. It's going to be okay."

But I couldn't forgive myself. I was engulfed in torment. There was nothing I could do now to correct my tragic mistake. I had to keep putting one foot in front of the other the rest of that night. With every step, I mourned.

CHAPTER 11

A SONG FOR THE JUNGLE

(Late July 2001)

Around daybreak, we arrived utterly exhausted in a small village. In fact, our single-file column was disintegrating as various people slumped down and instantly fell asleep, only to be roused by others to keep going.

A small shelter came into view. As we got closer, we saw a welcome sight: some ripe bananas on the ground. Suddenly energized, I ran to grab as many as I could, even stuffing some into my pockets for later. Martin and I sat on the ground and savored every bite of nourishment.

The people of that village must have felt very safe, because they openly came around to sit with us and talk in their language. They looked at our wounded and made clucking sounds of sympathy. They arranged for Ibno and the other two wounded men to be evacuated on a boat to Zamboanga, where they could get medical attention.

And then, who should show up in the middle of this small village but Sakaki's wife! As a Muslim woman, she was totally covered from head to toe with the black garb; I couldn't even see her eyes through the netting. Her hands were covered with black cloth as well.

But to us, she might as well have been an angel in shining white, because she carried with her a big green bag for us with a long strap. She handed it to Solaiman, who pawed through it, removing several items before he brought it over to Martin and me.

Inside were *malong*s and soap and toothpaste and

sanitary napkins. As I sorted through the items, I realized
the bag contained everything I had lost the night before!
I gasped with joy. It was as if God had already planned
ahead to erase my disastrous loss. Suddenly the tragedy
of our horrible night on the trail was reversed. But the
bag contained an even greater treasure: letters for us!
They were our first contact from loved ones after two
months on the run. How in the world had she received
these? We had no idea, but we didn't care. We were just
grateful to hear from our children.

Jeff's letter said:

> *Hey my cool parents,*
>   *We are having fun here with Grandma and
> Grandpa and all our cousins. Aunt Felicia took us to
> rent movies just now. It was great. I didn't really enjoy
> the movie we got but that's okay. I just wanted to say hi
> and that I'm looking forward to seeing you again. I'm
> praying for you. Bye.*
>   *Jeff (the cool one)*

He then added a happy face. I don't think Martin
and I had smiled this broadly in weeks. What a thrill to
hear from our firstborn.

Mindy wrote about going to the animal clinic and
all the dogs and cats she had seen. She concluded by saying,

> *I just want you to know I am praying for you. Bye
> Mom, bye Dad.*
>   *Love always, Mindy*
>   *P.S. Happy Fathers Day dad.*

It was so sweet.
Ten-year-old Zach's was short and to the point.

> *Dear Mom and Dad,*
>   *How are you? I am fine. We went to Wal-Mart today.*
> *It is fun here. At Mega Mall we bought two computer*
> *games.*
>   *I will write you back.*
>   *Love, Zach*

We just screeched with delight, laughing especially about his last line about writing us back. "No! We don't want to be here long enough to get another letter from Zach!" we said. We wanted instead to go running into that house in Rose Hill, Kansas, and sweep that little guy into our arms for a long, long hug.

There were letters from Martin's parents, my parents, each of Martin's siblings, and others as well. We sat reading them aloud to each other again and again. Some of the letters had pictures. We gleefully showed them around.

And finally, the bag contained a pair of replacement glasses for Martin. We figured that Francis or Chito must have called our New Tribes Mission colleagues and explained Martin's need. So here was a new pair of his prescription from the same optical provider in Manila's sprawling Mega Mall.

"I can tell what these people look like now!" Martin exclaimed to me, a big smile on his face. For nearly two months he had been living in a haze.

The dear woman had also brought along a second big bag of bread rolls. The Abu Sayyaf looked at them but were skeptical about the ingredients. So Joel, Martin, and I had a whole bag of bread to eat. We dove right in.

I went over to Sakaki's wife and gave her a big hug. "Thank you so much for coming," I said. "Sakaki is a good guard."

She nodded, and we talked briefly. She told me she was an elementary schoolteacher.

A while later, Fatima, who fancied himself one of the religious leaders of the Abu Sayyaf, called over.

"Hey, Martin, let me see your new glasses."

"Why?" Martin asked him.

"I just want to see them."

Martin took them to Fatima. The man held them in his hand, turning them one way and then another as he studied them. Then he announced without warning: "We'll keep these. If you had them, they would help you escape."

No! I wanted to scream, or jump up and dig my fingernails into Fatima's flesh. Martin was finally enjoying clear vision after all this time. We stared at the man. Martin's shoulders sagged with disappointment. Finally, he said, "Well, you might as well have the case, too. I don't want them getting messed up, in case I can ever have them back."

Fatima took the case, saying, "Yes, maybe someday." He passed the glasses along to Haija, who put them in his backpack.

We never saw those glasses again. Martin had worn them for less than two hours.

::::

Sakaki, of course, was delighted to see his wife. He asked if he could have a one-night leave with her. He'd be back in the morning, he promised. Permission was granted.

After he left, the others noticed that Sakaki had taken his gun with him. Everyone got upset—especially Zacarias. After all, why did he need his weapon to go home for a visit? Some of the other Abu Sayyaf had no guns at all.

The villagers volunteered to kill a cow and throw a

feast for us. The meat was being cooked in pots over an open fire, and delicious smells began to waft through the air. My mouth was watering as I imagined what that fresh beef was going to taste like. We hadn't had beef since . . .

"Sundalo! At the school! Everybody pack up!" There would be no feast after all.

We did manage to collect some of the pots and the half-cooked meat to carry with us up the hill and into the woods. Martin proudly carried the new green bag with all our goodies.

Curiously, we never saw Sakaki again. His overnight leave request turned out to be a permanent defection from the Abu Sayyaf.

This left Martin and me without an official guard, so Hurayra was appointed to take on this responsibility. This was nice for us, because Hurayra had such a gentle spirit.

A brand-new recruit from the village joined us in our trek. His English was quite good. Although I never did catch his name, I remember him because of something he said while we were sitting on top of the hill. Wearing only a T-shirt, shorts, and *tsinelas,* he said with uncommon frankness, "I never wanted to be a soldier. I never wanted to be in jihad. But these guys said they needed me."

It was a brief but poignant testimony to the fact that coercion was not just a tactic for hostages. It was apparently standard practice throughout the Abu Sayyaf.

Later that day, Sabaya came over to where Martin and I were sitting. "They're asking for a 'proof of life,'" he told us.

"Who's 'they'?"

"We're not sure."

But then later, Solaiman appeared to know more.

"It's that guy who's always smoking a cigar on TV," he volunteered, referring to the trademark pose of former Philippine president Fidel Ramos.

Soon Martin and I were ushered in front of a camera. Sabaya had assumed his beloved hard-guy image: dark sunglasses, knit cap, weapon in hand. Bro took the shots. Then the film was removed from the camera, and Sabaya told him where to deliver it in town.

They also asked us to make a tape recording. Martin was told what to say, of course: "Please bring this matter to a swift end. Please appoint a mediator."

Next, I was asked to record something for President Arroyo—sort of "mother to mother," they said. So I put together a little speech, pleading with her as a woman to work something out with this group, because I really wanted to see my children again. "Please do whatever you can, and have mercy on us," I concluded.

This tape was sent out along with the photo film.

As we walked away, I found myself coming to terms with the thought that this captivity just might be a long thing after all. Others had been ransomed—Reggie and Rizza, Francis and Tess, Letty and Kim and Lalaine, even Chito—but no such hope existed for us. The days were going on, there was always another trail to hike, another hill to climb . . . this wasn't going to end anytime soon. I began to be depressed.

In the days that followed, the depression really took hold. I thought about all that Jeff and Mindy and Zach must be going through without me, and the tears started to flow. A pall settled in around me and I just sat and cried, which was new for me. I had never been the weepy type—until now. The captors hated to see me crying. I tried to be quiet about it, and I hated to have Martin see me in this state. He had known me for many years and he knew I wasn't the type of person to be sad or upset for long. He was especially concerned and did his best to lift my spirits. But I just couldn't seem to snap out of it.

I didn't see Reina at all during our stay on that mountaintop. The poor girl had been through an awful ordeal with her face wound. She asked Joel to clean out the shrapnel, and he tried. But with no anesthesia, the pain was just too great. Finally, she took the forceps from the medical bag, got a mirror, gritted her teeth, and did the job herself.

It turned out not to be shrapnel after all. It was a splinter from a tree that had been shredded by a mortar during the all-day battle.

::::

Sabaya came to Martin one day and said, "You've told us you were never in the armed forces. Did you lie to us?"

"No, I didn't," he replied. "I got out of college and went right into mission work."

"Then why is Fidel Ramos calling you a 'brother'?"

"I don't know," Martin replied with puzzlement.

"Well, you must have been in the army with him!"

Martin thought for a moment and said, "Actually, for one thing, I'm a lot younger than Fidel Ramos. If he called anyone 'brother,' it would more likely be someone the age of my dad, who was a paratrooper in the army, for whatever that's worth."

The interrogation continued. "Tell us why he's using that term for you," they insisted again.

"It's my understanding that Fidel Ramos is a Protestant," Martin suggested next. "Maybe that's what he means; we're 'brothers in the faith.'"

"Oh, that must be it," they concluded. We both relaxed.

The Abu Sayyaf were in fact encouraged by this bit

of news and thought the negotiation stood a better chance as a result.

Not too long after this conversation, they announced, "We're going to take you back to rejoin the other hostage group."

Thus began a several-day walk. As always, Martin was tied with a rope to one of the captors while walking. And, as before, we were both chained to a tree at night. One morning as we were up building fires to ward off the cold, Solaiman called us over and said, "Your kids are going to speak on the radio here in just a minute." We quickly huddled around the battery-powered radio, which was tuned as usual to Radyo Agong.

Sure enough, we heard their voices!

"Hello, this is Jeff Burnham, the oldest son of Martin and Gracia Burnham. I just want to ask the Abu Sayyaf not to hurt my parents. They really weren't doing anything wrong when they went to that resort for their anniversary. There's no reason to harm them. Mom and Dad, I'm doing okay. I love you."

Then came Mindy. She introduced herself and again gave a message directly to the Abu Sayyaf, similar to Jeff's.

Even young Zach did a good job. As his mother, I could tell that he didn't really want to be making a speech, but he carried through for our sakes.

We were so happy. To hear their voices was an unbelievable treat and dispelled the chill from our hearts.

Meanwhile, Solaiman looked at Martin and me with amazement. "Those kids are talking to us!"

"Yes, they are. They don't want you to hurt us."

I sensed just a hint of softness in that moment. After all, he was a father too, with kids at home. Filipinos love their families very deeply. I think his heart was touched.

::::

Finally, we arrived at our destination, which turned out to be House 125. I was disappointed when I saw it, because it meant we were just going in circles, wearing ourselves out for no purpose. The striking force that had left us six weeks before was waiting for us. Sure enough, there was no Guillermo Sobero. The force had gathered a crop of new hostages: thirteen boys, some as young as thirteen years old, from a coconut plantation called Golden Harvest. Two others had tried to run away and been shot to death, they said. All the others had supposedly converted to Islam.

This was our first clue of things to come.

The house had been thoroughly trashed in our absence. Junk was everywhere and the place was filthy. I found an old rag in the corner and brushed the debris out of the room where we would be sleeping.

But as it turned out, we didn't stay there after all. Near the end of that day, we were put back on the trail again, destination unknown as always. The Abu Sayyaf were especially concerned that we not leave footprints, even when we came upon a stash of sugarcane that some of the guys very much wanted. We hiked all that night, and toward dawn, we arrived at a camp.

To reach this camp, which was along a beautiful river, we had to descend a steep cliff. This was the toughest terrain we had dealt with yet. At one point I lost my footing and went sliding toward the edge. At the last second, I caught a tree.

Hanging down over an expanse below, I managed to climb back up the trunk. We continued inching downward. At the water's edge, we began moving from one rock to another in the river for a while, then up a hill, finally arriving at the camp, which belonged to the MILF

(Moro Islamic Liberation Front). Their dialogue with the government was going better than the Abu Sayyaf's, we learned. They had recently been granted amnesty for past episodes.

By this point, we were all exhausted. My littlest toes were absolutely ruined. I could barely hobble along.

We found ourselves directed in the darkness toward a thatched-roof house about eight feet square, with a porch of equal size. Once inside, we were shocked to find Angie, Fe, Ediborah, and Sheila waiting there to greet us! What a reunion that was. We hugged each other and all jabbered at once, thanking God that we were back together again.

"Why do you think our two groups have been brought back together?" I asked.

"Well, someone in Malaysia is negotiating a release," one of the girls said. "They want to release us all together."

That sounded great to us, of course. We told the girls about all our adventures, the battle in the field, how hard we'd hiked, and how we'd been starving a lot of the time. Then they told us their side of the story—that they had been taken to a really nice location and sat for three or four weeks, with plenty to eat and no soldiers nearby. It made for quite a contrast.

"Reina—where's Reina?" they wanted to know.

"Well, she's with Janjalani," I reported.

"Oh. So it's true—she's been *sabaya*ed. We didn't believe that would happen."

Reina, who shared a house with Janjalani, was in fact ashamed to come over and talk to the others for several days.

After some more catching up, I turned to Fe and Angie to do what I knew must be done. "This is going to be hard for you to hear," I began, "but I feel like you need to know. I don't know what you have been told, but we've been told that Guillermo is dead."

"No, no one told us!" said Fe, her eyes starting to cloud up.

"Well, they did tell," Angie admitted, "but I didn't think I should say anything."

Fe stopped for a moment, then said with tenderness, "He's not really dead. He's alive in my heart. I won't ever forget him."

She wanted details about his death, of course, but I didn't have any.

Hardly a day later, however, Haija bluntly informed her that he had been the executioner. He spared no feelings. "It would have been harder for me to kill a dog than to kill Guillermo," he announced with some satisfaction. "He was a bad guy."

Fe was furious, of course. "What right does he have to judge Guillermo?" she stormed. None of us knew quite what to say. We just tried to comfort her as best we could.

::::

We were informed that Sheila and Ediborah had converted to Islam during their time away from us. Apparently, they had been told that if they converted, they would be released. So they had done all the prayers to become Muslims.

To their great disappointment, they didn't get released after all, but their daily treatment began to show a marked improvement. They were given more to eat, and they received a more steady supply of deodorant, shampoo, and other amenities. Omar, the leader of their group, also seemed to be showing a personal interest in Sheila, so he was especially looking out for her welfare.

All of this, understandably, did not sit well with

Angie, who held to her Catholic faith, and Fe, who was Mormon.

"There are six of us here, but only four of us are hostages," Angie complained to me one day, speaking of the six of us in the house.

"Well, Sheila and Ediborah are still hostages," I replied. "They obviously can't leave. Angie, we all need to stick together; we can't afford to be at odds with one another. We've got to live in this little tiny hut."

"We're already at odds," said Angie. "Fe and I think that at night, you and Martin should sleep in the middle, and the two of us can sleep on one side of you, while the two of them sleep on the opposite side. That way we won't have to even be near each other."

But soon that plan was discarded, because the Abu Sayyaf weren't going to let a man sleep beside a woman who wasn't his wife. So they put Martin tight up against a wall, then me, then Angie and Fe, followed by a wide space, with Ediborah and Sheila against the opposite wall. Again, I found myself pushing all night long trying to get a decent amount of room.

As time went on without proper sleep, my emotional state continued to deteriorate. It was our tenth week in captivity, the time I had set in my own mind for our release back on the speedboat. *Worst-case scenario, we'll spend the summer with these guys and be out by the time the kids go back to school,* I had told myself. Now August was nearly here, and I could see no hope for progress. The feelings of despair were overwhelming.

I often found myself sitting on a rock by the river, staring at leaves caught between rocks in the water. Whenever a leaf would break free and start floating down the river, I would be happy for that leaf. I'd just sit there and watch it, wishing I could go down the river with it and be free.

In the constant rumble of the river, it was like I could hear Satan laughing at me, saying, "You trust in the Lord—but you're still here." I found myself beginning to believe Satan's lies.

Sometimes Martin would come and sit with me by the river. He'd say, "I just hate to see you giving up your faith like this."

"Oh, I'm not giving up my faith," I'd tell him. "I still believe that God made the world, he sent his Son, Jesus, and Jesus died for me. I haven't given up my faith—I'm just choosing not to believe the part about God loving me. Because God's not coming through."

"It seems to me that either you believe it all, or else you don't believe at all," was Martin's gentle reply.

Music had always been such a big part of my life; I sang softly to myself all the time. Now, I found that I could still sing songs like "I Sing the Mighty Power of God" and other majestic anthems. But I refused to sing "O Love That Will Not Let Me Go." I was really mad at God.

After about three days of living with this torment, I was totally miserable. When I wasn't at the river crying, I was in the house crying. Finally, Martin learned not to say anything, because he knew this was something I had to work through myself.

One day as I was sitting at the river, I thought about some of the things Martin had said. I realized that my depression and anger against God weren't doing anything to make our situation more bearable. In fact, they were only making it worse—for me as well as for everyone around me. I knew that I had a choice. I could give in to my resentment and allow it to dig me into a deeper and deeper hole both psychologically and emotionally, or I could choose to believe what God's Word says to be true whether I felt it was or not.

This was a turning point for me. It was as if God

were saying to me, "If you're going to believe that I died for you, why not believe that I love you? Why don't you let me put my arms around you and love you?"

And I did. I simply gave in and handed all my pain and anger over to the Lord right then and there. I didn't have a Bible or anyone but Martin encouraging me. But from that day on, the Lord somehow let me know in my spirit that he was still faithful.

::::

Back at the cabin a day or so later, I apologized for the way I had been behaving and said that God and I had come to an agreement: He loved me and I was choosing to believe it.

Gradually, my singing increased. Fe knew some of the same hymns I knew and so we sang together. "How Great Thou Art" became our favorite. I'm sure the song-writer wasn't thinking of Basilan Island when he penned those words. But living in the jungle under the open sky, we could certainly identify with them. Angie didn't know the song, so we borrowed a pen and paper and wrote out these words for her:

> *O Lord my God! when I in awesome wonder*
> *Consider all the worlds* Thy hands have made,*
> *I see the stars, I hear the rolling* thunder,*
> *Thy power throughout the universe displayed.*
>
> *Then sings my soul, my Savior God, to Thee:*
> *How great Thou art! How great Thou art!*

The second and third verses expressed our circumstances even better:

> *When through the woods and forest glades I wander*
> *And hear the birds sing sweetly in the trees,*

When I look down from lofty mountain grandeur
And hear the brook and feel the gentle breeze,

And when I think that God, His Son not sparing,
Sent Him to die, I scarce can take it in;
That on the cross, my burden gladly bearing,
He bled and died to take away my sin.

Then sings my soul, my Savior God, to thee:
*How great Thou art! How great Thou art!**

Within a day, Angie knew the words by heart. I was able to harmonize with them, and we sounded quite good. We sang this song every day, sometimes several times a day.

The Abu Sayyaf never hissed at us for singing it. It sounded beautiful, and they liked music. More than once, Martin said to me, "Maybe God has us here just to praise him in this very dark place."

Gradually, my crisis of faith passed. I realized it would do no good to be angry with God. He had neither inspired the Abu Sayyaf to abduct us nor would he force them against their will to release us. Instead, he would sustain us day by day, night by night, mile by mile, for as long as it took.

Martin sometimes helped me get to sleep with his favorite hymn, "Wonderful Peace." He would hold my hand and quietly sing:

Far away in the depths of my spirit tonight
Rolls a melody sweeter than psalm;
In celestial-like strains it unceasingly falls
O'er my soul like an infinite calm.

Peace, peace, wonderful peace,
Coming down from the Father above!
Sweep over my spirit forever, I pray,
In fathomless billows of love!

And in that divine peace, I could rest.

CHAPTER 12

JUSTICE OR MERCY?

(August–Early September 2001)

Throughout our captivity, our days ran to one of two extremes, it seemed. Either we were mobiling to the point of exhaustion, running for our lives . . . or else we were sitting with absolutely nothing to do, bored stiff. The weeks in the MILF camp along the river were definitely the second of the two.

For some reason, our little shack became the place for our captors to hang out and try to pass the hours. Way into the night, Abu Sayyaf members sat around on the porch just talking and laughing. We woke up each morning to the sight of wall-to-wall guys just lying around asleep.

By now, we were pretty familiar with our captors so I really didn't mind having them so close, except when they got out their Korans and started their required reading aloud. They used a nasal, singsong chant, and there could be twenty different mumbly melody lines going on at the same time—each person on a different passage. It got so grating I used to tell Martin, "I've just got to get away from the 'choir practice.'" I'd pick up my water jug and a *bolo* knife and pretend I was heading off to go to the bathroom, whether I needed to or not.

One of the guys, while reading the Koran, turned every few lines and spit. I started wondering if it was forbidden to swallow while reading the Koran!

Meanwhile, the rest of us were trying to figure out what we could do to stay entertained. We amused ourselves with contests to see how many flies we could catch with our hands. Martin usually won.

Sometimes we sat and watched the ants, who were

always busy. We got a kick out of watching them move some pretty amazing loads.

Another insect that fascinated me was the water strider. I loved to watch them walking across long distances of still water—I could never figure out how they did that. They always seemed like such cheerful insects.

At times I told myself we were getting downright lazy. I'd look at Martin and say, "Do you want to brush your teeth now?" And he'd say, "Nope. I'm just going to sit here." It was pretty pathetic when the most exciting part of our day was deciding whether or not to brush our teeth.

Angie and Fe and I sometimes braided each other's hair. One day I said to Fe, "Would you like a back rub?"

"No," she replied.

Later, I posed the same question to Angie.

"Sure." So I started rubbing her back.

Soon Fe was interested after all. "Is that what a back rub is? Yeah, I want one of those!" So we added back rubs to our list of things to do.

In the absence of any grooming tools, I learned to pluck my eyebrows and chin hairs with my fingers. It sounds hard, but it can be done. I simply pinched the hair between my forefinger and thumbnail as hard as I could, then jerked.

It was even tougher to take care of my fingernails and toenails with no clipper or nail file. Actually, my preferred method for fingernails was to chew them off, but of course my hands were almost always dirty, and Martin said, "Don't chew your nails!" The only other option was to let my nails grow out to a certain length,

August 7
The Philippine government signs a cease-fire with the Moro Islamic Liberation Front (MILF) but continues to stonewall the Abu Sayyaf.

then get them as moist and soft as possible in the river, and *carefully* tear off the top edge.

Toenails, we found, were far more treacherous to tear than fingernails. One little slip, and we would be down into the quick. Ouch! Every step for the next few days was painful.

About this time I realized that my ears weren't pierced anymore. Weeks before, during a quick getaway, I had left my earrings lying on a windowsill. Now I found that the holes had closed up.

Whenever Martin's mustache grew long enough to be offensive by Muslim standards, we borrowed scissors from the guys. Martin was mostly bald but the back of his neck still needed to be kept clean. Several times we ordered razors so I could shave it for him. I'd already been his barber throughout the years, having learned that skill back in mission boot camp in order to save money. We actually kept him looking pretty good out there in the jungle.

Ordering supplies from the guys sent into town was always a hit-and-miss proposition. We never knew if they understood what we wanted, or whether they'd follow through. I giggled at the thought of sending these tough warriors out to bring back sanitary napkins, but I figured that was their problem rather than mine. That's what they got for holding women hostage, right?

Their main purpose in town, of course, was to buy food. The term they used for groceries was "budget" (in the sense of quota or allotment). When the meal was ready on the fire—rice and maybe something to go with it—they'd yell, "Budget, budget!" and we'd all run to the fire with our banana leaf or a plate or pot or whatever we had to hold our little portion. On other occasions, the captors brought the budget to us.

One time Martin cracked a joke by saying, "When we get out of here and back to Rose Hill, I'm going to have so much fun driving down to the IGA [supermarket] for the budget!"

By now, I was totally sick of rice. I like rice—but I'd never had to eat it morning, noon, and night, seven days a week. Often we had nothing to go on top of it, not even salt.

One day I threw a little fit. I told the other hostages, "I can't stand any more rice! Every time it comes, I'm so hungry and know I need to eat some—but I'm so sick of it."

The next morning I announced to Martin, "I'm going to skip my meal. I'll be at the river." I stayed there for a long time so I wouldn't even have to smell the rice.

When I came back to the cabin, Martin didn't say anything. But waiting there on my plate was a big round *apam*—the Muslim version of a pancake made from flour, water, and sugar! We had never received one of these before. In fact, I couldn't remember getting anything made with flour at all. I was totally humbled and felt awful for complaining. I prayed, *Thank you, Lord. You knew I truly couldn't handle any more rice, and you sent me a pancake!*

Fe and Angie, on the other hand, had their own ways of adding variety to their diet. I told them they had "sticky fingers," an English expression they found amusing. One evening, they went off and didn't return for a while. When they finally came back, they were laughing.

"We've just been over at Musab's fire, and as we were leaving in the dark, we stole these sardines!" They proudly showed four cans.

Throughout August
Jones family members want to raise public awareness but are persuaded by New Tribes Mission to keep quiet for the time being.

"You guys!" I exclaimed. "You're gonna get in big trouble!"

"No, no, people steal food all the time. We were just taking our share."

Soon after, when our rice was brought around, Martin was off talking to Solaiman for some reason. The three of us found something to pry open the cans and poured tomato sauce on the sardines.

"Do you want to pray for the meal?" they asked. I agreed.

"O Lord, I thank you so much for these girls with 'sticky fingers,'" I prayed. Everybody burst out laughing.

Angie and Fe had another talent that I could never quite master. We called it *langaw*ing, from the Tagalog word for housefly. If, for example, you have some food, and others come swarming around saying, "Can I have a bite?" you're obligated to feed the *langaw*. It is not culturally acceptable to refuse.

These two girls were really good at *langaw*ing, while Martin and I couldn't bring ourselves to beg. Occasionally, I swallowed my pride and tried it, however— and often the person said no! After all, I was *(a)* not Filipino and *(b)* a woman, so they felt no cultural pressure to share with me.

Sometimes I got really tired of being viewed as incompetent and stupid—a lower life-form—all because I didn't *langaw*, know how to build a fire, or like going to the bathroom in the open.

When it got to be the right season for marang fruit, we all were happy. One of the boys climbed trees all over the place and brought back the fruit for us. Marang are green with spiky skin, and they hurt if you grasp them too hard. But if you stick your thumbs in at the right place, they kind of fall open. Inside is a gooey mass of little white pods, and in each little pod is a black seed.

You stick each pod in your mouth and spit out the seed. What's left is wonderfully sweet.

I forgot to mention that when the guys went out for budget, they'd pick up ammunition as well. You may wonder how such a group as the Abu Sayyaf always seemed to be well supplied with weaponry. Were their al-Qaeda friends sending them supply boats in the middle of the night?

No, no—nothing so exotic as that. The Abu Sayyaf told us their source was none other than the Philippine army itself. More than once I heard Solaiman on the satphone calling Zamboanga, talking to a lady named Ma'am Blanco. He would give her all his specifications for guns, bullets, you name it.

"Who are you ordering from?" we asked him one day.

"Oh, the army," he replied. "We pay a lot more than it should cost, of course. So somebody's making a lot of money. But at least we get what we need."

I was amazed. The fact that such firepower could quite possibly wind up killing one's fellow soldiers seemed not to matter at all.

:::::

Solaiman was just as bored as we were, so he had ample time for theological discussions. He really wanted us to understand Islam as a religion of justice.

"We are trying to get justice for everything bad that has ever happened to us," he explained. He recited all the atrocities against Muslims starting back before the Crusades and explained how they were seeking retribution.

He talked about how awful the Philippine army had been to Muslims. Years ago, he claimed, the government couldn't get control of the southern Philippines because Muslims were such fierce warriors, so they sent down Christians (his term) to colonize the area. They eventually outnumbered the Muslims and took away their land, he said.

He described AFP atrocities against Islam. He claimed there was a radar station on a high hill on the Zamboanga Peninsula, accessible only by helicopter, where AFP officers held Muslim women captive for their personal pleasure. (I couldn't help wondering how this, if it was true, differed from Reina's present condition with Janjalani.)

All of this, said Solaiman, was the justification for jihad.

Martin said, "Well, I guess Christianity is a little different. Jesus told us not only to love our neighbors but also our enemies. 'Bless those who curse you, and pray for those who despitefully use you [Luke 6:28].'"

A big sneer came across Solaiman's face. "Where's the justice in that?!"

Muslims fully accept the fact of sin and believe everybody is going to be judged. We had already agreed on that general concept. So I said, "I, for one, don't want justice, because I am a sinner. I believe Jesus is God and came to earth to die for my sins. I don't have to pay for my sin, because it is already paid for."

He looked at me and said, "I don't want *anybody* paying for my sin. I'll do my own paying."

Later on, Martin reflected on this remark and said to me, "You know, that's exactly what Solaiman is going to do. Someday when he stands before God, he's going to pay for his own sin, and it's not going to be pretty."

We had already been praying for our captors every day, but now we felt an even greater concern to pray for their salvation—that somehow the offer of God's grace would break through.

In this connection, it was interesting to hear Allah described as Most Merciful—"more merciful than there are bubbles in the ocean," Solaiman said. Yet Muslims weren't expected to imitate this quality. To them, a merciful person was a weak person. Allah could be merciful if he wanted, but his followers had to be tough warriors in search of justice.

Martin said at one point, "You know, Solaiman, I hope my children don't take up the same attitude you have. I hope my kids back in the States don't ever go get a gun and shoot some Muslim because of what you have done to us."

A look of shock crossed Solaiman's face. "Done to you? What's my sin against you? I've never done anything to you!"

Martin looked at me incredulously, as if to ask, *Can this guy really not see? He's taken us at gunpoint from our families, forced us through the jungle, starved us, subjected us to gun battles—and he thinks his record is clean?*

We talked with Solaiman about the Koran and how only two of our Abu Sayyaf captors seemed to have read it completely through, even though it is only a couple hundred pages long, shorter than the New Testament.

"If I were betting my eternal destiny on the teachings of the Koran, I'd sure want to know what it said," I told him.

"Eternal destiny? Okay, let me explain for you how Judgment Day is going to be conducted." Solaiman then proceeded to tell us that everyone will stand facing in one direction, like Muslims do when they start their prayers. Everyone who has ever been born in the entire universe will stand, *totally naked, for forty thousand years,* waiting for Allah to pronounce his judgment of whether they go to paradise or hell.

People will understandably get impatient during this long wait. They will start going to the various prophets. First, to Adam they'll say, "Please go to Allah and tell him to judge us. We can't stand it anymore."

But Adam will reply, "I'm not worthy."

Then they will go to Abraham. He will say that he isn't worthy, either.

They will go to David, Solomon, and even Jesus. "Please ask Allah to hurry up and judge us now; we can't stand it anymore." Jesus, like the others, will say, "I'm not worthy."

So finally they will go to Muhammad, the final prophet.

Success at last! Muhammad will intercede with Allah, who will judge humanity, consigning those with good deeds to paradise and condemning those who fall short to hell—unless they were fallen *mujahideen,* those who had died in holy war and were thus already rewarded.

With this way of thinking, clearly the odds of reaching paradise were slim to none. The Abu Sayyaf didn't mince words when speaking of those who had "fallen short," those who didn't see eye to eye with the Abu Sayyaf and were therefore "not really true Muslims." This included even such notables as Muammar Qadhafi of Libya and the Saudi royal family. In fact, Saudi Arabia was especially scorned for being soft on Muslim principles, as evidenced by allowing the infidel troops of the United States and other Western nations to use Saudi military bases.

It was tough to argue with such logic. Whether or not Solaiman's information was theologically correct, to him it was entirely reliable. Of course, when it came to personal holiness, the Abu Sayyaf had their foibles, too. On the one hand, they complained, "Why does Hollywood make all this junk, all this immorality and violence, and then send it around the world?" We tried to tell them that many Americans feel the same way and don't watch a lot of those movies.

But then, someone would say, "Hey, Martin, have

you seen *Silence of the Lambs* [or another film of that stripe]?"

"No. That's way too gory, from what I hear."

"Oh, we loved that movie! It was great!" they would reply.

Nor would the Abu Sayyaf ever think of turning away from a tempting situation. Temptation, in their view, was something to be eradicated from the world by rules, not something to resist through personal discipline. That's why they wanted an Islamic state. In such a place, there would be no bad movies, prostitutes, stealing, or cheating, because the rules would be so stringent that people would be afraid to do anything wrong. All the women would be dressed in such a way as to eliminate seduction. Thus, nobody would sin, and society would be perfect. To put it in Fatima's memorable phrase, "If you remove the temptation, there will be no sin."

Martin tried to counter this view by replying, "Scripture tells us that everyone is tempted, but you have a choice about what to do with that temptation. God always works on the heart of a person. It's not outside temptations that make us sin; it's our sinful heart, and God wants to change that heart.

"Christianity isn't a big list of rules. We don't have a manual for fasting or almsgiving," he'd tell them. "These things instead are supposed to come from your heart. That's what salvation is: a change of heart, rather than a change of environment."

They were not persuaded.

Our porch was almost the only level, clean place in the camp, so when it was time for sundown prayers, this became the location of choice. If Martin and I were sitting out there talking, we'd have to move. It was always nice to be out in the fresh air, so sometimes we'd just stand at a distance rather than go inside.

Then as darkness fell, Omar began his Arabic and Koran lessons for the benefit of the new converts, Sheila and Ediborah. We had no electricity, of course. He'd bring an empty soy-sauce bottle filled with kerosene and a rolled rag as a wick. I called it "the bomb" because it seemed so dangerous to me.

Of course, we, being infidels, weren't allowed to touch a Koran or even get near it. If it was inside someone's backpack, we weren't allowed to step over it, because that would pollute it somehow. More than once I was reprimanded for that. I finally got the point: Watch out for backpacks, and step around them.

:::::

The month of August and the first half of September turned into a longer and longer stretch of hiding, waiting, getting noticed by outsiders and having to move up the river, then back down the river, then somewhere else again. Days turned into weeks, and the hopes we had placed on departing hostages who had promised to work for our release grew dim. We were stuck with our lot; nothing seemed to be happening; the daily grind and Martin's nightly confinement on the chain became a never-ending cycle.

One time, Martin became very sick with a high fever and nausea. His joints ached. *Could he have malaria?* I worried. We had no way to tell.

In the medical bag was an antibiotic called Augmentin—a name neither of us recognized. But Ediborah, being a nurse, said it was okay and might help him. Of course, her practice of medicine wasn't exactly what we Westerners were used to; we had once heard her tell another hostage to take "two ampicillin tablets."

When I asked her if he needed to take the pills for seven days, she responded, "Well, you're supposed to, but when people are poor and the supply is short, we just take a couple so we can start feeling better." That seemed to be common protocol for her.

Nevertheless, in this case, Martin took a five-day course of Augmentin—and did start to feel better.

Fe dipped into the medical bag for an entirely different reason. One day I saw her coating her lips with iodine as a substitute lipstick.

"Fe, are you trying to make yourself look good?" I asked.

"Yeah. I just feel so ugly here, you know? There's no way to make yourself look pretty."

"Oh, Fe, look what happened to Reina. Don't try to make yourself look prettier than you already are. You don't want to get *sabaya*ed, do you?"

::::

Whenever the order would come for us to pack up, a deathly silence would fall upon the camp. My heart would begin to pound, and all conversation would stop as we began jamming stuff into our packs. I often found myself shaking uncontrollably, so much that I could hardly pack my things.

If we finished and the leaders hadn't yet decided which way was safest to move, we would just sit, terrified that a barrage of bullets would come flying at us any second.

The Abu Sayyaf never really had "a plan," it seemed. They just made it up as they went along. Sometimes we would get up in the morning, be told to pack up for mobiling, walk half an hour—and then sit three or four hours while they discussed what to do next.

One night after we had been walking for hours, we stepped off the trail shortly before dawn into a grove of banana trees. They put down a tarp for Martin and me, because it had been raining. We collapsed onto the tarp. I didn't even take my boots off; I was so tired and my feet were all muddy and awful.

In my exhaustion, I looked at Martin and said, "What is going to become of us?" Hot tears were streaming down my face.

Martin's next words just amazed me. With complete composure, he said, "We are going to get out of here, and we are going to go home." I heard that sentence from his mouth on more than one occasion. Every time it calmed me down. On this night, Martin grabbed my hand and we prayed together. We prayed for the strength we needed to keep up with the group. We asked that the Lord would shed his mercy on us and that he'd touch someone's heart to pay ransom for us. And then we went to sleep.

The next night, we were mobiling through the jungle when we came upon a river. We had no other choice but to wade into the water and walk to the other side. At one point, the water was more than chest-deep. Once we reached the other side, we were totally soaked and freezing. I found myself falling more and more as I tried to keep pace with the group in the dark. I tripped on a rock and landed down on my knees and hands so hard that it rattled my teeth. I just stayed there for a minute, while the whole group waited for me to move.

Oh God, I prayed, tears streaming down my cheeks, *how much longer can this go on? Is there a certain line that they need to cross, a breaking point where you say I've suffered enough? Where is it? Have they crossed that line yet or is this just going to go on and on?*

I heard no answer and somehow got up on my feet again to keep walking. A little way down the trail, I realized that I no longer had my *malong.* I cried all the harder.

When we were back at the river several days later, I saw one of the men with my *malong;* he must have picked it up when I fell. Of course there was no way I was going to get it back. For weeks I went without one, until Joel found a new one somewhere and gave me his old one.

::::

I was doing laundry in the river when Hurayra approached me.

"A new striking force has been commissioned, and I've been named the leader," he told me. "I'll be leaving tomorrow and I may never come back. I was wondering if you would sing me a song as a parting gift."

He had been so kind (relatively speaking) to Martin and me. I wanted to please him, but I knew I couldn't. "No, no, I can't sing for you, Hurayra," I said. "I'll just cry."

But he kept pressing me. My mind was racing, *What do I sing? A hymn or something secular?* I asked if he had any favorites.

"No, it doesn't matter. You just pick something."

So I started to sing the old John Denver song:

Almost heaven, West Virginia,
Blue Ridge Mountains, Shenandoah River . . .
Country roads, take me home
To the place I belong . . .

I suddenly realized what I was singing, and that's when I lost it. I made it through the chorus and then just quit, weeping in my heart.

"Continue, continue!" Hurayra said.

"I'm sorry, Hurayra, I just can't."

He walked off then to his mission, and I didn't see him again for several weeks.

::::

One evening not long after that, a young guard came to see Martin and me quite late. "Solaiman and Sabaya want to talk to you."

We followed the boy up a steep, slippery trail, finally arriving at a little house. Solaiman began the discussion.

"We want you to make an audiotape for the Muammar Qadhafi Foundation." This was the same organization that had put up (or at least passed along) $25 million the year before for the Sipadan hostages. This was a handy way for them to appear magnanimous and caring in the eyes of the world while simultaneously financing their Muslim brethren's jihad.

"There are several phrases we want you to use," he continued. "You should say that the Philippine government and the American government aren't doing anything for you. So even though the Foundation hates the U.S., maybe they would choose to help you personally, as individuals. And be sure to include the phrase 'We would be forever grateful.'"

We had been hoping and praying for some source of ransom money, but the strongman of Libya wasn't exactly who we had in mind. This certainly raised an interesting moral dilemma.

Of course, they weren't giving us a choice. This was an order: Make the recording.

Martin took his turn first. I noticed he conveniently forgot to say the American and Philippine governments were not doing anything for us. When he finished, Solaiman said he thought that it was okay.

Now it was my turn. He reminded me to include the comment about governments. Well, at that point, I more or less agreed with him; I didn't see any action being taken on our behalf. So I gave my little spiel, saying,

"I know that our countries don't see eye to eye, but maybe that would not stop you from helping us personally." I told them how much our children needed us. Then I said that we would be eternally grateful if they would help.

On the way back to our place, we walked hand in hand in the dark. "Do you think we've done anything wrong, asking Libya to ransom us?" I asked Martin.

"We did what they ordered us to do," he reasoned. "I've been told you are not held accountable for anything you're forced to say under duress. So I think it was okay."

Of course, when we got back, everyone wanted to know how it had gone. We gave a little review.

Ediborah then said, "You didn't mention the Filipino hostages, did you?"

No, we hadn't, we said. They had told us just to talk about ourselves.

"Well then, you know what is going to happen, don't you?" she continued. "You'll be ransomed out, and we'll be left here, and everyone will forget about us, because Filipinos don't matter. You are the ones the world cares about."

"No, no, Ediborah!" we protested. "We weren't trying to leave you out. We just followed their instructions!" Martin and I felt horrible.

August 21
Paul Jones first raises the topic of paying ransom in a phone call to Oreta Burnham. No conclusions reached.

August 25
Zach's football team wins its first game of the season; Mindy's soccer team loses its first game.

August 30
Jeff plays wide receiver for the Rose Hill Rockets freshman team as they win their opening game.

Two days later, we were called back for another meeting. This time they had us write out pretty much the same thing we had said on tape. Martin wrote:

August 15, 2001

To the Muammar Qadhafi Foundation:
   I am a citizen of the United States of America. For the past fifteen years I have been residing in the Philippines as a missionary with the New Tribes Mission.
   On May 27, 2001, my wife, Gracia, and I were abducted from Palawan where we had gone to celebrate our wedding anniversary. For the past 2 1/2 months we have been held by the Al-Harakatul Islamia on the island of Basilan. We are well, but we desire to return home. We remember that approximately one year ago your foundation was instrumental in the release of the European hostages taken from Sipadan. We are requesting that you would consider helping us also. I realize that our two countries have not been on friendly terms in the past but I hope that this will not hinder you in helping us as individuals. As parents we would really like to be returned to our family. They and we would be eternally grateful for your help.
   Thank you for your kind consideration of this request.

They put it in an envelope and said they would send it out with the next messenger. Maybe this would be the key to unlock our door of freedom.

CHAPTER 13

SEPTEMBER 11

(Rest of September 2001)

Muhammad had made it clear, our captors explained, that slave owners were to treat their slaves with respect and feed them well. This was part of the Muslim code of honor: "What we eat, you eat," they said.

"Muhammad even said that if we are eating corn grits [a less desirable food], our slaves should be eating rice [the preferred food]."

It sounded good. But as time went on and the budget supplies got low, we started hearing a new term: "personal." People would show up with extra goodies and, when questioned, would say, "Oh, this is 'personal.'"

Janjalani and Reina's hammock was strung fairly close to us, and I began noticing that whether there was food in the camp or not, they always seemed well-supplied. I would watch them enjoying their meal, and feelings of jealousy would swell up. By this time, hunger was a constant companion.

One time on the trail, we had stopped to rest, and Solaiman and Martin were having one of their substantive conversations. We had left our bags just a little ways back in the long grass. The next time I checked, I realized that some of the young Abu Sayyaf guys had gone through our stuff and helped themselves to a bag of little bite-sized candy bars we'd been given a few days earlier! I was incensed.

Martin and I had been so disciplined to ration those out, even though we wanted to scarf them all down at once. We split one early in the day—just a bite, really—and then split another one at night. And now they were all gone!

The next time I saw Reina, I unloaded on her. "These boys! I thought the Abu Sayyaf didn't steal! Didn't Muhammad say if you steal, you get your hand chopped off? If that were true, these guys wouldn't have any hands left!"

She must have told Janjalani, because the next day those boys were reassigned to a different group.

It helped that every once in a while, Joel brought some coffee or something else he could spare from his group. I'd always say, "Oh, Joel, don't bring us things! We feel so guilty because we never have anything to share with you."

"I want to do it," he replied. "My group always tells me, 'You can take this to the other hostages if you want.'" Apparently there were still a few fragments of kindness in the camp.

I think it was the hunger that made me start to see myself the way I really am. Instead of being happy that others had food, I was jealous and covetous. Or to cite another example: Haija—the one who had been especially cruel to us, the one who had beheaded Guillermo—had lost his hammock in a battle and was now having to sleep on the ground like us. I could tell his bones were hurting—and I sort of relished the fact that he was experiencing hardship, too.

I realized that when everything is stripped away from you and you have nothing, you find out what you really are down deep inside. What I was starting to see was not pretty.

(Soon after that, Haija and Daud were chosen to go to Jolo Island on a "secret mission" in connection with Sabaya's younger brother. We found out later that it was some kind of an arms deal. Soldiers spotted them there, and when they ordered the three to halt, Haija opted to run rather than be captured. He was shot and killed on the spot. The other two were taken into custody. I couldn't help wondering whether Martin's glasses were still in Haija's backpack.)

I felt even more conflicted about food one time when a fresh supply came into the camp, but the guys who had brought it were visibly upset. Someone asked what was the matter.

"Civilians—we killed civilians."

"How many?"

"Oh, eight or nine."

There wasn't time to continue talking; we quickly hit the trail again. Late that night when we finally stopped, Joel filled in the details. He was really good at keeping his ear to the ground and knowing what was going on.

Their initial plan, he said, had been to stop any jeepney and take whatever food was on it. Well, the next one to come by was loaded on top with sacks of rice for the AFP, but it also had a number of civilians inside. Sitting on top at the front was a *CAFGU,* a civilian who is deputized to help the Philippine troops. This kind of person gets a very small salary from the government and is supposed to maintain peace and order in a given territory.

The *CAFGU* was holding a gun. When the Abu Sayyaf stepped out from the woods to stop the jeepney, he raised his weapon. So the guys opened fire—not just at the *CAFGU* but the whole jeepney, mowing people down with their M16s. It turned into a massacre—men, women, children, everybody.

And when they finally took the weapon from the dead *CAFGU,* they found out it wasn't even loaded.

They then gathered close to twelve bags of rice—the ones that didn't have blood on them. They also carried off the passengers' purses and bags. In one they were excited to find a big can of milk. In another, which looked almost like a diaper bag, they pulled out a little girl's clothes, some panties, a washcloth, and a little towel. All of this was brought back to camp.

Martin and I sat there in shock that night when a captor brought us hot milk with sugar in it. We were so hungry we felt we needed to drink it—but our hearts ached. Martin prayed, "Lord, we don't know at what cost this food has come our way. We just pray that you would have mercy and give strength to the families of these people who have died." I sat there looking down into the cup and wondering if that little girl had survived—the girl whose milk we were holding now.

A few days later I found out that she had not. And to make matters worse, she had been the niece of one of the Abu Sayyaf raiders. He had helped gun down his own sister-in-law and niece.

When I learned this, I just gasped at the ruthlessness of it all. I asked Solaiman, "What did this guy think of that? Wasn't he devastated when he found out who he had killed?"

"No, that was just their destiny," he calmly replied. This was the standard explanation for any casualty, it seemed. No big deal. It was just to be accepted.

But if anyone else harmed a Muslim, they didn't dismiss it as the person's destiny at all; rather, it was an atrocity for which they vowed to seek justice. I thought to myself, *Isn't this a double standard?* But by now, I was learning to control my mouth a little better, so I didn't press the debate.

The gun skirmishes continued, sometimes briefly, other times at greater length. The random firing of artillery kept coming, terrorizing us all. At the end of one scary day, during the captors' evening prayers, my nerves were shot from the constant bombardment. Martin and I were sitting on the ground along a rocky trail, and I said something that may sound strange: "Martin, I just need to tell you good-bye officially . . . so when I get killed or you get killed, I'm not going to have any regrets."

He understandably looked up in surprise. What in the world was I saying?

"I'm serious, sweetie. We have had a wonderful life together. I've totally enjoyed being married to you. We've gotten along so well; our goals have been the same; we both love the Lord with all our hearts. I have never for one second regretted marrying you."

I went on to tell him he had such a wonderful sense of humor. I said although I couldn't claim God had called me personally to be a missionary, he had called me to be Martin's wife, and that was enough to make me happy.

Finally, he responded, "Honey, this is weird. I'm not sure it's even real healthy for you to be saying this."

"Well, it makes me feel better," I replied. "I hope we get out of this alive, but if we don't, I don't want to have missed the chance to say good-bye to you and tell you how much you've meant to me."

We longed to embrace each other for a tender moment as husband and wife. But with the Abu Sayyaf no more than ten feet away, we had to settle for just looking deeply into each other's eyes. And with that, we got back to the business of setting up for another night of sleeping under the stars.

:::::

Somewhere during this time, word arrived that ransom had been paid for Angie and Fe. "But we're not going to release you quite yet," Sabaya told them. Why not? His response didn't really make sense.

As soon as he walked away, the two girls justifiably showed their anger. After all, they had been living for this day. Now the money had been paid, and the Abu Sayyaf was reneging on the deal.

I finally said to them, "Just pretend he never said that to you. For one thing, he lies all the time and tells us to lie all the time. This could be just a little joke of his. You'll be better off not to worry about it."

At about the same time, we learned that Reina had finally succumbed to Janjalani's pressure and agreed to marry him, as opposed to being just his mistress. She had been told, "If we get married, then you aren't Abu Sayyaf property anymore; you're mine. I can release you whenever I get ready."

So a little ceremony had been convened, with either Musab or Fatima officiating. Martin and I were not invited.

Implicit in this, of course, was her becoming a Muslim. She didn't overtly choose to renounce her Catholic faith, but it was explained to her that this was just part of the package, and she would now receive tutoring in how to pray properly and read the Koran.

Meanwhile, no word came back from the Qadhafi Foundation, and about this time we started hearing about a wealthy Manila physician named Doctora Rose. She had been instrumental two years before in freeing a group of teachers and schoolchildren whom the Abu Sayyaf had taken. Now she was negotiating for our release, they said. She was going to pay $3 million for all of the hostages, not just the Americans.

Of course, Martin and I started getting excited. Finally, someone was going to break the deadlock.

She would call Solaiman, or Solaiman would call her to ask how things were going. She said that it would take two weeks to get everything together, and then we would be released. She was going off to a Hong Kong bank to get the money and would be back in one week.

After seven days, Solaiman called; she wasn't back yet—something about her needing seven *working* days to get the money, and Saturday and Sunday didn't count. But be prepared and be safe, she said; the money is coming.

A couple of days later she reported, "Yes, I've got the money. You guys start heading for the coast. I'll turn this money over in Zamboanga, and you arrange for a speedboat. We'll tell you where to meet up."

Solaiman began trying to line up a speedboat, but they didn't have enough cash. We heard him talking to an old classmate, saying, "Bring us the boat, and I'll just give you an OPM. I'll pay you when I can." (Solaiman told us that OPM stands for "oh promise me," a Philippine term for an IOU.)

Sure enough, the boat driver we hadn't seen since landing on Basilan showed up again in camp. We started slowly moving toward the coast. Our hopes began to rise. Maybe we would be able to rejoin our kids for the start of school after all. . . .

::::

And then on Wednesday morning, September 12 (Philippine time) . . . Solaiman was sitting in his hammock, listening to the news from Voice of America on his little radio. He often did that—either VOA or the BBC.

He called Martin over to his hammock. The two of them sat there, motionless, for a long, long time. I watched from a distance. *What is so engrossing on the radio?* I wondered.

Finally, my curiosity got the best of me and I could stand it no longer. I ventured over to Solaiman's hammock. By this time, Zacarias had come around, too.

Martin motioned me close to him. "Something terrible has happened in the United States," he said quietly.

He then described how two planes had hit the World Trade Center in New York, and another had hit the Pentagon. Thousands were dead. The world had been plunged into crisis.

Oh, no. How ghastly! Our hearts just sank.

Of course, the word spread rapidly through the camp. Guys huddled in little groups, talking and laughing and congratulating one another. Everybody was really happy that Muslims had done something treacherous to the U.S.

Martin and I retreated to sit quietly under our little tree. We had so many questions, so few answers. What would happen now? How would our country respond? Were the numbers of casualties exaggerated? Maybe it wasn't as awful as it sounded.

That night as we lay down on the ground to sleep, we quietly sang "The Star-Spangled Banner" together and prayed for the victims so far away.

The next morning, of course, Martin was over listening to the news again. At the end of the newscast, the VOA played our national anthem. The guys asked Martin to repeat the words for them, so they could know what the song said.

Martin got choked up as he began to recite, "Oh, say can you see, by the dawn's early light . . ." Everyone listened carefully. When he got to "the land of the free and the home of the brave," a sneer came across Solaiman's face, as if to say, *Ooooh, you think you're so brave? America has a lot to learn.* He made a snide remark along the lines of "We'll see how brave you are," or something like that.

The full impact of the horror could not reach us, of course, living in the jungle with no CNN or newspapers. What was riveting the rest of the world twenty-four hours a day in living color, we were catching only faintly as through a keyhole. Still, we knew it was a serious turning point.

Up until this time, our situation had seemed to be local, not global. Everyone had thought of us as just a couple of Americans in the Philippines (of course, there are many) who happened to be in the wrong place at the wrong time. Now, the geopolitical lines were more clear. A worldwide showdown was brewing, and Martin and I were clearly on the side of the enemy of Islam, in their view.

A few days later, after the buzz in the camp had settled down, we went to Solaiman. "This seems like a very selfish question for us to raise," we said, "given all that people in other parts of the world are going through right now. But we must ask: Has this attack changed our situation in any way?"

"Not at all," he calmly replied. "We already have a deal with Doctora Rose to exchange you guys for $3 million. Our word is our word, and we will not change that."

So again, we waited in hope.

::::

The following Wednesday would be Martin's forty-second birthday. I asked God to please, please get me something I could turn into a present for him—a candy bar, anything.

A few days before his birthday, some guys went out to get the budget and once again were spotted by soldiers. They ducked out of sight, but the soldiers fired a few rounds to scare them away. Right after that, the heavy artillery started up. We all went running down to the river and hid behind one of the banks while shells exploded on all sides.

We ended up mobiling to a place in the mountains where we had been before, spreading out our empty rice sacks to sleep. When I sat up the morning of Martin's birthday, out from under the rice sack crawled a little brown snake, heading for the woods! I sarcastically said to myself, *Oh, goody, we provided a warm place for him.* Then I told myself, *It's not worth worrying about. If I let my mind run wild, it WILL!* I pretended it didn't even matter. But I did wake Martin up and tell him that a snake had shared our sleeping space that night.

That morning our group had nothing to eat. We packed up to mobile again. As we were walking along, the Abu Sayyaf started saying, "Happy birthday, Martin!" Muslims don't believe in celebrating birthdays and are, in fact, quite proud of that. But they didn't mind saying happy birthday to Martin.

"How did you know it was my birthday?" he asked, perplexed.

"People have been calling in to Radyo Agong wishing you a happy birthday," they said. They even gave the names of Bob and Val Petro, our friends from Aritao.

At noon, the only thing to eat was salt from a bottle that was passed around the circle. We kept walking the whole day. As it got closer to evening, we stopped along a trail, and for some reason our group of captors didn't want us with them. So Janjalani and Solaiman had us moved to another group, which fortunately had some kind of soup. They shared with us, providing a little nourishment on Martin's birthday after all.

But I was disappointed that the day ended without anything I could give my husband as a present. I told him how badly I felt. He just smiled and said, "You can make it up to me when we get out!"

That evening I remember he had an interesting conversation with a captor named Ustedes Hail. This man was one of the most embittered fighters, passionate about regaining the Muslim homeland. He said the Abu

Sayyaf didn't want to have to do things like the recent massacre at the jeepney, "but the Christian world has just pushed us too far, and we're sick of it. When people are oppressed, you can't hold them back. It's just going to be this way until we are given what we want."

Martin kept his cool, as always, and gently probed for specifics. "Let's see—just what all is included in your homeland?"

"Tawi-Tawi, Sulu, Jolo, Basilan, southern Mindanao . . . ," he began naming off the islands in dispute.

"So, if you got these—if the government decided, for the sake of peace, to give them to you—would that be the end of your struggle?"

"Oh, no, no," came the quick reply. "That would be only the beginning. Then we would be obligated to take all of Mindanao; after all, it's a wealthy island.

"And then once we took Mindanao, we would take all of the Visayas [referring to the midsection of the Philippines, such islands as Cebu, Samar, Leyte, Negros, and Panay].

"Then when we were done with the Visayas, we would go next to Luzon.

"When all of the Philippines belonged to us, we'd move on to Thailand and other countries where there is such oppression. You see, Islam is for the whole world."

::::

We pressed on toward the coast, following Doctora Rose's instruction. We walked day and night for several days, until my feet were totally raw. Every time we walked through a stream, water and sand leaked in through the holes in my blue boots. Before long it felt just like sandpaper rubbing the skin off my feet.

At every rest time, I rinsed out my boots and shook out my socks. But still, my feet began to look awful.

We walked through several Muslim villages that were totally deserted. Some of them were quite nice; they even had paved streets. But the civilians had fled, knowing that wherever the Abu Sayyaf came, bloodshed followed. In fact, this pattern became so established that the military had begun using it as a clue: abandoned villages meant the Abu Sayyaf must be nearby. The terrorist leaders had even resorted to bribery at times, sending messengers to say to the village leaders, "Please don't leave. We'll pay you to stay in your area, and we promise not to harm you. But please don't give the *sundalo* a signal that we're here."

About this time Reina announced that she was pregnant. She told Janjalani, "If you want this baby to be healthy, I've got to be getting better food than I'm getting here." That was enough to get her released.

We got to a place where the Abu Sayyaf had stayed before. We could tell by the trash left behind: old, sun-bleached candy wrappers, fire pits, general garbage. Solaiman was on the phone, as usual, and also getting text messages, which is a big thing in the Philippines.

"Hey, let me read this one to you," he said to us. "See if you think you can guess who it's from." He then read: " 'Do you think I could come and spend some time at your place? Everyone is terribly upset with me right now, and I really could use a friend.' "

I looked at Martin and had no idea. He didn't, either.

"We don't know," he said. "Who is it?"

Solaiman read the message again, and then gave the sender's name. "It's from Osama bin Laden."

Could it have been true? Was the al-Qaeda mastermind feeling the heat in these days right after September 11 and looking for an obscure refuge somewhere? (I later learned that this same text message had been sent as a joke to millions of cell-phone users in the aftermath of

September 11, but at the time we had no way of knowing that.)

::::

That same day, we found out that Janjalani, Solaiman, Fatima, Bro—almost all the leaders—were leaving for "important business" on the outside.

I told Solaiman in tears, "You guys are going to leave us here and we'll have no leadership and no communication!"

"No, no, no—this is a good thing," he reasoned. "I'm going out to arrange for everything with Doctora Rose. The speedboat will come and get you. You'll be out of here in no time."

"Well," I said, "it's just really hard for me to stay in this camp of enemies. You are an enemy, but at least you have been an enemy we could connect with. You told us some of what was going on outside. Now you're leaving, and we're going to have nobody."

The look on his face said that he was completely amazed that I called him an enemy. In his mind, he was just a wonderful fellow.

Soon they trekked off on their "important business," which I thought was probably no more than finding a grocery store. They took two of the three sat-phones plus Janjalani's stash of money, which funded our food supply. We were left to the tender mercies of Musab, Omar, and Sabaya.

There was one silver lining, however. Janjalani gave us his hammock as he left. After three and a half months on the ground, we could finally be a little more comfortable at night—although two people trying to sleep in the same hammock is not exactly luxurious. We found out that two sets of shoulders at the same end was next to impossible. So we had to put our heads at opposite ends in order to get any rest.

Only on extremely cold nights did I start out with my back against Martin's chest, just to help us both stop shivering. Then before long, I needed to pivot the other way. A few nights I even retreated back to the ground in order not to be so cramped.

We stayed a few days there on that hill right beside the water. Looking across the valley, we could see a finger of ocean coming in toward a river. Across on the other bluff, we noticed AFP troops moving in and setting up. Meanwhile, all was now silent from Doctora Rose.

Could it be that the military had been using her to lure us to the coast so they could flush us out?

In fact, that is exactly what seemed to be the case. I personally don't think there ever was any $3 million, or that she ever intended to ransom us. The whole thing was a ploy to get us to a vulnerable place where the army could move in.

Martin's love affair with flying machines began on weekend trips home from boarding school.

The man of my dreams

A special place for a special question

Our wedding in
Kansas City, Missouri

Whenever Martin was in the air, I was at the radio, maintaining contact.

Jeffrey and I often visited Dad's "workplace" —the hangar.

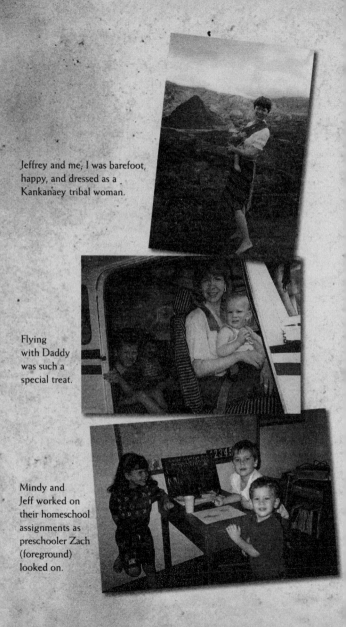

Jeffrey and me, I was barefoot, happy, and dressed as a Kankanaey tribal woman.

Flying with Daddy was such a special treat.

Mindy and Jeff worked on their homeschool assignments as preschooler Zach (foreground) looked on.

Filipino children loved the man with the red-and-white airplane.

In the tribal areas where we worked, kids come up with their own ways to have fun. In the background stands a typical tribal home.

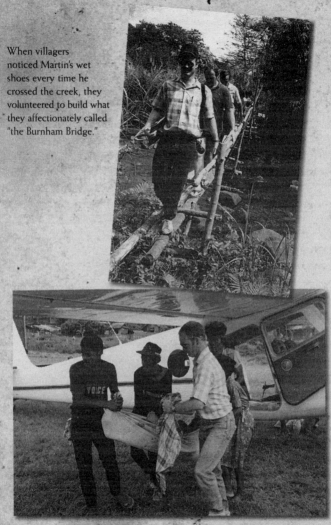

When villagers noticed Martin's wet shoes every time he crossed the creek, they volunteered to build what they affectionately called "the Burnham Bridge."

One of Martin's responsibilities was transporting patients to medical facilities.

Martin and me on our porch in Aritao

Dos Palmas Resort

Our first "proof of life" photo, taken in July 2001.
Sabaya is in full jihad regalia, Martin is wearing a scrub from the
Lamitan hospital, and I'm in my one-and-only long-sleeved shirt.

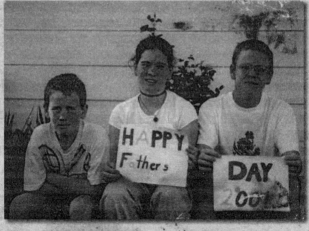

Zach, Mindy, and Jeff continued a family tradition of documenting each
Father's Day. This photo actually reached us in the jungle and we carried
it with us for the remainder of our captivity.

When Calvary Bible College named us "Alumni of the Year" in absentia, Martin's parents (left) and mine accepted the plaque in Kansas City.

My sister Mary in the Radyo Agong studio to make her appeal. When this photo was taken, we were fewer than twenty-five miles away!

Various writings that we
saved during our year of captivity

MGA KIDNAPPER!
MGA MAMAMATAY-TAO!

Abu Sabaya

Hamsiraji Sali

Khadafi Janjalani

Abu Solaiman

Isnilon Hapilon

PREMYO PARA SA IMPORMASYON
HANGGANG $5,000,000

The U.S. Government is offering a reward of up to $5,000,000 for information leading to the arrest or conviction of the terrorists responsible for the kidnapping of Martin and Gracia Burnham, and the kidnapping and murder of Guillermo Sobero. If you have any information about any individuals committing acts of international terrorism against U.S. persons or property, please contact the U.S. Embassy.

PREMYO PARA SA KATARUNGAN

www.rewardsforjustice.net

1-800-10-739-2737 (Manila)   1-800-877-3927 (USA)

Kung cell phone ang gagamitin ay tumawag lamang sa 02-526-9832/9833/9834

LAHAT NG IMPORMASYON NA MATATANGGAP NAMIN AY ITUTURING SIKRETO

The U.S. government offered a reward to pressure the Abu Sayyaf leadership. (Isnilon Hapilon is Musab's given name. Hamsiraji Sali is not mentioned in the book because we knew him only briefly. We called him Hamsi.)

Sheila (from left), Fe, and Angie celebrated their freedom in Manila. Our captivity continued another six and a half months after this photo was taken.

Ediborah Yap (center, seated) in happier days at the Lamitan hospital where she worked

SPECIAL EDITION

The Wichita Eagle

JUNE 7, 2002

- GRACIA BURNHAM MOVED TO HOSPITAL
- WHITE HOUSE CALLS FAMILY IN ROSE HILL
- BURNHAM FAMILY THANKS COMMUNITY FOR SUPPORT

MARTIN BURNHAM KILLED; WIFE GRACIA RESCUED

Filipino nurse also dies in firefight with rebels

Within hours of being rescued, I arrived at the U.S. embassy in Manila.

Woman to woman: President Gloria Macapagal-Arroyo wanted to hear the story of my rescue and Martin's death.

60A

Home at last! Zach (striped shirt) and Jeff met me at the Kansas City airport. My sister Mary was my wheelchair driver.

My wonderful, all-grown-up daughter, Mindy

It was so good to see everyone at the groundbreaking for the new home being built for us in Rose Hill.

The Martin Burnham family today . . . we continue to move forward with gratitude for one another.

In Loving Memory of

Martin Burnham

High Flight

Oh, I have slipped the surly bonds of earth
And danced the skies on laughter-silvered wings;
Sunward I've climbed, and
joined the tumbling mirth
Of sun-split clouds - - and
done a hundred things
You have not dreamed of - -
wheeled and soared and swung
High in the sunlit silence.
Hov'ring there,
I've chased the shouting wind
along, and flung
My eager craft through
footless halls of air.
Up, up the long, delirious
burning blue,
I've topped the windswept
heights with easy grace
Where never lark, or even eagle flew.
And, while with silent, lifting mind I've trod
The high untrespassed sanctity of space,
Put out my hand, and touched the face of God.

John Gillespie Magee, Jr.
September 3, 1941

The funeral program included this quote from Martin's last message in his home church: "I wasn't called to be a missionary. I wasn't called to the Philippines. I was just called to follow Christ and that's what I'm doing."

CHAPTER 14

WEDDING TIME

(October–Mid-November 2001)

It was about this time that my ever alert husband, being mechanically inclined, discovered that his handcuffs didn't stay shut anymore. Something had rusted through.

We didn't tell the Abu Sayyaf, obviously. We let them think they were locking him up securely every night. But in Martin's mind, he knew he was free.

"What would people think," he worried, "if they knew I could have escaped any time from here on, and I didn't? Would they think I'm a coward?"

I just smiled and said, "They would know you were staying with your wife until the opportunity presented itself for both of us. And they'd respect you for that."

Now in hindsight, I suppose there was one night when we maybe could have gotten away if we had really been on our toes. They put us in a farmer's little shelter on the very edge of the camp. Right beside us was a big hill that went straight down to the ocean.

Could we have slipped out in the middle of the night, gotten down the hill without being noticed, and somehow fled to a town or army camp? It's hard to say. Anyway, we were exhausted that night and went to bed as usual. We woke up the next morning and hadn't given it a thought.

We always asked the Lord, "If there is an opportunity and you want us to try to escape, please make it clear to both of us, and give us the courage to act." That time never came. We never sensed it was what we were supposed to do.

I do remember one conversation about the fact that

I wasn't guarded nearly as closely as Martin. "Maybe I should just go off for a walk and not come back," I hypothesized. "You could follow me whenever you got the chance." I wasn't entirely serious about this, but it was something to mull over.

Not long after that, I stood up to go to the bathroom out in the woods. I ended up staying there for a while just to cry. It must have been half an hour before I returned.

Martin's face was as white as a sheet. "I thought you were gone!" he exclaimed under his breath. And then he confessed, "In fact, I believed it so much . . . that I ate your share of the rice!"

We broke up laughing. But in that moment, I saw how afraid for me he was, and how we both needed to be careful not to do anything foolhardy.

Meanwhile, the daily dangers continued. The AFP was clearly on to our scent. One day the firepower jumped to a whole new level, beyond automatic rifles and artillery shells. Helicopter gunships with big machine guns blazing out the sides swarmed over our heads. What an ominous sound they made as they swooped down. Every pass seemed like it would mean our last breath.

And as if that wasn't enough—a group of A-10 Warthog attack planes then came screaming across the sky dropping real bombs. How in the world we avoided getting hit I will never know. Out of this whole battle, the Abu Sayyaf suffered no deaths and only one injury.

It rained that night, and there were no trees to which we could rope our *toldas*. So we just dragged the plastic

October 5
Abu Sayyaf defectors lead AFP troops to the remains of Guillermo Sobero.

over us for a little protection. We awoke the next morning totally soaked.

We walked much of that day, then returned to the same place to sleep the next night. The following morning, we were walking down toward a riverbed when, all of a sudden at the front of the line, shouts rang out, followed by new gunfire. We all hit the ground. The Abu Sayyaf were not intimidated in the least; they plunged ahead to see what was up. Soon we heard a scream. In time we learned that they had encountered three men at the river and managed to behead one of them, a *CAFGU*. The other two had run away. Just another normal day of jihad, apparently.

Whenever there was going to be a battle, in fact, Musab took out a little piece of cloth to make a headdress. He wanted to be sure he looked like a warrior. No matter what we were doing or how much we were running, he'd take time to arrange his headdress so he'd look cool if he died.

We just kept going and came to a farm where a young boy was working. I couldn't help thinking he was about the age of Jeff, our son. We all rushed for the ripe bananas that lay on the ground—all except Martin, that is, who was roped to a guard. I stuffed about four or five bananas into my pocket.

Meanwhile, they tied this poor kid up with his hands around a tree. I could see he was absolutely petrified. A little bit later, one of the nicer guys ordered that he be loosed. But they couldn't afford to let him go, now that he knew who we were. So—we had ourselves a new hostage. I felt so sorry for him.

::::

We walked all that night and the next day. Once when we sat down to rest, Sheila came and sat down beside me.

This was a bit unusual; she normally sat with Ediborah, both of them being Muslim now.

"I have a really big problem," she began.

"What is it?"

"Omar is *sabaya*ing me." Her face dropped.

I said, "Sheila, you're already married! How can they do that to somebody who is already married?" My heart really sank, because if this came to pass, it meant that none of the rules applied.

"I don't know. But I have to move in with him tonight. I just don't know what to do about it."

"Sheila, I am so sorry," I said. "I suppose you have to do what they tell you to do. But if I can help you, I will."

::::

A few nights later, as we were walking in absolute darkness, Martin and I were allowed to proceed without a guard for a change. I was hanging on to his shirt so I wouldn't get lost. The artillery kept getting closer and closer. I was praying out loud, "O God, save us. O Lord, keep us safe. Please keep us safe. Don't let bombs hit us. Lord, keep us safe. O God, help us," over and over. I know Jesus talked about not needing to babble on and on, repeating yourself in prayer. But I couldn't help it. I was just too strung out.

On another night we walked until three-thirty in the morning. Totally exhausted, we lay down in a field. All of a sudden there was a big thump, like an artillery shell, but close. Suddenly the sky lit up with a bright light, and then a parachute opened up as a light floated to the ground right near us. Anyone watching could have seen our whole group.

"Oh, no, they found us!" Martin said, leaning toward me. "They're just confirming that we are here."

But we were so tired that we just lay there. Early the

next morning, we heard the rumble of what are called "6 by 6s"—huge trucks with flatbeds on the back. These were full of soldiers. We got up and began moving out of this sheltered area toward a big field in a valley. Within minutes we heard somebody yell, "There they are! Hoy! It's Abu Sayyaf!" The guns started blasting.

Well, this is it, I thought as we ran and dropped, ran and dropped. Assad, the guard assigned to us, was handcuffed to Martin. They began running straight for a tree—and I saw what was going to happen, like it was in slow motion. Sure enough, Assad headed for one side of the tree and Martin the other.

"Stop!" I yelled. Just then they hit that tree. Both of them went flying.

Assad's side of the handcuffs (the rusted side) came off, of course, but still left a huge gash on his wrist. Martin badly wrenched his shoulder. They both just lay there for a minute.

Sabaya came running up and said, "What! What! Are you trying to escape?" He began chewing Martin out right in the middle of the battle.

Martin answered, "Sabaya, calm down. We are with you. We are not trying to go anywhere. We just had an accident. We are with you. We are with you. Don't worry about us."

They quickly put the handcuffs back on, still not realizing that they were rusted. Martin shot me a look, and I breathed a quick prayer of thanks to God. Soon we resumed running, as bullets kept whizzing past our heads. We eventually got into some woods. Along the way I lost my black *terong,* which had always been so hot and oppressive. I thought, *Yes! Finally I can start wearing something else on my head.* I really hated that thing.

Once again, the AFP didn't actually pursue us. We walked less than an hour and stopped to set up camp. By now the exhaustion and fear were nearly more than I could take. I sat just bawling my eyes out along the trail, with my legs pulled up and my arms around my knees, sobbing.

Angie came up to me and blithely said, "Gracia, what's wrong?"

How can she ask that after we've just been through a horrible battle? I thought to myself. At that moment, I'm afraid *Gracia* didn't respond very *graciously.* I looked at her and said in a snippy tone, "Nothing's wrong, Angie. Everything is fine. It is just such a beautiful day. There's nothing to worry about, no reason to cry." Angie looked surprised, then sat down quietly beside me.

The next day, Martin was asked to write a letter to an AFP colonel that would be read over Radyo Agong. It said, in essence, "Please negotiate for us, because even if you kill some of these Abu Sayyaf in battle, you are not going to kill them all. With God as my witness—and I have been a witness here during this whole thing from our capture last May until now in October—only nine have died. It is not the big numbers that you are publishing."

We had heard on the radio that the AFP claimed to have killed twenty-three Abu Sayyaf back when they called in the A-10s to bomb us. That made no sense from our vantage point; there weren't more than ten or twelve Abu Sayyaf to target in that particular place and only one of those was hit. What really happened, I heard, is that the AFP ended up bombing their own people on the ground, so that there very well may have been twenty-three casualties, but twenty-two were caused by friendly fire.

October 10
The outside world gets its first photo of Martin and Gracia. They sit beside a smiling Sabaya who flashes a *V* for victory.

"Even if you do kill off all these Abu Sayyaf around us," Martin concluded, "there are lots more, and they cycle in and out. They go on a break, and then they return. So we must get down to negotiations in order to solve this problem."

::::

Soon after that, the three remaining Filipino women in our hostage group had their own crisis to face. It was announced that all three would be *sabaya*ed.

Musab had chosen Ediborah.

Moghira, a leader in charge of the "blocking group" that brought up the rear whenever we mobiled, had chosen Fe.

And Sabaya had chosen Angie.

All three of these men were already married, of course. Musab had two wives and Sabaya had three, although he had recently divorced one of them. But that didn't seem to limit the men's appetites for current companionship.

The girls were all so upset. Angie's and Fe's ransoms had already been paid. Ediborah, meanwhile, was a married woman (as Sheila was). What a horrible thing this was for them. We had prayed and begged God not to let this happen. Yet here it was. I could not understand God's way in this. I was just sick.

When the time came to move, Fe sat holding on to me and saying, "I'm just not going to go. I'm going to stay here with you."

"Yes, Fe, you can do that," I replied.

Soon one of the guys came and told her to move over to Moghira's place.

"No, I'm not going to go."

The guy took the message back, then returned to say, "Well, he just wants to talk to you."

So she went. She begged Moghira, "Let me stay with the Burnhams tonight up in the house—please, please!"

Soon she was back all excited. "He said I can stay with you! I don't have to go with him."

But in a few minutes, the messenger was back. "He wants to talk to you again."

Fe never returned to us that night.

When you are in a hostage situation, you just do what you have to do. You put the emotions of it all in the back of your mind and don't let yourself get carried away with how you are doing or how you are feeling. Otherwise, you would go crazy.

Since I have been back in America, people have often asked me, "What were you feeling at this time or on that occasion?" To be quite honest, I can't remember. My defense mechanisms had risen up to block the feelings. I was disciplining myself *not* to put feelings into words. My job was rather to put one foot in front of the other, to stay alive one more day. We just kept going and praying that we could get back to our children. That's all.

::::

By this time, everyone was miserable from the cold. Musab and Ediborah had some extra plastic with which they would make a little windbreak.

I went to see Fe every day just to make sure she was doing okay. Bless her heart, she always had some food for me—perhaps a banana, or what they call *bianbons,* which are green bananas that have been roasted, then mushed up and put into a banana leaf, then roasted again. They were really good. She was always happy to see me coming, and we enjoyed talking together.

One night she brought us a big Tupperware cup of hot soup made of sweet coconut milk with little flour balls (like dumplings) in it. The mixture also included corn, some kind of dried beans, and I think some bananas. It was really, really good—what a wonderful gift. We enjoyed it so much that night.

Before she left, we prayed with her. The next day, she came back to tell me something, although I could see that she was reluctant. Finally, she got it out.

"You know that soup I brought you last night?"

I nodded.

"Uh, that was from my wedding feast. Moghira really wanted us to get married. I didn't want to, but . . . like he says, if I'm his wife, he has the say about what I do. He can release me, and it doesn't have to be a committee decision."

"Well, thank you for telling me," I replied. "If you felt you had to do this, we're behind you. You hang in there."

We prayed together then as we had before, but this was the last time. We didn't want Fe to put herself at risk with Moghira. As far as religion was concerned, Fe always told me, "I'm still a Christian. Even though I do their praying and everything, I haven't converted to Islam in my heart."

The same scenario unfolded with Angie. She was quickly put to work as Sabaya's secretary, bringing us letters she had prepared for him so we could check the English. Some were about the Golden Harvest boys, wanting the local Muslim organization to send them on *hajj* (pilgrimage to Mecca) and also to college. All of the Golden Harvest boys had converted to Islam, or so they said.

Occasionally, one of the guys even tried to solicit Martin's interest. "Are you ready to convert to Islam?" they would bluntly ask.

Whenever I heard this, I started framing a dramatic rebuttal in my mind, something along the lines of *Christ is my only Lord and Savior, and I will never deny him no matter what you do to me!*

Martin was much more astute. The Abu Sayyaf already knew where his loyalty lay, and so he elected not to pick a fight. "Hmm, well, you know, my father is a Christian. His father before him was a Christian. Going even further back, my family has always been Christian. . . ."

At about this point, they would give in, saying, "Yes, I understand that you have a long heritage." And the subject would be dropped.

Sheila never married Omar. I'm not sure he ever asked her; I think he was afraid his other wife would be upset. Musab, however, started pressuring Ediborah to be his wife. But she held out for a while.

(Months later we learned that Solaiman, who was supposed to be out finishing arrangements with Doctora Rose for our release, had instead headed to Jolo Island and picked up two more wives in addition to the one he already had. The rest of the Abu Sayyaf were pretty upset about that. "He's off having fun while we keep suffering in the jungle," they complained.)

Whenever Martin mentioned how much he missed his children, Musab brushed him off with a comment about the hardship of being away from his own much larger brood. "It's harder for me," he said. "You miss your children three. I miss my children nine."

::::

More battles, more running in the rain, more missed meals, more desperation. During those days, I began to notice the weight just falling off Martin, especially in his shoulders. I could see his shoulder blades sticking out. Never a big man to start with—he weighed 72 kilos (158 pounds) when we were captured—he was now turning into a scarecrow.

We stopped for the Muslim prayers one evening and

then kept going. We came to the road and began walking along it in the darkness—something that always made me nervous, because it left us too exposed. But by this hour, we were all just kind of brain-dead, putting one foot in front of the other.

All of a sudden, right in front of us, shooting started. There were soldiers on the road. We ducked out of their sight. In the ensuing chaos, Joel was lucky enough to escape, which reduced the main hostage count down to six. Several of the Golden Harvest Plantation boys also got away, one of whom was carrying the medical bag. We were glad for them, of course, but also depressed that once again, we were still in captivity.

The loss of the medical bag meant that now we didn't have medicine or scissors—a serious loss for us all. A few days later, the one remaining sat-phone quit working; Sabaya's rather lame explanation was that "the thunder hit it." (Thunder?) Whatever the cause, we knew we were steadily losing our connections to the outside world.

My biggest physical problem at this point was with my feet, which had begun to ooze a clear pus. I put them out in the sun whenever we stopped. I tried to think of something else to make them heal.

In my backpack I had been carrying a bit of sunscreen. I was tempted to throw it away, because we really didn't need protection from the sun, what with all the clothing I was required to wear. Martin also had to keep his head covered. But I began reading the ingredients on the sunscreen bottle, and noticed aloe as well as vitamin E.

I told Martin, "Okay, maybe this will help my feet. It's going to sting like the dickens, but I'm going to try it anyway." I grimaced as I put it on, but it did seem to help.

Another thing that helped my mental outlook, if not my body, was remembering Scripture I had memorized long ago. I would have given anything to have had an actual Bible, of course. But that obviously was not going to happen.

One Sunday I found a piece of paper and began writing down all the promises of God that I could recall. My wording wasn't verbatim in every case, but I came up with quite a few:

> I will never leave thee / He careth for you / Will supply all your needs / I'll prepare a place for you / I'll come again / Honor parents & your days will be long / If we confess, he will cleanse & forgive / Ask & it shall be given to you / He that believeth in me, tho dead, shall live / Acknowledge Him & He'll direct your path / If any man open the door, I will come in & sup w/ him / I've loved you w/ everlasting love / When He appears, we'll be like Him / He'll perform a good work in you / I will not leave you comfortless, I will come to you / And lo, I am with you always / He that believeth in me shall not perish but have everlasting life / Delight in the Lord and He'll give you the desires of your heart.

What a comfort it was to review these eternal truths. In the face of the most dreadful circumstances, these were the words of the One I could depend upon.

A couple of days later, when I was in a slightly less spiritual mood, I thought of another divine promise to add to my list!

> Vengeance is God's. He'll repay.

Early on Monday morning, October 15, Sabaya came over to tell Martin to get ready to do a live radio interview. Although the sat-phone had gone dead, we did still have one cell phone that could be used if we could find a transmission tower close by. In addition to giving a prepared speech, Martin would respond to questions from the outside. Of course, Sabaya outlined five complaints against the West that he wanted made, which Martin duly jotted down on a banana leaf, since nobody seemed to have any paper that day.

1. United States support of Israel against the Palestinians
2. Oppression of Muslims everywhere
3. World sanctions against Iraq and Libya
4. Continued presence of Western troops in Saudi Arabia
5. Support for the Philippine government's goals in Muslim Mindanao

Soon the phone connection was made and the discussion began. When asked how he was faring, Martin said, "Well, I'm very tired and weak, and frightened. My wife is very tired and weak. We've both lost a lot of weight from walking a lot."

In a few minutes, the interviewer asked what message the Abu Sayyaf had for government officials, both in the Philippines and the United States, since the broadcast was being widely heard. Martin duly went through the list, as instructed.

But before the interview ended, he managed to get in some personal notes: "We would like to wish our daughter, Mindy, a happy birthday. She has her birthday in two days on October 17. So, this is our first opportunity to send them news that we are alive."

He also got a chance to address the AFP's rescue attempts: "Please stop. . . . Our lives are often in danger. Unlike the local hostages, it's impossible for me to escape. . . . I'm always tied up. I am always in the center of the group—not like the locals who are often sent to get water or sent to do small errands. The repeated rescue attempts and especially the artillery and the air strikes have been very frightening because they're so random. They cannot rescue me with an artillery attempt, and they cannot rescue me with an air strike. We will only be killed, and our children will only be orphans."

At the end, he summarized: "The Abu Sayyaf is going to survive this operation, but the hostages will not. Eventually, the hostages are going to succumb to sickness, and eventually some of the hostages are going to be killed." Thus, he conveyed that negotiation was the only sane answer.

Sabaya, meanwhile, took his turn on the air to keep up the bravado. He noted that President Arroyo would head to Washington the following month for a state visit. "It would be very embarrassing if she goes to the U.S. with the bodies of Martin and Gracia," he observed.

The only response to the interview in the days to come, as far as we could tell, was more pursuit by the AFP, more shelling, more raids. Things were not pretty. Everyone wanted this to be over, even the Abu Sayyaf. It had already dragged on much longer than anyone expected. With increasing frequency, guys in the Abu Sayyaf went AWOL. They headed to town for supplies and never returned.

October 17
Mindy's twelfth-birthday parties are held at school and home. Her best present: a tape (from Radyo Agong) of Martin wishing her a happy birthday.

November 12
U.S. Representative Todd Tiahrt comes to Rose Hill to visit Martin's parents; he also stops at the middle school to address students.

The lack of leadership skills became more and more apparent. We ended up back in the general area where the jeepney massacre had taken place. Apparently, our leaders thought that the people, being loyal Muslims, would feed us and take care of us—forgetting that just about everybody in town had lost a son, a daughter, or a cousin in the shoot-out. These people were so angry with the Abu Sayyaf that they not only refused to help us but also went straight to the military asking for protection.

The crazy part was, the AFP didn't believe them, because there had been no recent reports of sightings in that area. So one night, some of the villagers went outside with their own guns, shot into the air all around town, and then ran back to the military claiming that the Abu Sayyaf had attacked them. Obviously, we didn't hang around this village very long.

::::

We began hearing that they wanted to release a good number of people—the rest of the Golden Harvest boys, the farm boy we had recently captured, and the Filipino women hostages. After all, Angie's and Fe's ransoms had already been paid, and the Abu Sayyaf were not hopeful of getting any money from the nurses' families back in Lamitan.

Sure enough, the rumors proved true. To mark the start of Ramadan, the Muslim holy month of fasting, on November 15, a major release was set up.

Oh, the emotional good-bye we had. I told Fe to call my parents and tell them I loved them. From my pocket I pulled out my wedding ring at last and pressed it into her hand. "When you get to Manila, give this to the New Tribes Mission office, okay? Tell them to send it to my daughter, Mindy, in case I don't get out. If you lose it, that's okay—don't worry. Just *don't* let the Abu Sayyaf get their hands on it!"

She promised she would. I gave her my dead watch as well.

Of course, Martin and I added, "You tell them out there that somebody needs to do something for us. Somebody needs to pay our ransom."

We had by then settled the debate—in our minds, anyway—of whether that was the right thing to ask. Martin had reasoned, "It is not our responsibility to figure out how a ransom payment is used. If we can trust the Lord for a million dollars, which is something totally beyond our reach, we can trust the Lord that that million dollars never buys a weapon or blows anybody up. These guys can just as easily send the money to their wives so they can live in luxury or something."

At the very last minute, Musab decided he wasn't going to let Ediborah go. He was a stubborn man and very proud. I think the only reason he made her stay was to show the group that he was the emir, the boss, and what he said went.

After many hugs and tears, the group began to make their way down the hill. But an hour later, they were back; they'd spotted soldiers at the bottom of the hill.

We mobiled to a different place where civilians were found who were willing to take the group into town. So

November 14–16
Paul Burnham and Gracia's sister, Mary Jones, travel to Washington to lobby their representatives as well as the Philippine ambassador for more action. Two New Tribes Mission executives also attend.

November 16
Mindy prepares a Philippine meal for a school project. She takes pictures to send to her parents.

we said good-bye again. I just wept when they left. I was happy for them, but I knew I was losing the companionship of girls I'd come to love.

Three or four hours later, they came back again! The civilians had failed to find out what time the jeepney left for town. So they would have to try again early the next morning.

We put up hammocks for the night. Martin and I were assigned a place right in the middle of all the activity—in fact, it was between two trees and directly over a big trash pile of banana peels, coconut husks, and marang skins left from cooking. Somebody decided this was a good place for our hammock. The flies were horrible. This only depressed me all the more.

Early the next morning when the girls left again, I cried, but I didn't make any more speeches or give them hugs. I just kind of waved at them as they went by. I thought about Job, of whom the Bible says, "He sat down among the ashes" after his whole life had crashed (Job 2:8). That is exactly what I was doing.

Everyone was very quiet the rest of that day. The excitement in the air turned into a real sadness. I could tell that Omar missed Sheila right away.

Meanwhile, the thought began to dig into my mind that maybe, just maybe, this kind of a day would never come for us. After all, time was passing by. Every scheme that had gotten our hopes up had dwindled away. What was it Solaiman had said back on the speedboat that first afternoon? "We will make demands, and we will deal with you last." We were indeed left for last now, along with Ediborah. The rustling of the wind in the jungle trees only reinforced the loneliness in my heart.

CHAPTER 15

THE PACKAGE

(Mid-November–Mid-December 2001)

Ediborah and I had not spent all that much time together up to this point. My social life had seemed to revolve more around the needs of Fe and Angie. All this changed now that Ediborah and I were the only two women left in the camp, surrounded by some forty male captors.

A capable woman about my age, mother of four, Ediborah had been a nurse supervisor at the Lamitan hospital. Her husband had left her shortly after the birth of their last child, a son, six years before. She talked most about her oldest son, Jonathan, twenty-four, and how reliable he was. He worked for a fishing company in Zamboanga and sent or brought money home whenever he could. I could tell she was really proud of him.

Ediborah and I both needed to get our minds off the fact that we (along with Martin) were the last remnant now, so we volunteered for jobs. The guys had stolen a cow and her calf and had begun to butcher them—a skill they seemed to just naturally know, like tying your shoes. I'd never done anything like this, but Ediborah had, and so we said we'd cut up the meat.

That was easier said than done, because *bolos* were in short supply, especially sharp ones. We worked together that day, with me holding the meat while she sliced it thin, so we could then salt it and smoke it on the fire to preserve it. We actually had a good time.

I wondered to myself, *Now how does stealing this beef fit into the* mujahideen *code? I thought they didn't do that.*

Musab came around at one point, and I decided to

ask him. Ediborah interpreted my words into the local dialect so he would understand better.

His answer was simple: "The civilian is nothing; the normal person is nothing. The *mujaheed* must go on." In other words, the fighter in holy war must have what he needs, regardless of the ramifications.

I pressed Ediborah a bit more. "But what if you get to the point of having an all-Muslim state? If people steal a cow in that situation, they would get their hand chopped off whether they're *mujahideen* or not, right?"

Her next answer was classic. "If we need it, it's not really stealing."

I thought back to June, at the Lamitan hospital, when hostages began looting that patient room of its supplies. The logic had been the same. Human nature seems to find ways to justify its wrongdoing, to move ahead with what serves its self-interests, and then to figure out an explanation so it doesn't sound so bad.

By the time Ediborah and I finished working with the meat, our hands were covered with blood, and we were sweaty. "Let's go to the river for a bath," she suggested.

"Well, sometimes they won't let us." The guys often didn't like to stop what they were doing and stand guard down at the river.

"They'll let us go," she said. "Just come with me and don't even ask." With that, she started off, and some of the guys scrambled to follow, as required.

November 19
President Arroyo arrives in Washington to assure President Bush that her military can handle the rescue. She also has lunch with Rep. Todd Tiahrt, who comes away "optimistic."

November 19
Jeff attends his team's football banquet.

::::

The month of Ramadan had begun, when Muslims are allowed to eat only before sunup and after sundown. That rule didn't apply to Martin and me, of course; they didn't care when we ate. They called us to the fire before sunup to get our food, and we just saved it until later. We ate half of it for breakfast and the other half for lunch. Then we ate supper with the group after sundown.

The odd thing was, although Ramadan is called a time of fasting, these Muslims ate *more* during this lunar month. Food preparation started in the early afternoon, and they were very meticulous about their cooking. They wanted to have everything ready right at dusk, so they could promptly "break the fast." They looked at their watches time and again, and they discussed whose watch was correct. But they all waited for the leadership's signal that it was dark enough to begin eating.

We began noticing that when they were divvying up the budget, they fixed extra treats, like bananas mixed with sugar, but we only got our normal little pile of rice. "We can't give you any of this," they said. "It's for us because we're fasting—so we need more." The logic of that always seemed to escape me.

But then speaking of treats—a day or so later, a box arrived for Martin and me! I was over at the fire with Ediborah when she said, "The emir has some glasses for Martin."

"What did you say?!" I thought I had misunderstood her.

"A package came in for you last night. The emir has your eyeglasses."

I went dashing off to find that box, because I knew if I didn't claim it right away, it would be pilfered by the

Abu Sayyaf. If it had any food in it, I knew I couldn't depend anymore on them stopping to screen the ingredients for shortening; they were too hungry now. I had to find that box immediately.

Sabaya had it. "Is that box for us?" I eagerly asked, even though I could see the New Tribes Mission marking on the outside.

"Yes, it is. But I have to look through it, because it might have some kind of microchip or homing device in it, so they'll know where we are."

"Sabaya, trust me—our mission would never do that!"

"Well, I have to look through it." With that, he turned away. A crowd began gathering around him.

I went back to where Martin was just being unchained from the tree after a night of sleep. "Martin, a box came in for us last night. They're going through it right now. Maybe you'd better go over there and claim it, or there is going to be nothing left!"

He immediately headed that way. When he got close, Sabaya said, "Oh, don't come over here; we'll bring the box to you."

"I just want to make sure that we get it," Martin said, standing his ground. Sure enough, he saw items starting to be removed from the box. One of the guys was already holding a package of Snickers bars.

Meanwhile, I went to get the glasses from Musab. He handed them over, a new pair from the same optician as before. When Martin put them on, a big smile came across his face; he could see clearly again, after so long! We were both so thankful.

November 21
President Arroyo calls Martin's parents in Kansas to express her concern.

In time, Sabaya finally brought us the box. "I had to take out the Cheez Whiz, because I really like that stuff," he said with a smile. "But the bulk of everything is still here for you."

We sat in our hammock and began pulling out our treasures—everything from cookies and crackers and peanut butter and bouillon cubes and soup mixes to letters and pictures. There was a *Newsweek* magazine with a cover story about the U.S. military buildup in Afghanistan. It had pictures of the weaponry they used—such as night-vision goggles and various guns. We knew the Abu Sayyaf would be interested in seeing the pictures even if they couldn't read the articles.

We began making little piles of all the wonderful things. But at the same time, we couldn't stop thinking about those Snickers bars. The bounty we had wasn't quite enough somehow. And then we looked at each other and said, "You know, this box has arrived from our mission out of nowhere—and we're complaining about what the Abu Sayyaf took? We should be rejoicing in the Lord's goodness."

We decided we needed to share. Martin began going from group to group, giving out spices, soup mixes, and cookies. I gave one of the two deodorants to Ediborah, plus some peanuts. She was very happy, and so were the others.

All of a sudden, Martin and I looked at each other again and realized something incredible: It was Thursday, November 22—Thanksgiving Day! We had asked the Lord earlier in the month to send us something nice for Thanksgiving, and he had done it!

November 22–24
The Burnham children spend Thanksgiving with Grandpa and Grandma Jones in Arkansas.

Of course, I had asked for things before—a gift for Martin on his birthday—and been disappointed. So I hadn't really expected God to do anything this time. But here was a whole box of food, and it was so humbling. The Lord showed us he could bless us even when we didn't have any faith. How we enjoyed that package!

We were a little apprehensive that the *Newsweek* might cause trouble as people began seeing how well-prepared the American troops were for battle. But it had the opposite effect. The guys eagerly passed the magazine from one to another, studying the pictures and even ripping out some of them to save. They were totally intrigued. Martin and I had to fight to get to read the articles ourselves.

By now, of course, President Arroyo had made her U.S. trip, and we were still alive instead of in body bags in the cargo bay of her plane, as Sabaya had threatened. Actually, she had said earlier on the radio that she would be escorting us back home as her gift to the American government. It sounded good to the Filipino audience, but obviously, it hadn't happened.

Over the months, we had heard so many rumors about our being ransomed. But because the president of a country said, "They are almost out; I'm going to take them to the States with me," we couldn't help but hope.

A day or two after Thanksgiving, she came back on the radio to report that her time in Washington had been very productive, and she had called our parents to say we would be home by Christmas. We just laughed when we heard that. We knew it wasn't going to happen.

::::

That Saturday, the guys brought in some gabi, which is a kind of stalk with a leaf on it, similar to rhubarb, only three or four times bigger. They cut it up and boiled it, then poured off the water because it was poisonous, then put in new water and boiled it again. Gabi is similar to cassava, which has a high arsenic content; if it's not fixed right, it'll kill you.

That night, the cooks must have been in a hurry and taken a shortcut, because while I was eating, my mouth began to itch, and my tongue started swelling. This had happened once before with gabi. I knew to back off immediately.

During the night, I woke up with severe chest pains. I wondered if I was having a heart attack. Then I thought back to the gabi at suppertime. I lay awake for much of that night and was glad I hadn't eaten more.

Early the next morning, which was Sunday, Sabaya called us over to say, "We've got a television reporter coming in. You are going to do an interview."

This was interesting. We didn't know whether to be glad or apprehensive.

"This is your chance to let the world know what poor condition you're in," he continued, "and that they need to ransom you. Gracia, if you could cry a little bit and be upset, that would help."

I looked at him and said, "How many days recently have I *not* cried?"

"Oh, yeah. That will be no problem for you."

Sabaya went on to tell Martin to mention two mediators: Sairin Karno, the Malaysian ex-senator, and somebody named Yusuf Hamdan. He rattled off those names like I'd say John Smith. Martin replied, "Well, when I start talking to a camera, I'm not going to remember." So Sabaya grabbed a piece of paper and wrote out the names.

🌐

November 30
Bryant Gumbel of CBS's *The Early Show* does a live interview with Martin's mother, daughter, and sister-in-law.

Within minutes we were ushered down the hill. On the way, I thought to myself, *This could be good. Maybe we'll get to say happy birthday to Zachary!* He would turn eleven in a couple of weeks, on December 13.

Waiting for us was a young woman in khaki pants and an Adidas sweatshirt, with her head appropriately covered, of course. She had no film crew; instead, she held a small video camera in her left hand. She introduced herself. "Hello, I'm Arlyn de la Cruz from Net 25 television."

I gave her a hug and said, "Thank you for coming." I was struck in that moment that someone like this had actually been able to find us! The AFP had been trying for six months, and all of a sudden, here was a TV reporter right in front of my face. What I didn't know at the time was that this young woman was a personal friend of Janjalani's. She prided herself on getting into dangerous places and coming out with gutsy, award-winning interviews.

Accompanying her was a man named Alvin Siglos, a boyhood friend of Sabaya's. He stood around the edges taking his own home videos.

The Abu Sayyaf, meanwhile, encircled us like a choir, brandishing their weapons. The heavy-gauge barrel of an M-57 mortar was intentionally placed right over Martin's shoulder. Sabaya stood with arms folded across his black shirt with the "No Fear" logo—a fitting mark for him—ready to throw in comments along the way.

Martin looked gaunt in his brown plaid pullover shirt and brown *pantos*. When he spoke, he clearly articulated the message that we were in desperate straits and needed help. "I would say to my own government," he said, "could you negotiate or talk to these people?"

Throughout the interview, his tone was controlled, almost flat, without flair of any kind. He seemed to be conveying to the viewer, *I'm walking a real tightrope here.*

I'm not telling you the tenth of it, but . . . fill in the blanks, okay?

Meanwhile, I did what Sabaya wanted me to do and what I felt inside: I let my emotions show. My voice quivered at times as I said, "We're always hungry; there's never enough food. This is no way to live. There's no way to take care of yourself. . . . We've been forgotten. We need someone to show us some mercy. Is there no one in this whole country who can help us?"

After the interview, Arlyn went over to sit by Sabaya's hammock for more conversation. Martin and I went back to our place.

"I really just want to talk to her for a while," I told Martin. "There's so much I want to say off camera."

"Then go over there. Tell Sabaya you want to talk to her, woman to woman. He'll understand that."

I did. We began to visit. Arlyn also promised me a day at a spa when I got out. I told her I'd never been to one and would look forward to it.

She told us that September 11 had really hurt our chances, because now the U.S. was mad at terrorists and would never pay anything. As far as other sources of money were concerned, the stakes had grown too big for ransom. And besides, the Philippine generals and government officials would need their cut. It was not very encouraging news.

She was hungry, and it felt good to be able to share crackers and peanut butter with her. She clearly sympathized with how awful our plight was. She ended up giving me a red sweater. I gave her letters to forward to our families. We had written them just in case we got a chance to send them out with someone.

While there, I learned that a new plan was being hatched. Sabaya said, "Arlyn, you can go out and sell this footage to CNN or some network for at least a million dollars—maybe two million. Just send it back to us directly for their ransom, and then we can let them go. You'll get to be famous, we'll get paid—everybody will be happy."

Sounded good to me! (None of us knew in that moment, of course, that the market value of the interview was not nearly so huge. CBS ended up paying fifty thousand dollars.)

"Even if I can't sell this to some foreign media," Arlyn added, "maybe my church, Iglesia ni Cristo, could help me put something together to help you." This is an indigenous denomination that's very large, with some unusual doctrines; for example, they believe that when Christ returns, not only will they rise to meet him but their *buildings* will go up as well, all of which have the same architecture across the Philippines. Attendance at weekly services is mandatory, complete with a sign-in procedure for enforcement.

Soon the reporter was gone, and we immediately mobiled out of that place, in case the military found out what had occurred. Would this interview get anyone's attention? So many other attempts had produced nothing to this point. We didn't expect miracles, that was for sure.

::::

The longer Ramadan goes on, the more irritable its observers become from the odd eating schedule. Someone told us that in some Islamic countries, there's a lot of road

December 7
Arlyn de la Cruz's jungle interview airs on Net 25 in the Philippines.

December 11
Mindy's school Christmas concert is held. A special video tribute is given to the victims of 9-11 as well as Martin and Gracia.

rage and street brawls near the end. It's as if people are just sick of the regimen.

I guess during Ramadan, you're also not supposed to have sex—although maybe that rule is like eating and applies only to daytime hours. Musab loaned me a rule book once that outlined all the requirements for those who disobey. I had to chuckle at one that said, "If you inadvertently have sex during Ramadan, here's what you have to do to make it right."

I looked at Martin and said, "Excuse me, but how does a person inadvertently have sex? I don't know!"

Meanwhile, of course, earning points with Allah had to go on. One day a captor named Lukman brought Martin and me a huge plate of bananas boiled in coconut milk. "Thank you!" we exclaimed. "How nice of you!" We assumed this was an act of almsgiving on his part.

It got to the point that there just was not enough food to support everyone. We were all scrounging for nutrition. At one point we had nothing but *carabao* hide for three straight days. They put the skin into the fire to burn it, then scraped it to remove the hair and soften it up, then burned it again, then scraped it again, over and over. At last they cut it up into chunks with a *bolo,* then boiled it for a long time.

What all this effort produces is a hunk of fat with extremely chewy skin on it. But by the time we put salt on it, it didn't taste as bad as it sounds. Of course, when a person is extremely hungry . . .

I found a piece of paper and, for the first time, began making some daily notes, like a journal. It was mainly a record of how long we walked, whether it rained or not, what food we managed to get, and how we slept. On Thursday, December 13, which was our son Zach's birthday, I recorded, "I feel like a dirty animal—muddy, wet, stinky. Asked God for a nice place to take a bath."

A day or two before, a delegation had been sent out to get budget. In the process, however, they had met up with the AFP. One person was killed, and a couple of others were separated from us for a while. The rest came back empty-handed. Now we would have nothing.

On that Thursday morning, I said to Martin, "It's Wednesday night in the States—midweek service time in at least some churches. People are praying for us right now."

"Yes, that's true," he replied.

Just then another group of guys came into the camp. They had leftovers from the night before. But they weren't allowed to eat them during the day—so they gave them to us! I believe God answered prayer to relieve our hunger that day.

Finally, we got to the last day of Ramadan, which calls for a huge feast. We had walked for three days straight, from early morning to late at night, to get to a certain farm that would have plenty of fruit and vegetables, they said. At last we came to the top of a hill, and there it was.

This farm even had a well, which made it possible for us to have our first bath in four weeks. Ediborah shared some of her soap with us. Everybody was in a much better mood.

We began preparing a feast. One of the guys brought a kind of large, light green squash to me, with a *bolo* knife. "Peel this and cut it up," he said.

I looked at the huge *bolo* and thought to myself, *How is this supposed to work on this squash?* Obviously, I

December 13
Zach's eleventh birthday. CBS manages to attend the party. Zach has to blow out his candles four times for the camera.

had no cutting board, and I could just see myself cutting off my finger trying to wield this big blade.

Someone had given us a spoon with a fairly sharp edge on it. Retrieving the spoon from my pack, I was able to skin the squash. It wasn't a pretty sight by the time I finished, but at least the job got done.

And once the sun set that Friday, we enjoyed a wonderful meal for a change. The only thing was, it was cloudy that night, obscuring the moon, so Ramadan was not officially finished after all. We got to do it all again Saturday night.

Martin and I were sharing a toothbrush, which didn't make for the best dental hygiene. When one of us got sores in our mouth, soon the other got them, too. My tongue always seemed to be sore. I don't know if it was caused by stress, lack of nutrition, or getting burned by the hot coffee because I was too hungry to let it cool down.

We finally learned to skip brushing if we thought we were just going to make the other person miserable.

I knew we needed to be flossing, too—but with what? We realized we could accomplish this by unraveling the rice sacks, which were made from a woven plastic fiber.

Water purity was not exactly a refined science. More than once we noticed that our rice tasted like soap, because one of the cooks had grabbed a pail of water from the same area of the river where people were bathing.

A popular shampoo brand in the Philippines is Sunsilk. We'd say to each other, "Hmmm—this is very good rice, with just a hint of Sunsilk!" Or, "This *viand* [anything that goes on top of rice, like a sauce] is really good, with just a sprinkle of Tide."

In fact, Martin's humor released my tension more than once. One day as we were walking along a river, I could hear Martin humming to himself. When we got to the next stop, I asked, "What song were you singing back there?" expecting to hear some great anthem of the faith.

"Theme song from *The Beverly Hillbillies*!" he replied. We both broke up laughing.

On another day, we were climbing a hill, and when we reached the summit, I was totally exhausted. I flopped down on the grass to cry. Martin looked at me, and instead of trying once again to comfort me with profound sentiments, he pulled a line out of a comedy routine by the Christian comedian and singer Mark Lowry in which he mimics a talk-show announcer: "What happens when two women love the same man, and that man is reaaally ugly? Stay tuned—we'll be right back!"

With tears still wet on my face, I absolutely split up. We just howled there on the hilltop and started telling each other more Mark Lowry jokes. I'm sure the Abu Sayyaf were wondering what on earth had happened to the American woman—she normally sits and weeps because her heart is broken and she's dead tired, but this time she's cackling!

Another time Martin entertained me by retelling a movie he had seen on his most recent long, trans-Pacific flight—only after all the big setup, he wouldn't tell me the ending. I was going crazy—"Come on, Martin! Finish the story!"

He never would.

CHAPTER 16

SILENT NIGHTS

(Mid-December 2001–Mid-January 2002)

Christmas was now only ten days away, although we had no outward reason to look forward to its coming. Our kids at home were no doubt busy with school concerts and parties and shopping—we could only imagine. We expected the twenty-fifth of December to be just another day of rugged mobiling through the steamy jungle.

About this time, Ediborah and I had several serious talks about Musab's pressuring her to get married. She always said, "Is it sinning for me to do this? I already have a husband [although she was estranged from him]. How can anyone have two? Of course, sooner or later, he's going to force me anyway."

As before with the other girls, there was no simple answer I could give.

Then late one night, somebody brought us some hot coffee and an *apam,* one of the little Muslim pancakes. How nice—a midnight snack! Sure enough, a day or so later, while Ediborah and I were making supper, she said, "Do you remember when they brought you the snack?"

"Yes."

"That was part of our marriage feast," she said with quiet resignation. "We're married now. Musab really wants to have a son."

"Well, Ediborah, you've done what you felt you needed to do."

The Abu Sayyaf had told her that this made her first marriage null and void, because her first husband had been a "Christian" (their term for any Filipino who wasn't Muslim).

It was hard to tell how sincere Ediborah's conversion

to Islam really was. She told me she hadn't truly meant it
in her heart. But then out came some phrase like "I do believe in the holiness of jihad"—whatever that meant. I
looked back at her with big eyes and mainly kept quiet.

::::

Sabaya, meanwhile, announced that he would be leaving
us for a few days to get the negotiations "wrapped up."
He was clearly unhappy that so many others had let him
down: Solaiman, Doctora Rose, and even Arlyn de la
Cruz, from whom nothing had been heard. Now he
would go get a boat and take care of things himself.

As much as we tried not to think about it, Sabaya's
trip did raise our hopes. Maybe President Arroyo's pre-
diction that we would be out by Christmas was going to
come true after all.

Several times he sent runners back to the camp with
instructions for Martin to write a letter of complaint
against Arlyn. The one dated December 21 read:

> Martin,
>   There is a good news you just wait for my announce-
> ment through Radyo Agong about your release.
>   And regarding the letter of complain against Arlyn
> & Iglesia ni Cristo just do it.
>   After your release just do something to help Alvin
> Siglos because Arlyn betrayed him after all the efforts he
> has done about your release, and you must also thanks
> to Sen. Sairin Karno because he is the real key of your
> release.
>   A. Sabaya

Martin composed a letter regarding the Arlyn de la
Cruz matter as instructed, even though we didn't understand the deal and didn't see how it would help. It was

carried out of the camp. Like so many other letters, we never saw any fruit from the effort.

::::

At every new place, it was necessary to clear out underbrush in order to string up our hammocks and have space to cook. In fact, the Abu Sayyaf were notorious for whacking down all kinds of trees, whether it was necessary or not.

In one particular place, there was a tiny bamboo tree growing right beside our hammock space. Martin was ready to chop it down. I said, "Oh, wait, wait! Maybe that can be our Christmas tree." Not that we had anything with which to decorate it, but still it would have been a nice symbol.

Unfortunately, we ended up having to mobile out of that place before Christmas anyway.

On December 23, two of the group went out again—and returned with a packet of letters for us from the mission! Bob Meisel and Jody Crain from the NTM office in Manila had put together a wonderful assortment in a box, complete with an inventory list that showed everything from peanut butter to chocolate-chip cookies to cheese to soup mixes to magazines. But none of the items made it to us; apparently, Sabaya's group was enjoying them while out "negotiating" for us.

We read the list to Ediborah and talked about how different Christmas would have been had we gotten the

⊕ ———————————————————————————

December 19–21
Paul and Oreta Burnham and Mary Jones go back to Washington, again with New Tribes colleagues. Two of them, Kathy Ryff and Margie Clark, deliver a petition to the White House with more than twenty thousand signatures calling for the Burnhams' release.

box. But we didn't mourn as before. We turned our attention to the letters, which were such a lift to our spirits—funny at times, poignant at others. Oreta Burnham had played stenographer for each of our kids, taking down their dictation so that we had a full single-spaced page from each of them. We found out the kids had gotten to go to my parents' place in Arkansas for Thanksgiving.

Mary, my little sister who lives in Ohio and is the spitfire of the family, hinted at her efforts with government officials to get some action: "I have lots to say. . . . We are working hard on this! Do you follow me? I want you to know that. Stuff is happening. You keep your chin up."

She also said she'd been to see our kids in Kansas. "I went to M[indy]'s basketball game this morning. She is also in the choir and has solos because of her great voice. She has good fashion sense and dresses cute. Z[ach] is a nut, and we have decided that we need to trade Z and myself [to the Abu Sayyaf] for you and Martin. We would drive everybody crazy, and be asked to leave!"

She also gave Martin and me an assignment: Think of appropriate boy and girl baby names, since she and her husband, Lance, were planning to start a family.

Martin's brother Brian and his wife, Arlita, wrote: "We feel guilty having so much when you are poor and hungry. . . . We wish we could send you a truckload of chocolate."

Our oldest, Jeff, after describing his football season, turned reflective: "I saw your videotape that the reporter took. I was happy to see your faces but VERY sad to see your condition. (Why do they cuff you, Dad?) . . . I want to tell you how proud I am of you. You guys are the best parents I could ask for. I'm looking forward to seeing you again. (By the way, Dad, that beard looks good on you.)"

A two-and-a-half-page, single-spaced letter from my niece, Sarah Tunis, included long quotations from Ephesians 1, James 4, Colossians 1, and Philippians 1, among others. This became our "Bible"—we read it every day.

Christmas Eve came, and I sat in the hammock singing carols, while Martin gathered firewood. Normally, that was my job because he would already be chained. But on this evening, he volunteered for the job.

It had rained hard that afternoon. As rainwater ran off the *tolda,* we gathered it to drink. Then that night, we had *sindol,* which is hot coconut milk that can be mixed with a variety of things: chopped bananas, chopped sweet potatoes, pieces of coconut. We also had marang, a banana, and rice with *viand.*

Eating in the dark was always difficult, of course—but we couldn't start the fires until sundown, the time we knew any soldiers in the area would have stopped searching for us and returned to their tents.

The night was cold. Lying there, I heard a plane go over. I heard some of the guys still up, cooking "personal" food, and it made me very sad.

At midnight on Christmas Eve, the Philippine custom is to have a little feast. Guess what: Ediborah came over at midnight to bring us crackers and cheese! Wherever did she get them? I have no idea. But we were grateful for her generosity.

In previous years I had loved planning ahead for Martin's Christmas gifts. Whenever I heard him talk about an author he admired, I'd go write down the name lest I forget, so I could buy the book.

December 24
Two million subscribers to *U.S. News & World Report* get the Burnham story, with a picture, as part of a three-page feature on Philippine terrorism entitled "Opening Up a Second Front."

He liked cowboy stuff. One day, before our capture, I was walking down the street in Malaybalay and saw a shop called Chico Craft. In the window I saw beautiful carvings. That sparked an idea. I happened to be reading the *Little House on the Prairie* books to the kids at that time, and the front of each chapter had a woodcut of an old Western main-street facade.

I took this in to Chico Craft and asked, "Could you make a shelf to mount on the wall with three pegs underneath for hanging things, and on top a carving of this scene?"

"Oh, yes, we can do that." It turned out marvelously and took its place in our living room. Martin was so pleased with that gift.

This year in the jungle, however, I had to face the reality that I would have no gift for my husband at all.

When we awoke the next morning, breakfast was plain rice with nothing on top—not even salt. I had begun brushing up on the Christmas story from the Bible, which I had memorized as a kid. So I recited parts of Luke 2 for Martin that morning: "And she brought forth her firstborn son, and wrapped him in swaddling clothes, and laid him in a manger; because there was no room for them in the inn. . . ."

We reread our letters from our family and talked about what they would be doing on this special day. On Radyo Agong our captors heard greetings from both Doug and Brian Burnham and told us, which warmed our spirits. We took a piece of paper and drew a checkerboard on it, turning little twigs and pieces of foil we had saved into the light- and dark-colored pieces, so we could play the game. We spent a lot of time singing and praying and talking together.

Lunch turned out to be a bit of fish soup, hot tea, rice, and roasted bananas. Martin started not to feel well after that and took a nap. We heard artillery even on this day, but not close to us.

In America, the postholiday question when everyone returns to work or school or church is "Did you have a good Christmas?"

Yes, Martin and I had a good Christmas. Why? (1) We had something to eat, and (2) we didn't have to pack up and hike. In our minds, that made the day positive.

::::

On December 30 or so, word came that we were to mobile to a certain place to meet Sabaya and the others who had gone with him.

Every relocation, of course, meant finding a new spot for our hammock. Martin used to drive me crazy redoing it. He would get it all set up between two trees and then say, "Okay, why don't you sit down and test this?"

I'd sit down. "Fine—it feels really good."

"Well, it looks to me like this end is a little higher than the other end. Why don't you get up, and I'll retie it."

After this process was completed, I would again pronounce it perfect—and he'd say, "Well, I may have gotten that just a bit low. Could you stand up again? I'll retie it."

This would go on and on until I'd say, "Enough

December 26 and following
Christmas presents for Martin and Gracia remain unopened in a corner of the Burnham living room in Kansas.

December 28
The Joneses and Burnhams gather at the Kansas City home of Gracia's brother, Paul. The families have an extended prayer time for Martin and Gracia.

December 29–31
Rep. Todd Tiahrt travels to the Philippines to meet with President Arroyo and military leaders.

already! The hammock is fine. You're just like my brother-in-law Bill!"

A few years before, I had gone with Bill one day to shop for apples. At the first grocery store, we walked through the fruit section, and he must have picked up every apple to examine it, but ended up buying only four or five. Then we went to a few orchards, where he used the same scrutiny. He felt the apples and hemmed and hawed. Sometimes he bought a few, and sometimes none at all. It was hilarious.

Now in the jungle, I joked with Martin, "I hope you never go apple shopping with Bill. You two would take weeks and probably buy nothing!"

Every time after that, whenever I got annoyed with his perfectionism, I said, "Someday you and Bill are going to go shopping for apples!" And we'd laugh together.

When we joined up with Sabaya, we learned that he had not been able to go to town as intended; too many soldiers were watching. But a negotiation was still proceeding, he claimed, and things were going to turn out fine regardless.

He told with some pleasure how the AFP had tried to poison him but failed. He had hired a man to get food for the group, and one day he had put in a request for fresh fish.

The man, however, had leaked this information to the military. The AFP had offered to provide the fish. The toxin they added had made the Abu Sayyaf members very sick. One of them named Bashir had almost died, in fact. But in the end, they were all alive to tell the story.

The next day we said good-bye to Moghira and another leader, Umbran, who took their groups off on a striking force. This left just fourteen of us: Ediborah, Martin, myself, and eleven captors.

While gathering up some marang under a tree, we

noticed an unusual airplane overhead. It wasn't the kind that usually tracked across the Basilan sky. All eyes turned to Martin.

"Is that the kind that's going to bomb us?" people wanted to know.

"Oh, no. That's a twin-engine plane, the kind flown by a dignitary or someone very important."

Sabaya looked at us and said, "Well, on the radio I heard that your congressman is here from the United States, from Kansas."

We looked up again, longingly this time. Could it be that Representative Todd Tiahrt, our congressman from the Wichita area, was actually so near at hand? A warm feeling came over us. Maybe he would be able to bring about a breakthrough where so many others had failed.

That night Ediborah came up with special treats to welcome the new year: tiny pieces of cheese and some crackers. The next day, a newspaper arrived in the camp. A new letter had arrived from "them"—again, we didn't know who—requesting another "proof of life." Sabaya somehow came up with a camera, and so we posed sitting together and holding up the newspaper with its date.

Martin had to show Sabaya how to load the film and where the shutter button was. With every attempt at pressing it, however, Sabaya jerked the camera wildly. We told him he needed to hold still, but we weren't very successful.

Ediborah posed with us for a couple of pictures, too.

::::

The coming of the year 2002 meant that we no longer had a calendar. We'd been referring to the small 2001 pocket calendar I had rescued from our identification on the speedboat, but now we would have to keep track of the date in our heads. More than once there was disagreement in the camp about what day it really was. But Martin, with his organized mind, invariably turned out to be correct.

Soon the military pressure increased again, and we retreated inland to the higher elevations. One evening, as the sun was setting, we were going through our nightly routine before bedtime—I would put on an extra shirt and extra pair of pants; we'd brush our teeth; we'd pray together; Martin would carefully stow his glasses in their case for safekeeping—when suddenly, we heard wood being chopped not far away.

"Sundalo!" came the word. "Just on the other side of the hill!" They were chopping down trees and setting up their hammocks.

We very quietly packed up and took off in the opposite direction, down to a river and then along a trail.

There, in a quiet moment, we heard a soldier talking into his radio! Obviously, there were more soldiers in that direction, too. We just kept walking. Late that night, we stopped along a river for a few hours of sleep. Early the next morning, we moved on into the mountains, where we spent a relatively peaceful four or five weeks.

Martin and I gave this place a name—"Camp Contentment"—because that is what the Lord was teaching us there.

"You know," Martin said to me one day, "here in the mountains I've seen hatred; I've seen bitterness; I've seen greed; I've seen covetousness; I've seen wrongdoing." I nodded my head vigorously, thinking back to incidents I had observed as well.

But then he surprised me. He hadn't been talking about the Abu Sayyaf as I had assumed.

"I've seen each of these things in myself. The Lord has been showing me how incredibly sinful I am." He then proceeded to go back through the list.

"Hatred? At times I have hated these guys so strongly. When we were getting cheated out of food, I'd sit and think, *Wow, I wish I had a big pot of rice, and they were the ones chained to a tree. I'd sit there and eat it all in front of them.*

"At other times, when one of them pulled out a 'personal' snack from their stash and ate it, I coveted it rather than being happy for that person."

He kept going through the list. We talked about how our hearts are wicked, and how we had rationalized that by saying we were the ones being wronged and so our feelings were only "natural."

"But Jesus said to love your enemies . . . do good to those who hate you . . . pray for those who despitefully use you," Martin continued. "He said we were to be the servants of all—and he didn't add any exception clause like, 'except for terrorists, whom you have every right to hate.'

"Let's just ask the Lord to work out some contentment in our hearts and teach us what he wants us to learn."

We decided to do that. We committed our situation to the Lord. I can't say we became models of saintliness after this. But we did get to the point where we could go stand at the fire and accept a lesser amount of food than everyone else without complaining or going back to our spot discussing our portion size. That had become a bad habit of ours, and we were able to stop it.

I saw Martin's servant heart with regard to one of the fellows we called "57," since it was his job to carry the

January 2, 2002
The Philippine government accepts U.S. offer of "training and logistical support."

January 3
Martin's sister and brother-in-law, Walt and Cheryl Spicer, return to their teaching at Faith Academy in Manila.

M-57 mortar. He seemed perpetually in a bad mood. I had said to Martin that I thought the name was fitting for him since he'd been a grouch for at least fifty-seven days in a row!

Only later did we find out that he suffered from chronic headaches.

Martin went over to him one day when he was sitting, just moaning from the pain. We had gotten some ibuprofen in a recent package, and Martin gave him one. "Here, this will help your head," he said. "I'm praying for you."

Not long after that, "57" was sent out on a mission of some kind. When he returned, he was totally different toward us. Even when he was cranky with others, he was always nice to us. Martin continued supplying him with pain reliever whenever he sensed the need.

::::

This resolve to be content, however, was put to ever increasing tests. In mid-January when the radio reported that American military had arrived in the Philippines to help train the AFP, it really made Musab angry. He took it out on Martin by "forgetting" to send someone in the mornings to unchain him from the tree.

If Martin, however, asked to be freed in order to go to the bathroom in the woods, they freed him and did not rechain him afterwards. He found himself debating whether to say he had to go even if he didn't, just for the benefit of getting loose.

It got to the point where if Martin didn't say anything, he was chained twenty-four hours a day.

Meanwhile, I was really craving privacy, especially while going to the bathroom. Finally I dragged all the branches that people had chopped down while arranging their hammocks and formed a barrier up against a hill so

Ediborah and I could avoid being watched. The only trouble was that the brush pile proved attractive to snakes. One day she showed me a snakeskin she had found.

I said with a touch of fatalism, "Well, good! If one of them bites me, that'll be the end of me, and I'll be outta here." At this point, death seemed a pretty good alternative to living the rest of my days as a hostage.

By then, both of us were getting so little to eat that our monthly periods ceased. In the earlier months there had been enough money to keep the women supplied with what they needed, and when anybody was ransomed out, she passed her supplies down to the ones remaining. Now the Abu Sayyaf were low on money—but it didn't matter anymore.

Ediborah was worried, however, that perhaps she had become pregnant, which Musab very much wanted. I told her, "Don't worry about it—my period has stopped, too. It's the lack of nutrition." In fact, I was right. Several months later, when the diet improved, our cycles resumed. Only then did we have to resort to using rags a few times.

As for toilet paper: I enjoyed a grand total of two rolls during the entire twelve months of captivity. I made them last as long as possible!

::::

Staring at the same tree day after day after day, Martin started planning businesses he might launch if we ever got back to Kansas or Arkansas.

"What if I set up a flight school? Or what if I lined

January 16
Brian and Arlita Burnham return to their mission work in Papua New Guinea.

January 17
Jeff calls Radyo Agong to wish his mother a happy birthday.

up weekend seminars for pilot certification?" He began estimating the income this might bring and the costs it would entail.

Several times Martin mentioned that when he got back to the States, he'd like to try to find the Taylorcraft single-engine plane that my dad had owned long ago. He wanted to buy it back if he could.

What about starting up a doughnut shop? We picked out a certain spot for it in the parking lot near the IGA and the Pizza Hut in Rose Hill.

One day we even talked about him running for mayor of Rose Hill! We outlined a campaign, complete with candidate qualities and local issues to be tackled. How about a town swimming pool? What would stimulate more business? It was stupid, given the fact that we'd never actually lived in Rose Hill but only stayed there during furloughs every five years or so.

On another day, Martin said, "Gracia, what would you think of me becoming a pastor?" That led to a long conversation. Soon he was telling me sermon ideas.

Sometimes we made vacation plans for our family. "Let's plan a camping trip out to the state park. We'll leave on Friday after the kids get out of school. Should we stay through the whole weekend, or should we come back in time for Sunday morning church?" We'd plan all the gear to take, what we would eat each meal—anything to occupy our minds.

Then on January 17, a Thursday, my birthday came. I had never expected to spend this day in the jungle. The Abu Sayyaf were aware of the occasion, and two days before, they had brought in a cake about ten inches across, baked in a special pan. We guessed that the ingredients were probably about the same as those in pancake batter, except the cook had used Royal Orange soda for some of the liquid.

On my birthday, the group stretched one tiny 170-gram can of corned beef (about six ounces), imported from Brazil, over two meals. We couldn't believe how flavorful it was. It went well with rice and Maggi noodles. When it was time to cut the cake, we got our share—two little squares about two bites each.

We managed to rig up a windbreak of branches to ward off the cold. That night we invited Ediborah over so we could visit and talk about birthday traditions. We'd saved a mini-size Cloud 9 candy bar, which we cut up with my spoon into three pieces to share with her.

After she left, Martin and I prayed together and then went to sleep. It certainly wasn't like any other birthday I'd ever celebrated in my life. No balloons. No cards. No gifts. No bedroom door to close behind us for a romantic ending. But in its own modest way, it had been a nice day.

CHAPTER 17

SO CLOSE

(Late January–Late March 2002)

One morning while in "Camp Contentment," Sabaya came up to me and asked, "Do you know someone named Mary Jones?"

My heart leaped. "Yes! That's my little sister!"

"Well, she's in Zamboanga, and she's going to make a statement on Radyo Agong soon. I'll bring my radio over so you can listen to it."

What in the world! My sister was just across the strait in Zamboanga City? I had never wanted so badly to fly like Superman in my life.

We huddled around the shortwave there under our *tolda.* Soon the announcer said, "We have today Mary Jones, sister of Gracia Burnham, who has a statement to make."

And there came the voice I knew so well. I listened intently with a big smile on my face as she spoke very forcefully for four or five minutes, expressing her concern for us. Our children were frightened after seeing the pictures of our deterioration, she said. She appealed to the Philippine government to do something. She also appealed to the Abu Sayyaf: "Please do not harm them. You have nothing to gain by doing so. They are peaceful people."

Then as she ended, she gave phone numbers for our captors to call.

"Wow!" I exclaimed to Sabaya. "Yep, that was my sister!" I turned to Martin and continued, "She said very nice things about us, didn't she?" We both laughed at that. We couldn't believe that she had gone to all this effort and travel for us.

The next morning, Sabaya was back with a frown on

his face. "They're airing part of her statement again—the part about the phone numbers. Why is she doing that?"

"I don't know," I replied. "Maybe she just wants to know how we are. Maybe she brought money with her." I figured that should get his attention.

He wasn't eager to respond, however. "Well, we don't have a sat-phone, so there's no way to call even if we wanted to. You write her a letter and ask what her real reason for coming was. Ask why she gave those phone numbers. Tell her we don't have communication, but in the meantime, Janjalani and Solaiman can speak for us; she can trust them.

"No one will see this but Mary," he added. "We will forward it to Alvin Siglos, who will take it to Manila and personally deliver it."

So I got some paper and began to write what I knew I was supposed to say:

Hello Mary,

It is the day after we heard you on the radio. Abu Sabaya came to us this morning. He is confused about your real purpose here in the Philippines. It is reported that you are being escorted by the FBI. You have given phone numbers to call. Does this mean that someone at

January 21
CBS airs a *48 Hours* feature built around Arlyn de la Cruz's footage taken back in November. Public concern in the U.S. heightens.

January 24
Six hundred sixty U.S. troops arrive in the southern Philippines.

January 24–30
Mary Jones and her husband travel to the Philippines, meet President Arroyo, and make an appeal on Radyo Agong for Martin and Gracia's release.

these numbers is willing to negotiate with the group for
our release?

The group wants you to know that we will never be
released without some concession. Their losses have been
great and they will never just give us up. They are asking for the return of their homeland, but since that
seems impossible just now, they are willing to take a
ransom, as they need to arm themselves for this fight.

A couple of paragraphs later, however, I began to
write more personally out of my heart:

Could you please send us a pkg. with Alvin? . . . Could
you send a couple thousand pesos [$40] for us personally
so we can get medicines, etc. I need boots. Martin gets
thinner & thinner. It is hard to watch, Mary!

This whole situation is so difficult. Everyone is being
stubborn . . . we are caught in the middle . . . the Abu
Sayyaf will not let us go w/out ransom . . . the governments say "no ransom." This is an endless circle, and to
be honest, we do not want to be rescued, as they come in
shooting at us. If someone can't give somewhere, we will
die.

Thank you for coming here and reminding the world
that we are people . . . we are being treated as only political pawns and it is very sad. You are kind and sweet. Tell
Mom & Dad I love them . . . and my kids. I love them so
much it hurts.

When I finished, Martin said, "Hey, I think I'll
write something."

"You're going to get us in trouble!" I warned.
"Sabaya said to keep it short."

"No way. I'm not letting this opportunity pass." So
he added a couple of pages. Among other things, he said:

*It seems as though something should happen soon . . .
but we've been saying that for a long time. We remain
encouraged in the Lord. Many of you included Scripture in your last letters—they have become our Bible
and we read them daily.*

*Jeff, Mindy, & Zach . . . it's hard to know what to
tell you except I love you so much and am praying I can
come home to you soon. Jeff, I wanted to watch the
World Series, then the Super Bowl with you (and all
the other bowl games), but I don't even know who
played! Isn't that funny? Happy Birthday to you!*

When we finished the letter, we took it to Sabaya.
Later we discovered that it did *not* go directly to Alvin
Siglos. It ended up at Radyo Agong and was read over
the air before it ever got to Mary! I would not have been
nearly so blunt had I known that would happen.

Needless to say, the Abu Sayyaf never called the
phone numbers. Sabaya was too busy worrying about
Mary's FBI agent. We should have told him that this was
standard practice in any kidnapping case involving
Americans; the FBI would have been involved from day
one. But even that wouldn't have relieved his fears.

Not long afterward, one of the captors' wives
showed up in camp with a story of having met Mary at a
congressman's home in Isabela, the provincial capital of
Basilan. She said Mary was crying, had "boxes of
money," and was pleading for my release. It sounded
good—but the truth, I found out in the end from Mary,
was that she was never in Isabela at all. Zamboanga City
was as close as she got.

::::

Our food supply at this time was actually quite good for
a most unusual reason: The armed forces were feeding

us! A group of them met our guys and handed over quantities of rice, dried fish, coffee, and sugar. This happened several times over the course of a few weeks.

Why in the world did President Arroyo's troops provide the Abu Sayyaf with their daily bread? We were told that it was because Sabaya was wheeling and dealing with the AFP general of that area over how to split up any ransom that might be paid. Arlyn de la Cruz had warned us about that. "You know, this is going to be a really big deal," she said, "and everybody is going to expect their share."

Sabaya was willing to give the general 20 percent of the action. But the messenger reported back that this wasn't enough. The general wanted 50 percent—when his own government steadfastly condemned the ransom concept altogether. We weren't really surprised at this, as over the years we had read newspaper articles about generals' wives installing floors of smuggled marble in Corinthian Gardens, an elite section of Manila, and about their children attending the best schools abroad. Those things don't happen on a Filipino general's salary.

We soon learned via radio that negotiations had broken down. Radyo Agong often uses coded messages in public-service bulletins. For example, if someone's father dies in the city, the station will let all the relatives and friends in the province know what has happened, since many don't have telephones.

One day, the announcer used a tip-off name for Sabaya and said, "The bank turned down your offer for the house that you wanted to sell, and they're going to come now and take the house by force. My advice would be for you to leave the house so you don't get in any trouble."

It didn't take too much sleuthing to figure out what that meant. Negotiations with the general had broken down, and we needed to move along.

Just at that time, another incident gave cause for relocating, too. Assad came running up the hill with the key to Martin's handcuffs and took them off. He was excited and talking nonstop, although we couldn't understand much of what he was saying. We figured out that our captors had caught a man who said he was out "looking for an ax" he had lost several years before.

But this fellow had found the Abu Sayyaf once before, and Omar had warned him, "Don't you come looking for us again, or we'll kill you."

Now they sat and talked with him a long time. They finally decided he was a scout for the army. So after moving us over to one end of the camp, they took the prisoner up the hill and beheaded him. We didn't see or hear the actual event, but we saw Bashir coming back down the hill trying to get the blood off his shirt.

A little while later, Sabaya stopped to tell Martin all that had transpired. "I'm sure this kind of blows your mind," he added.

"Well, you know my views on it," Martin replied. "You know I believe it's wrong, even if you call it 'holy war.'"

Again came the standard explanation: "This was just this man's destiny. He should not have come looking for us. But he did, and now we have to find a new camp." This was what upset Sabaya most—the inconvenience of moving.

We remembered a recent conversation we'd had with Sabaya about a Muhammad Ali interview that had appeared in the December *Reader's Digest* we had gotten in our pre-Christmas box. The magazine's writer had been scheduled to talk to the famous American boxer at his Michigan home back on September 11, of all days. They went ahead with the interview that morning and of course the journalist began by asking Ali for his reaction to the attacks.

"Killing like that can never be justified," he had said. "It's unbelievable. I could never support hurting innocent men, women and children. Islam is a religion of peace. It does not promote terrorism or killing people."

The interviewer then asked how Ali felt about the claim being made already on the news that Muslims were responsible for the World Trade Center and Pentagon disasters.

"I am angry that the world sees a certain group of Islam followers who caused this destruction, but they are not real Muslims. They are racist fanatics who call themselves Muslims, permitting this murder of thousands."*

We showed the article to Sabaya and asked what he thought about it.

"Well, of course Muhammad Ali would denounce this; he's living the good life in America! As long as he has plenty of money, he's not going to say he agrees with us, because that would ruin his prospects.

"But I can assure you that if he's truly a Muslim, he knows about jihad, he understands jihad—and he appreciates jihad."

::::

We walked for hours up the river where we had to be more careful than on a normal trail. We always had to take the hardest route, usually through thick foliage. We would see trails and know to avoid them, for fear of civilians spotting us. From a hilltop, the Abu Sayyaf would point out a village in the distance and say, "We're going over there. On the trail it would only take a few hours"—but we'd end up taking two days to get there, up and down, up and down.

We walked through water up to our waists, with

*Howard Bingham, "Face to Face with Muhammad Ali," *Reader's Digest* (December 2001): 92–93.

mud and gunk at the bottom. We'd carry our boots rather than risk having them suctioned off.

We estimated that by this time, Martin was carrying close to fifty pounds of gear: his odds and ends of clothing, our hammock, the chain with which he was bound every night, some budget, plus one or two big mortar rounds, which they called "M-90 mortars." These are canisters at least three feet long that fit into a mortar launcher. He came up with a long strip of cloth somewhere (perhaps from someone's discarded hammock) and tied it to each end of the "mortar," so he could sling it over his shoulder and thus have his hands free. A lot of times when scrambling up a hill in a steep place, we really needed our hands to grab onto a branch.

Meanwhile, I was carrying perhaps twenty-five pounds, including a couple of what they called "M-60 mortars." These weighed four or five pounds each and were about the size of a Pringles can. I noticed my arm and calf muscles getting very strong from all the exertion, even while the rest of my body was weakening.

And the crazy part was, these heavy "mortars" never got used! We just lugged them around the jungle week after week. In a firefight, there wasn't time to set them up and fire them; guys just grabbed their assault rifles and began blazing away.

Given the loads, Martin and I had more than one debate about which personal items were essential. Back in June when the schoolteachers had been so kind to me, they had given me a pair of jeans. But Martin asked me not to wear them, because Muslim men object to seeing a woman's figure; I was supposed to be in the baggiest thing possible.

So I stuck to *pantos* while still carrying the jeans around. After a couple of months, we discovered that Martin had lost so much weight that *he* could wear the jeans. He decided he wanted to hang on to these for his release day, whenever it came. He also had a nicer, heavier shirt with a collar he had been given at the hospital. Together, these made up his special outfit.

We carried those around for months. One day I said, "Martin, this is not going to be a quick captivity. We're carrying all this extra weight through the jungle; what do you think?"

"Man, I hate to get rid of them. I just keep thinking we're going to get out soon. If I could walk out of here looking decent, I'd really like it."

A few days later, though, we gave up and buried the jeans behind some rocks. He was very sad about this, and so was I. We kept the shirt, however, for warmth at night.

Sometime in February, as the food supply kept shrinking, I began noticing that when I sat up in the morning, I could feel the blood pulsing through my head, *boom— boom—boom!* That went on for weeks, until the diet improved again. I didn't know if my blood pressure had gone crazy or what. It was scary.

When I was really down and feeling sorry for myself, I would think about what I might have wished had never happened.

Did I wish our family had never come to the Philippines in the first place? No, we'd had a wonderful fifteen years before the capture.

Did I wish I'd never married Martin? Absolutely not.

Did I wish I'd never become a Christian when I was a little girl? No.

The only thing I could agree to wishing was that I'd never been born. I sounded like Job when he said in his agony, "May the day of my birth perish. . . . That day— may it turn to darkness; may God above not care about it; may no light shine upon it" (Job 3:3-4).

Obviously, my mental state was becoming shaky.

Several times I said to Martin, "I would rather be dead than live anymore in this situation."

"Gracia, you can survive. What do you think the kids would say if you could pick up the phone and call them?"

I had to admit, "They'd say, 'Just keep going, Mom, because maybe you'll get to come home someday.'"

"That's right. And that's what you need to do. Don't let your mind think long-term. Just keep walking until the next rest break. All this will seem like such a little while after you're out."

Poor Martin—he was so good to put up with my emotions. If we were in a gun battle and I was falling apart, he would say, "Gracia, this isn't the time to cry. You're wasting energy. You need to get ahold of yourself—you can cry later, okay?"

But he never reprimanded me for crying. It made me think back to earlier days, when I was homeschooling the kids, and I pushed Jeffrey so hard to perform that he would burst into tears. On more than one occasion I had said, "I don't want to see you cry, because you're just trying to get your way." I was really impatient and unfair with him.

Now in the jungle, I thought to myself, *How would you feel if someone walked up to you right now and said, "I don't want you crying, because you're just trying to get your own way"?* I promised myself that if I ever got back to Jeff, I would sit him down and apologize for pushing him so hard. He was actually a good student, and so were the other kids. I just expected them to be perfect little adults instead of kids who were learning to make their way in the world.

::::

I also learned to lighten up a bit with one of the captors named Akmad. He was about fifteen years old, like our

Jeff, only chunkier, and could be happy-go-lucky sometimes. But he was very moody at times—a normal teenage boy, I guess.

He found ways to divert our food to his own benefit. Sometimes he claimed that the group food was "personal." He was the one who had invented the strange line "You can't have any of this—we need this food, because we're fasting." (The Abu Sayyaf generally "fasted" on Mondays and Thursdays—during daylight hours, that is. They ate before sunrise and after sunset, of course.)

One day Akmad and a couple of others were chosen to supervise our bathing and laundry process at the river. We knew this wasn't a favorite job for them, so we tried to hurry up and do exactly as we were told. "Faster, faster!" Akmad barked. Soon he began throwing rocks at me to get me to hustle even more.

Upset, I swung around and said, "Okay, then I *won't* hurry! Go ahead and throw them at me!" He didn't understand all of my English, but the rocks kept coming.

Still not getting the results he wanted, he cocked his gun.

"Fine—go ahead and shoot me," I said. "I really don't care."

Fortunately, he didn't take me seriously, but the rock barrage continued until Martin finally said, "No! Don't do that!" Only then did he stop.

A few days later, Akmad happened to see a picture of our daughter, Mindy, who was only twelve. Of course, Filipina girls are small, and so Mindy appeared quite mature in Akmad's eyes. He began saying he'd like to marry her.

"No way," I replied, "after the way you've been treating me!"

Ediborah translated what I said to Akmad. He just grinned and said back to her, "How do I tell her in English that I'm a 'good boy'?" She taught him the English phrase.

But whenever he tried to use it with me after that, he got confused. I'd go to the fire, and Akmad would say brightly, "You are a 'good boy'?"

I'd smile and say, "Yes, Akmad, you are a 'good boy.'"

He would then push his luck by saying another English term he'd learned from Ediborah: "Mother-in-law?" At this, everybody would laugh.

I would shrug my shoulders and say, "Maybe—if you are a 'good boy'!"

Several times when I saw him stealing dried fish, I'd scold him, "Akmad! You are a 'bad boy'!"

He would just smile at me and insist, "I am a 'good boy'!"

I remember thinking more than once, *This kid should be coming home from school to warm cookies and milk, not traipsing through the jungle with an M16.* Instead, he and the other young ones were more like the "lost boys" in *Peter Pan.* Martin and I even used that term for them once in a while when talking in the late evenings.

In a gun battle later on, Akmad ended up taking a bullet through his thigh. He could not just lie down, however; he had to run with the rest of us for quite a distance. We went through a swamp with water up to our waists, which of course infected the wound.

At the first chance to rest, I noticed some of the guys picking up leaves from the ground and putting them into their mouths to chew. I didn't know what this was all about until they then began stuffing the masticated leaves into Akmad's wound as some sort of medication. Martin and I gazed at this in disbelief and decided to keep quiet. Then the wound was bandaged to stop the bleeding.

Martin gave up his long *malong* for use as a stretcher. Akmad was then carried along the trail with the rest of us.

Before long, however, infection had produced a high fever. He began talking out of his head. Late one night, we heard him repeating himself over and over in his language. The only parts we could understand were the intervals of *"Allah akbar! Allah akbar! Allah akbar!"* Then he began to growl in a low voice, "Personal! . . . Personal! . . . Personal!" I felt so sorry for this young man.

The days wore on, and there were too many soldiers in the area to risk sending Akmad out for medical help. His ranting became more frequent as his condition worsened. Naturally, he needed help going to the bathroom, and others were not always nearby to assist him.

One day, he had soiled his *malong* and sleeping mat, and I could see that he was upset.

"Hugasi bani?" I said in my fractured Cebuano, which means "May I wash this for you?"

He nodded.

I took the two items to the stream and washed them out. As I hung them up to dry, the thought came to me: *If this were Jeff, I'd want some lady to show kindness to him.*

::::

Jeff's birthday (February 11) came and went, as did Valentine's Day. We tried to make cards for each other. In my log I wrote: "If we ever get out of here, Martin wants

February 11
On Jeff's fifteenth birthday relatives gather for another party.

Mid-February
The Bush administration adopts a "subtle, but very important" shift in U.S. policy on civilian hostage situations, from "no deals at all" to case-by-case consideration, with an openness to ransom if it would in some way bring terrorists to justice.

February 21
A U.S. Chinook helicopter goes down in the sea off Zamboanga; ten soldiers die. The Abu Sayyaf hear this news and rejoice.

Valentine cookies (sugar) w/ frosting and cupcakes w/ frosting. . . . How I wish I could make him some. I love him so much—and we are hungry."

For the time being, however, we made do with the local snacks if they were available. The three "official goodies" of the Abu Sayyaf were:

- Magic Flakes, which are three saltine crackers with icing between
- Cloud 9, a candy bar sort of like a Milky Way, but with no shortening (or at least none listed in the ingredients)
- Bingo cookies, similar to Oreo cookies

Martin even kept the empty wrappers so he could smell them when there was nothing else to eat. The left-over aroma dampened his hunger pangs a little.

Meanwhile, we were learning to appreciate a different kind of delicacy: eel. The river had lots of eels, and the guys built beautiful fish traps with vines and other materials to catch them. Eel is really good to eat; it has a lot of fatty skin, and the meat is excellent. We thanked the Lord every time somebody brought us a slice of eel for supper.

We learned to avoid dried squid, however, which is something Filipinos seem to love. Martin quickly found out it made him very sick. One night they forgot to hand-cuff him for sleeping—which turned out to be convenient when he needed to go vomit in the woods. He was careful to call out, *"Sakit ako! Sakit ako!* [I'm sick! I'm sick!]" so they wouldn't think he was trying to escape and shoot him.

That was the last time we ate squid; from then on we skipped those particular meals.

The first few times I faced little dried fish, complete

with heads and tails, I took off the head, then carefully picked the rest apart, throwing away each tiny bone in order to get at the meat. I then sprinkled the meat on our rice to give it flavor.

But as time went on and we began to starve, we decided the fish heads probably had good protein. Everyone else was eating them, and we started to as well, along with the bones of the skeleton—we just chomped down everything.

Sometimes bigger fish would come, and we would be given only the head. We learned to chew it up and be grateful for the nutrition. Fish-head bones are not as hard as one might think; the only part that can't really be crunched, believe it or not, is the eyeball. It's hard as a rock. Martin just swallowed his whole and let his stomach do the work. I couldn't make mine go down, so I'd throw it away.

One day about the time I did laundry for Akmad, I was at the babbling brook again. I looked down at a tiny pool formed by the rocks at the edge and saw a little fish about an inch and a half long.

I didn't think I could catch it, but I reached down anyway—and grabbed it by the tail. I held it up to Martin.

Early March
Gracia's uncle approaches an American philanthropist for ransom money and gets a favorable response.

March 11
The *Wall Street Journal* runs a front-page article on the widening war against terrorism and reports, "The most ambitious U.S. military action outside Afghanistan is taking place on the small island of Basilan." The article attributes to U.S. officials the opinion that "the Philippine troops are poorly organized and have yet to learn how to move with the stealth and speed they need to rescue the Burnhams and Ms. [Ediborah] Yap."

"Look! I caught this fish!" I exclaimed, very proud of myself. "Do you want it?"

"No, that's okay."

So I popped it in my mouth and ate it raw. After all, if I carried it around with me until a cooking fire became available, it might rot. Better to get the nutrition now. In fact, it tasted very good. Who says God had to supply our needs the same way every time?

By now my hair was getting long and needed to be in a ponytail to stay out of my eyes. My *terong* wasn't enough to do the job. Obviously, I didn't have a scrunchie or a rubber band to use. What to do?

Lord, can you figure out something for me to use to tie back my hair? I began to pray. That may sound silly to others, but when we had absolutely nothing, we learned to pray about things as mundane as this.

I was learning the truth of the Scripture that says, "Every good and perfect gift is from above, coming down from the Father" (James 1:17). If somebody walked by and handed us a tiny boiled banana only two inches long, our immediate response was *Oh, thank you, God! We need this.* Every bite was a gift.

Soon after, I glanced down at the ground—and there lay a strip of black rubber, like from a bicycle inner tube. I picked it up, tied the ends together in a knot, and gleefully pulled my hair back. This became my scrunchie for a long, long time.

When I lay down in the hammock on my back, however, I'd have to take it out to be comfortable. I was always afraid of losing it. So I would carefully stuff it into my pocket. I needed to guard this prized possession.

::::

Sabaya had an unusual question one day: "Are there a million Christians in America?"

"Oh, certainly," Martin replied.

"Well, then, couldn't they give a dollar each and get you guys out of here?"

We just groaned. I said to Sabaya, "There are a lot of Americans in the States who wouldn't give you a single dollar, Sabaya. You are a bad guy, and people don't give their money to bad guys!"

He looked at me, shocked, as if to say, *What? Me? A bad guy?* This was preposterous, to his way of thinking.

Whenever he saw me upset or crying these days, he tried to patch me up by saying, "There's a negotiation! There's a negotiation!"

I wanted to reply bluntly, "No, Sabaya, there isn't. You've said that dozens of times now, and it's never produced anything." But I held my tongue.

CHAPTER 18

RANSOMED!

(Late March–April 2002)

If you're ever tempted to go camping in a swamp of mangrove trees—don't. Mangroves are fairly short tropical trees with much of their root system *above* the ground, forming a picturesque tangle of limbs that eventually converge into a trunk some three feet or more into the air. They flourish only in places with abundant water.

A mangrove swamp is a great place to hide, if a person doesn't mind the smell of rotting leaves and the dampness. We spent two nights in one just before Easter and about went crazy. When we got out of our hammock, our feet sank two inches into the goo.

Of course, I must admit it was a tiny improvement over the previous week, when we'd lived in bunkers the Abu Sayyaf had dug into a steep hilltop. With no more than five feet of headroom, we crouched in the darkness, forbidden to go outside for fear of discovery. Martin and I had to share a bunker with Musab and Ediborah, which meant I couldn't communicate openly with my husband. Martin seemed more depressed here than at any other time.

At least in the mangrove swamp, we could see the sun through the trees.

Being close to the ocean meant we weren't far from civilian fishing activity. In the Philippines, a common (although illegal) way to catch fish is simply to throw a stick of dynamite into the water. When it explodes, the dead fish float to the surface, where the fishermen can collect them and take them to market. It's not exactly friendly to the environment, but it works.

Whenever we heard a big *ba-boom!* I cringed in fear

of an incoming AFP mortar. The others calmly listened a few seconds, analyzing the sound, and then declared: "Fish bomb." In other words, no problem.

Another *ba-boom!* I held my breath and then someone else announced: "Fish bomb." I never did learn to tell the difference.

One evening, the guys who had gone out for budget came running back with news. Their excitement was obvious, even though we couldn't understand their dialect. Everyone quickly began packing up to mobile. My immediate thought was that soldiers had found us again. We began packing, too.

Then Martin looked at me and said, "You know, I don't think this is a soldier thing. People are too pleased about all this."

We hiked out of the swamp and came to where Sabaya and Musab had gone for a meeting. They had us sit down. Then they spoke.

"Someone has paid a ransom for you—15 million pesos [$330,000]. So this is really, really great."

At last! Our hopes had finally been realized. We'd be going home!

We both held our breath for the next line.

"But—we are going to ask for 30 million pesos more." They had always said they wanted a million dollars for Martin, and they were sticking to that figure.

I remembered, just a day or two before, hearing Sabaya on the phone telling someone in town, "Take anything they offer, because we are ready to get this over with." But now I studied their faces and could just see the hardness settling in.

March 14–19
FBI director Robert Mueller visits his Manila staff to review their efforts and to encourage action.

"Please, please do not do that," I pleaded with Sabaya. "Take the money and let this be over!"

"No, no—the person who paid this ransom said that if we require more, they'll come up with it. This won't be a problem."

I thought to myself, *Well, okay, if that's true, go ahead and ask for the rest.* Meanwhile, all the Abu Sayyaf guys were celebrating. "The money's been paid, the money's been paid! You're going to get out of here! *Allah akbar!*"

"Okay, we're going to leave this island now," Sabaya said. We began an hour's walk toward the sandy beach, where we sat waiting for a boat while the captors kept several cell phones going.

Mosquitoes were everywhere, of course. I had a tiny bit of Off! in my backpack, but I didn't want to get it out for fear that the zipper would refuse to close again, as it often did. So we just sat there getting bitten.

In time, someone said, "The boat's here. Move up close to the shore." We heard the engine sound drawing near.

A spy plane was also circling overhead during all this. We had come to ignore them, however, because they had been circling for months, and nothing ever happened. "Why don't they do something useful with those things and spray for mosquitoes?" Martin said ruefully.

Someone gave a flashlight signal from the shore, and a small boat called a *banca,* maybe twenty or twenty-five feet long, pulled up. We began wading out to meet it in chest-deep water. We awkwardly pulled ourselves aboard and sat down. The Abu Sayyaf began loading their guns and bazookas on board, then climbed in themselves. Soon the boat was full, and more people kept coming.

I turned to Musab. "There are too many people on here; it's going to sink," I said. "You've got to get some of them off."

He looked at me like I was crazy.

But in fact, the boat began to take on water. People tried to bail with their hands. I got a little bowl out of my backpack to help. Even Akmad was bailing with his hands from his *malong* stretcher as he said over and over, "No panic! No panic! No panic!" When they saw we were sinking, a number of guys disembarked.

The spy plane kept circling above. *If they can't see us now, they really are useless,* I thought to myself.

Finally, with some fifteen of us on board, the boat took off toward the bright lights of Zamboanga. This little, out-of-the-way island of Basilan had been our abode for ten months. Now at last, we were finally making headway toward freedom. I was so grateful. The open breeze was freeing for me, after so much hiding in foliage.

Several weeks earlier, I had gotten frustrated with praying for release; it just wasn't happening no matter how I prayed. So I had said, somewhat childishly, "Okay, I'm going to pray for something else: a hamburger!" I even told Martin what I was doing and said, "The only way for us to get a hamburger is to get out of here, right? Maybe God will answer that prayer instead!"

Now in the boat, Musab looked at me with a big smile and said, "We're going for your release!"

"Tonight? Will we be released tonight?"

"Oh, no, no. Maybe a week. Maybe two weeks. Maybe a few days."

My heart plunged. So this was not going to be our big moment after all. *Here we go again,* I thought. *Why did I let myself expect anything more?* It seemed that we were being toyed with once again.

::::

We rode the waves all night. Poor Ediborah, who didn't swim, was terrified. Martin just held on to her hand and said, "We're going to be fine; we're going to be fine."

The Abu Sayyaf were not about to venture directly into Zamboanga City, of course, with its AFP Southern Command headquarters and all the other security forces. They stayed in the shadows and worked with intermediaries.

By morning we had landed at what they called Island 11. A war between two tribes fighting over a water source was underway. The AFP generally stays out of such conflicts. Hence the Abu Sayyaf assumed we would be safe.

Most of the civilians had fled the island, leaving many abandoned houses for us to occupy. The available water was very sulfuric, and Martin and I both got sick right away. Diarrhea raged, and we vomited as well. Yet we weren't allowed outside, Sabaya said.

Well, that simply would not work, given our condition. So they moved us to a different house that had a bigger room. They put up a big tarp divider to keep us hidden from any visitors. Martin pried up a piece of the floor in order to make a place for our wastes. It was totally gross.

We found a big box of the absent homeowner's clothing that, I am sorry to admit, we basically stole to turn into rags and use as toilet paper. Occasionally the captors brought us water for washing.

Meanwhile, of course, money was still flowing freely—our ransom money. (After my return to America, I read various reports that the ransom money had been diverted and never reached our captors. Not true.) Every night a boat came from the mainland with supplies. Every captor had been given 10,000 pesos ($200) to spend as he wished.

Ayub, probably eighteen years old, spent a tenth of his wad on cookies! He had huge sacks of Bingo cookies and sat down for a feast.

Lukman spent a lot of his money on clothes, especially a few classy motorcycle shirts. A handsome fellow, his long, straight hair was quite striking.

One evening late, after the supply boat had come and gone, the room began to fill with the most wonderful smell as Martin and I sat behind the tarp. We peeked around the corner, and there was Assad with a big tub of hot fried chicken! He looked up at us, grinned—and tossed us a thigh, like he would toss something to a dog!

"Oh, thank you, Assad!" we cried.

"I'm spending my money!" he said with glee.

He also bought a tape player and some music, which was supposedly "forbidden." When scolded for this by another captor, Assad told the fellow off and said, "Leave me alone—it's good Muslim music."

Soon the Abu Sayyaf came to realize that this island was not as safe as they had thought. The AFP might not be there, but the tribal war was just as dangerous. Word quickly got around that the Abu Sayyaf had arrived, and nighttime skirmishes flared up.

The first time, we had to leave our stuff behind and run out of the house for a while. Through the darkness we ran to the only cement structure on the island, where Martin and I slept on the floor in the far corner. No blanket, no *malong*, nothing to fold up as a pillow. That was a long night, especially with the gunfire continuing. Just before dawn, they sneaked us back to our house.

The next time hostilities broke loose, we began packing immediately. Someone came running into our room. "Get your things! We're going!" And soon we were loaded back onto another *banca*.

March 25
The Philippine military turns down an Abu Sayyaf offer to release a hostage in exchange for a temporary cease-fire and medical care for one of its commanders.

We were surprised to see a woman already on the boat when we got on. We were even more surprised when we learned it was Musab's first wife. Where had she come from? I had no idea. I didn't get a good look at her, because it was dark, and she was covered in black except for her face. She did have a baby girl with her.

In the middle of the night, we pulled up to a little Muslim fishing village near Zamboanga. They sneaked us under the houses built on stilts over the water and then hauled us onto a plank sidewalk with a number of boards missing. We had to walk very carefully. I was barefoot, not wanting to lose my boots in the water.

When we got to a house, Ediborah was put into a room with us, while Musab and his wife were in another room.

Soon the Muslim call to prayer began ringing out across the village. It was mournful but also beautiful in a sense. When the sun came up, someone was dispatched to find breakfast. Oh, my! We had *banana-cue*—ripe banana pieces rolled in brown sugar and fried in oil. We had deep-fried doughnuts! We had ripe mangoes. What a feast! We were glad the Abu Sayyaf had lots of money again. The money hadn't gained our freedom, but at least it was improving our diet.

Even so, Musab couldn't bring himself to divide up the twelve doughnuts equitably. Martin and I received one each, while Musab kept the others.

Previously, when we had gone without adequate food for a time and then got relief, we tended to wolf things down too quickly. Food would get stuck in our esophagus, and we'd gag. We'd almost forgotten how to swallow.

This time we ate very slowly and chewed each bit a lot. I tried to make each mouthful last for forty chews, so my throat could swallow easily.

At lunchtime, there was fried chicken with rice! We had gravy for the rice, and some fruit salad.

For a snack that afternoon, we got *halo-halo,* which is crushed ice with sweetened condensed milk that has been mixed with fruit, sweet corn, and even garbanzo beans. It tasted so good!

The group called civilians to bring us freshly cooked fish. Twice a day, someone brought hot tea with sugar in it, as well as rice. We really enjoyed it.

Omar had brought his wife along on this journey, and during the day, she decided to go shopping. When she stopped by our sweltering little room to get Ediborah's list of items, however, she made a mistake. She had a friend with her, whom she carelessly allowed to follow her into the room, thus exposing the presence of us two Americans. The captors became irate, and Omar's wife got a royal chewing out. She turned as white as a Filipina can turn.

For supper, they bought a hunk of beef, which was prepared over a small kerosene cookstove the Abu Sayyaf had bought. Again, we feasted.

Toward evening, Sabaya asked us, "Is there anything you'd like to have?"

"Well, Gracia's been praying for a hamburger," Martin offered.

"Hey, I'll send my guy to Jollibee [the Philippine counterpart to McDonald's]."

Sure enough, around nine o'clock, some hamburgers arrived with French fries and Cokes. We shared one with Ediborah—but that got her in trouble with Musab. After all, Jollibee hamburgers might have pork in them.

"You realize we're going to have to move now," Musab announced, "because a civilian saw you." Everyone began packing up, and guides from the local area were called to assist. I was swathed with *malong*s so as not to be identified.

Just before we left, something happened that simply broke my heart. Our group was still carrying along the injured young Akmad, who by now was growling and screaming a lot of the time. We could tell he was slowly losing his mind.

Ediborah, being a nurse, had been urging Musab to figure out some way to help the kid. After all, Akmad was his nephew. We joined in as well. "Somebody really needs to do something," we said. "Why is he continuing to suffer like this?"

"It is the will of Allah," came the response. "He has been confessing his sins: stealing food from the group, not saying his prayers, not reading his Koran. So this is Allah's punishment for him."

I wanted to scream back that the suffering had nothing to do with Allah; it was all the fault of the Abu Sayyaf leaders. They had control of Akmad's life.

Now, just as we were walking out of this house on stilts above the ocean, I peeked in another room and caught my last glimpse of the boy. A baseball cap was pulled down over his eyes. He was so skinny I could see the bones of his elbows through his skin. His arms and feet were tied down to anchor points in the floor and wall, and a sock was tied into his mouth with a bandanna to gag him. He thrashed pitifully against the restraints.

My heart just went out to him. The irritation of weeks before when he had thrown rocks at me was long gone. I felt nothing but sorrow for the agony he was now enduring.

Later I was told that the AFP raided that house, captured him, and tried to question him. Where is Akmad today? In an insane asylum somewhere? Or has he died? I doubt I will ever find out.

::::

Another long night on the sea. Martin and I realized we had a serious problem to manage: our diarrhea. I thought to myself, *This situation is going to get very embarrassing.*

Would you believe that we traveled across the water all night long, and neither of us ever had to go?! By the time we got to the peninsula coast, daylight had come. As soon as we stepped onshore and found a log to hide behind, the need struck us both with full force. I believe that was just the Lord's goodness—a small shield from needless humiliation.

The night had its terrors, however, in that we were out on the open ocean in the darkness, and whenever another boat got close to ours, we had to crouch down and stay covered under a tarp. At one point, a government patrol boat, complete with cannons poking over the side, was spotted. My heart began to pound as I thought, *This is it. This is the end of us. In just a few minutes we're going to get blasted into the sea, and we'll drown.*

I pled with God to spare our lives. I found myself repeating one phrase over and over: "O God, save us! O God, save us! O God, save us!"

Our captain turned on one small light at the back that shone down into the water, thus pretending to be a fishing boat. His ruse worked, and the patrol boat passed by without investigating.

We soon learned that an older man aboard our boat named Mirsab, who was about fifty-six years old, knew the immediate area from his earlier days with the Moro Islamic Liberation Front. He became our guide.

Once we landed, we set up camp in the jungle once again. We hadn't been there long when a group of civilians arrived unannounced to talk to Musab. This was problematic, because they obviously saw the white faces of Martin and me; there was no chance to hide us. Who knew what this group would do with that information?

We promptly moved again, but the pattern kept repeating itself: discovery by civilians, another march to another place. Talk of negotiation and release faded; we were back to the same old grind as on Basilan, only in this case, it became apparent that the Abu Sayyaf didn't really know where they were going. Once we mobiled beyond the territory that Mirsab knew well, we just wandered aimlessly in the jungle.

At this time, Martin developed worse intestinal problems than ever before. His need to go into the woods was unceasing. He worried that at night he wouldn't be able to get someone to unchain him fast enough so he could go. Bless his heart, as a precaution he began wearing some of the rags we had brought from Island 11, almost like a diaper, just in case he had an accident. *Oh, what I wouldn't give for a single bottle of Pepto-Bismol or a few tablets of Imodium A-D to help him,* I thought. But there was none.

Meanwhile, we pleaded with the Great Physician for relief. And within a few days, the worst of it passed.

By now his weight loss was obvious to everyone, not just me as his wife. The Abu Sayyaf needed to keep him alive for obvious reasons, so his food budget was improved. He began to regain a little weight. At least his bones weren't protruding to the point that they were visible through his T-shirt.

We would look at each other and sigh. I remembered back to our early years of marriage, how we would romanticize, "Won't it be nice to grow old together someday?" Well, that was exactly what we were doing there in the jungle. Only we weren't in our seventies or eighties. We just looked like it. For a time, we weren't allowed to bathe in the river for fear of being discovered. We were so awful and messy from the diarrhea. I finally went to Sabaya one day and said, "I can't go on like this. I need to do laundry, at least. If you don't start treating us differently, you just may as well go ahead and shoot me."

Martin, of course, kept trying to get me to calm down and be less dramatic, but that is truly how I felt. He went to Sabaya and said, "You know, really, if you'll just let us get back to bathing and taking care of ourselves, we won't be so dejected. Our depression is coming from being so filthy."

This succeeded in getting us back to the water on almost a daily basis, but not during the daylight hours. We had to bathe at twilight or even after dark, when they thought civilians were probably elsewhere.

One day I said to Sabaya, "Remember that book about almsgiving that Musab loaned me a while back? I read something very interesting in that—in fact, I even memorized the page number.

"On page 65 it says that some people asked Muhammad one day, 'How can a man be closest to paradise and the furthest from hell?' Muhammad said, 'Free a slave or let a captive go.'

"What about this? That's how the Prophet, may his name be blessed forever, answered the question." I thought I was really being clever by using their verbiage.

Sabaya was not impressed or convinced. "Oh, he was talking about some Muslims who had taken other Muslims captive. That passage refers only to a Muslim-Muslim thing; it has nothing to do with you."

So much for my efforts at theological persuasion.

But Martin wasn't making a lot of headway, either. One time Sabaya confided that he missed his wives. He said he also missed Angie, his "booty of war." That led to a discussion of American courtship.

"We try to teach our sons the biblical standard of staying pure until marriage," Martin explained. "I wish I could be home teaching that to my teenage son right now, in fact. Boys need to learn to be responsible when dating."

"Well, men think about women all the time," Sabaya countered. "It's just ridiculous to think a man would restrain himself. 'Boys will be boys,' you know. But if a girl sleeps with someone before marriage, she is to be put to death. Or at best, she is only good enough to be a slave the rest of her life. That's just the rules." The blatant injustice of this setup apparently didn't cross his mind.

::::

Days dragged on. We heard Sabaya on the satellite phone threatening to take matters into his own hands if the intermediary didn't start producing results. Where were the other 30 million pesos? he demanded.

What neither he nor we knew was that among the American advisers, the tide had turned against making further payments. Their intelligence seemed to indicate that the first money had only produced squabbling within the Abu Sayyaf. The conclusion was that to pay more would simply be throwing good money after bad.

Finally, Musab decided to go to the city and take charge. This would also give him a chance to see his family again, which was a priority for him. We got our hopes up once more; after all, Musab was the second-in-command of the whole organization.

He said he would be gone only a few days. Time passed, and we all waited. Musab didn't return.

We kept waiting.

In fact, he never returned. Sabaya was furious. "Here Musab was always our preacher," he complained.

"He was the one to get us together on Fridays and tell us we all needed to be tough and endure hard things in our struggle for Allah. And now he abandons us!"

Every once in a while, Musab called on the sat-phone to talk to Ediborah. "I'm going to send for you this coming Friday," he would promise. She would get all ready to leave, parceling out her stuff to others. I would get her deodorant, perfume, and soap.

"Ediborah, why don't you just keep these until you actually leave?" I would say.

"No, no—he's promised me a boat is coming this Friday."

The day would pass, and no boat would show up. I would give her back her belongings. Others, however, did not; she ended up losing a long-sleeved shirt, among other things.

Obviously, Musab was not going to play the liberator role for either her or us.

Martin and I were journaling nearly every day. The Abu Sayyaf had even started ordering pens and paper when they saw us writing so often. Martin's journal entries pretty much convey the mood:

April 25, Thursday
It's hard to feel like something is really going to happen even though they say it will. We've been promised before. Sometimes it's as though we're just being strung along. There is nothing else to do but just keep going. . . . The Lord is faithful, and he is our strength.

April 24
Another family statement of encouragement airs on Radyo Agong but is not heard by Martin and Gracia.

April 26, Friday

The boat didn't come last night, so no new treats (or anything). There was the usual Friday [Abu Sayyaf] meeting that turned into a surprise when one of the members was taken into custody for expressing some form of dissent. Not sure what his fate will be. . . . One of the guys came running at me with his gun and a rope. I thought maybe things were over, but they [only] wanted my handcuffs for the new prisoner who has been declared more dangerous than I. First time I've had the cuffs completely off since I don't remember when. Feels kind of funny. It's like I forgot to get dressed or put on my watch.

We're still waiting for news. No idea what will happen.

April 27, Saturday

Who would have thought we'd still be here after 11 mos.? It just keeps going on. The boat didn't come again last night—engine trouble again. I was not chained last night because they're chaining their member. Good thing, as I had bad LBM. Many trips up the mountain. Not too much sleep for me as I didn't trust myself.

April 28, Sunday

The boat arrived finally last night. More rice and re-inforcements, although 2 did go out. My "personal" was new handcuffs. Just what I wanted! . . .

Sabaya did a radio interview. He denies that our ransom has been paid. We'll have to see what the story is when we get out. I still believe it will happen. Just don't know when. Maybe next week.

In a letter to the kids at this same time, which was written but never dispatched, Martin wrote:

Jeff, are you driving yet? I have been wondering. If we take a family vacation you can help with the driving now. That should be strange.

We have been trying to imagine life outside for some time now. We wear the same clothes all the time. They're like pajamas. . . . Someone gave me a button shirt and that has been nice.

. . . We will never get back this lost year, but hopefully we will all be stronger for it. Your mother has had a hard time with all this—more than I, I suppose. She just wants a friend. I need to keep trying, and we all need to be supportive of her. She still thinks sometimes that this is her fault because she made the plans for Dos Palmas. God has much to teach us about forgiveness, but the place to begin is forgiving ourselves. This is the fault of the Abu Sayyaf, and no one else.

God has a purpose. I will never understand why he has allowed it to go on so long. Guess we still have need of patience. I will say that my faith has been strengthened. I think your mother's has as well. We do struggle, though.

Love, Dad

CHAPTER 19

ONE RAINY AFTERNOON

(May–Early June 2002)

With each move, we seemed to be heading inland into the higher, more remote elevations of the Zamboanga Peninsula. We knew this was not good because it portended more hiding out and a continued stalemate.

At least the Abu Sayyaf had new phones, thanks to the ransom money, which allowed us to order supplies. One day when Alvin Siglos asked what we wanted, I said, "How about some new boots for me?"

He did try to get the boots, but every time a new pair arrived in camp, they were pilfered by others who wanted boots, too. Finally, on the sixth try, I got my boots.

Since the money was still available, we decided to ask Alvin for a Scrabble game. We were looking forward to some friendly competition to keep our minds sharp. I heard later that three or four Scrabble sets had been bought, but none of them ever reached us.

At times, we were forced to hike on terrain that was so steep we could hardly keep our footing without hanging on to a tree. Once on a steep hill, I dislodged a rock that rolled down and hit Martin's leg. He limped for the rest of the day, and I felt horrible about that.

One night when the guys went down to wait for the *banca* that would be carrying our supplies, a boat pulled up and started to unload. Our guys went out to greet them with the usual *"Salam alaikom!* [Peace to you!]"— only to discover that these were AFP troops! We hadn't seen the armed forces for weeks, ever since leaving Basilan. Now they were back on our trail.

The guys took off running in a panic and managed to get away. But the soldiers had obviously seen them and could no doubt follow their footprints. We wondered if they'd be able to find us, and so we spent the next days on alert.

In this area were lots of *kalaw,* or duckbills—beautiful, big birds with bright red bills. Since we couldn't go to town for food now, the Abu Sayyaf shot several *kalaw* for us to eat.

On a bright Sunday morning, some of the guys began building cooking fires so we could prepare the *kalaw.* But suddenly, a hand was raised and we all got silent. One of the guys thought he had heard something down the hill. We quickly began to pack up our stuff. Mirsab, the guide, spotted soldiers heading up the hill and again motioned for us to be silent. My heart began to pound loudly. I never did get used to these confrontations.

All of a sudden, shots were fired from one side of the ridge. Ediborah began running down the other side.

I thought back to a conversation she and I had had a few days earlier.

"What if this negotiation doesn't go through?" she had asked. "What if we're here for a long, long, long time? Can we keep doing this?"

"We have to," I replied. "We don't have any other options. Are you thinking we should try to escape?"

"No. I'm just asking if we're strong enough mentally and physically to keep on." Now that she was alone, without Musab, she seemed so much more vulnerable.

Later we learned that Musab was trying to get one million pesos ($20,000) from a Manila senator for her release, but the senator kept stalling. This made Sabaya look bad, since he had announced over the radio that Ediborah would soon be released as an act of good faith on the Abu Sayyaf's part. Now he couldn't make good on his promise, thanks to Musab's wheeling and dealing.

I watched as Ediborah ran off, and I decided to follow her.

"Stop!" Martin called after us. "You need to stay here! We'll get in trouble." But we kept running.

Along the trail, I slid in the mud, scratching up my arm and wrenching my back. Martin stayed behind Ediborah and me, following us closely. Finally we reached the river, where we hid behind a rock overhang. I expected that the Abu Sayyaf would withdraw here as well and we'd all head upriver. I had assumed wrong.

"Hey, Martin!" came a call from high on the ridge. "Get back up here! Where's Gracia? Where's Ediborah?"

"We're all here," he called out. "Don't shoot at us!"

We had to climb back up the hill, and by the time the three of us reached the top, we were spent. Nevertheless, we joined the rest in mobiling along the ridge. It proved to be a hard trek.

When we finally stopped for a rest, Sabaya confronted Martin. "Why did you run?!"

"I ran because the ladies ran."

I figured I'd better speak up, too. "I ran because Ediborah ran."

"Were you trying to escape?"

"No, honestly," Martin replied. "I was just concerned about the women."

Sabaya's eyes narrowed as he said, "If you ever run again, I will shoot you." Turning to his comrades, he added, "If he ever runs again, you shoot him."

Everyone got quiet then, and from that point on, security was definitely tighter. After nearly a year in the jungle, Martin's bravery and optimism finally began to crack. He wrote:

May 6, Monday

Slept on the ground. I'm so discouraged. Usually I'm not, but today I am. PTL [praise the Lord] for Gracia. She's saying all "my" lines [of encouragement] and I'm thinking all "her" thoughts from the past. Only dif[ference] is (I guess) I'm too dumb to stop, but I really feel like I'm going to die here. I think the ladies will get out because it's the "right" thing, but not me. . . . We're going to walk and walk. God, please give us strength for the journey.

If I was any encouragement to Martin, it was more through the songs I sang rather than anything I may have said. I would go through the alphabet trying to sing a song whose title began with each letter: "Abide with Me," "Blessed Assurance," "Calvary Covers It All," etc. One morning as the sun came up, I rolled out of the hammock to give him more room and sat on a sack of rice, singing songs for the occasion:

"When Morning Gilds the Skies"
"Precious Lord, Take My Hand"
"Reach Out to Jesus"
"When We All Get to Heaven"

Among the most uplifting songs was "His Strength Is Perfect" by Steven Curtis Chapman, which begins, "His strength is perfect when our strength is gone."

I modified the words for a second and third chorus: "His will is perfect" and "His way is perfect."

I had to sing quietly for two reasons: The Abu Sayyaf

🌐
May 7
A two-page article in *People* magazine features the Burnham plight.

didn't think singing was appropriate (although they had tolerated it in the past) and none of us wanted to be discovered by the AFP. So my singing voice, which in the past had been trained to project well, became quiet and quavery. *Will I ever get to cut loose and sing strongly again?* I wondered.

Assad had been wounded the day that we had run from the soldiers, but he was still able to walk. Good thing, because for a week or so, we hiked and hiked. Our captors had a destination in mind, they said, and when we got to that village, they would release us to the barrio captain. *Oh, really?* I thought. *I'll believe that when I see it.*

Meanwhile, food was harder to get here on the peninsula because it wasn't a farming area. It was more given to logging. Whereas on Basilan we always knew that bananas and coconuts were nearby, here we were at the mercy of the *banca* deliveries. What this region lacked in food supply, however, it more than made up for in mosquitoes. They were ferocious.

We pressed on with difficult hiking, not sure where this village really was. Occasionally a guy was sent to climb a tree and look for it amid the sea of green. We mainly wandered through the forest.

Rumors abounded. Supposedly Malaysia was still going to pay a ransom for us.

On May 20, Martin got up the nerve to ask to borrow Sabaya's shortwave radio. Searching the dial for Voice of America to get the news, he happened upon KNLS, a Christian station out of Alaska. A short devotional came on, only two or three minutes. The pastor, named Andy Baker, read from Romans 8:

> *If God is for us, who can be against us? He who did not spare his own Son, but gave him up for us all—how will he not also, along with him, graciously give us all*

*things? Who will bring any charge against those whom
God has chosen? It is God who justifies. Who is he that
condemns? Christ Jesus, who died—more than that,
who was raised to life—is at the right hand of God and
is also interceding for us. (vv. 31-34)*

What an amazing selection—the first spoken Scripture we had heard in almost a year.

"If you are in the midst of a hard situation," Pastor
Baker said, "and if you could hear Christ in the next
room praying, you wouldn't be afraid of thousands of
enemies. He would be calling your name."

Martin and I looked at each other with tears in our
eyes. The speaker then began to lead in prayer—for people who were oppressed, people on the West Bank and in
Afghanistan, and people who were being treated
wrongly because of their faith in Christ. It seemed like he
was praying for us. We were overwhelmed.

:::::

One of the many target dates we had set in our minds for
release was Saturday, May 25. We knew from a letter received long ago that my niece Sally would be married
that day in Indianapolis, the first of my nieces to be wed.
All the family would be gathered for the festive occasion.
Earlier, we had hoped to be there as well, of course.

Instead, we passed this day in the jungle, praying repeatedly for Sally and Tom, that God would bless their

May 27
To mark the one-year anniversary of captivity, Radyo Agong
plays an appeal for release from Martin's parents.

May 28
A candlelight prayer service is held in front of the U.S. embassy
in Manila.

new life together. We tried to imagine what all was happening. We knew that this was the last marker on our mental calendar; we had now run out of information about what anyone was doing back home.

The next Monday, May 27, marked our one-year anniversary of captivity. The day came—and went. Long ago, we would never have believed we'd be in captivity this long. But there we were.

By now we had heard that several shiploads of soldiers had landed on the Zamboanga Peninsula. It was clear that the noose was tightening around us.

One day while walking along, the leader of our group suddenly ducked down. Not knowing what was ahead, the rest of us ducked as well. Across the next hill, we spotted two soldiers eating their lunch, talking and laughing. From the conversation, it sounded like other buddies of theirs would be coming along soon. We quickly changed course.

With this change in direction, our supply line had been cut entirely. We were on our own to find food and even water. Life got very hard, harder than it had been our entire time in captivity. The hiking was tough as we tried to stay high in the mountains; the soldiers seemed to prefer the lowlands. Struggling along the trail with the heavy pack on my back, I silently recited from Hebrews 12:1-2:

> *Wherefore seeing we also are compassed about with so great a cloud of witnesses, let us lay aside every weight, and the sin which doth so easily beset us, and let us run with patience the race that is set before us, looking unto Jesus the author and finisher of our faith; who for the joy that was set before him endured the cross, despising the shame, and is set down at the right hand of the throne of God.*

We were still carrying some rice, but we'd lost our cooking pots that Sunday morning when the *kalaw* meal got interrupted. Everyone was hungry. (Sabaya, in the same battle, had lost his cherished Colt .45 pistol. I silently rejoiced, because all along, I had figured he would use that to finish us off if he got into some desperate spot.)

Martin remembered that a year before, our son Jeff had gone on a survival week sponsored by Faith Academy. He had come home telling us how to cook rice in bamboo. We could take a section, he told us, drill a hole in the side, fill it with rice and water, then heat the bamboo over the fire.

Martin explained this to the guys. We got to a river where some bamboo was growing, but were reluctant to try it because soldiers were all around and chopping down bamboo can get noisy. In the end, however, hunger overruled caution, and soon we had something to eat. Martin and I had to smile at this turn of events, thanks to the insights of our son now so many thousands of miles away.

However, at other times there was no bamboo available. We eventually came down to just our remaining salt and raw rice. When we couldn't stand the hunger anymore, we resorted to chewing on the raw rice. It was supposed to be group food, but I confess I ignored the rules and helped myself more than once. I had adopted the excuse "If I need it, it's not really stealing" at last.

Some of the boys ate so much that Sabaya grew worried about the dwindling supply. He gathered up everyone's remaining stock and committed it to Martin to carry—the only person he could trust not to devour it. This meant Martin wound up with an even heavier load than before.

After several days, the leaders announced that we would have an easier time hiking on the logging roads than the trails. That concerned me; it meant that the chances of being discovered by a logger or other civilian were much higher. I voiced my reservations but was overruled.

We set out in the morning. Suddenly the two men at the head of the line wheeled around and came running back in our direction. *"Sundalo! Sundalo!"* We all turned around and began to run the opposite direction.

The soldiers must have had radios to communicate with each other, because off in the distance, we heard trucks start up the mountain, heading our way. We darted off the road, scrambling over the piles of leftover branches and brush, called "slash." This wasn't a fast process, of course. As we began climbing the mountain-side, my heart was racing from both the exertion and the danger, but I didn't dare stop.

By this time, Ediborah had lost her shoes and was walking barefoot. We ended up walking the rest of the day.

We were still in search of the village where, alleg-edly, more ransom would be paid, and then all would be well. That evening we came to another logging road. We sat in the forest waiting for the cover of darkness, then got organized to dash across, three at a time.

When it was Martin's and my turn, we made our run, along with a guard named Sarin. In the middle of the road, I glanced up—and there was a civilian coming right toward us! I couldn't believe it.

A commotion followed as the Abu Sayyaf took this fellow hostage; they couldn't afford to just let him keep walking down the road. I felt so sorry for him, especially when he was chained to a tree for the night. As I lay down to sleep, I could just imagine what was going through his mind: *Why did I have to come along at just that moment? How did I get into this mess? Will I ever get out alive?* It turned out that he worked for the logging company and knew the area much better than Mirsab did. This qualified him to be our guide up at the head of the line.

::::

It had now been nine days since our last true meal. We were reduced to eating leaves. I would pick a leaf and ask the others whether or not it was safe to eat. We tried to keep drinking plenty of water that we gathered from rivers or collected when it rained.

As we hiked, we came to yet another logging road. Since it had been raining, we couldn't help but leave tracks in the mud. I appealed to Sarin again. "Is there any way you could talk to the guys and point out how dangerous it is to be on these roads?"

He ignored me. Again, we waited until dark to cross.

When I got to the other side, I misstepped and fell about three feet down into some of the slash. A couple of others did the same. As I worked my way back up, I scraped my back and wrenched my arm. Nevertheless, we kept walking, eventually crossing a river before we were allowed to stop, totally exhausted, around two or three in the morning.

There was no moon; it was an especially dark night. We couldn't see what we were doing. We put up our hammocks as best we could and lay down to rest.

I thought we would at least get to finish the night

May 29
The United States offers up to $5 million in reward money for information leading to the arrest of Janjalani, Musab, Sabaya, Solaiman, or Hamsiraji Sali, another of the captors.

June 3
The Burnham children head to Arkansas for a summer visit with Gracia's parents, her brother, and his family.

there. But an hour or so later, we were aroused to get moving again. "Dawn is coming soon, and we have to be out of here." We were groggy and disoriented as we fumbled around in the darkness for our belongings.

On the trail Ediborah said to me, "I felt really alone last night. Nobody helped me set up my hammock, and I couldn't find two trees that were close enough. I just had to sleep on the ground."

"Oh, Ediborah, I'm so sorry that happened," I told her. "You're really all alone, aren't you?"

"Yes. Actually, that wasn't the worst of it. I ended up on an anthill. I didn't sleep at all."

After the sun had come up, we ran into, of all things, a farm! It had nangka trees and marang and coconut. Soon we were all shoving this unripe fruit into our mouths as fast as we could and drinking the coconut milk. We gorged ourselves, then hit the road once again.

About eight that morning, we stopped to set up our hammocks. Apparently our captors intended to spend the day in this place. Up on the hill, we could see the logging road we had crossed. A truck came along. It stopped at a point I calculated to be about where we had been during the night. We could hear voices talking excitedly, and then some shouting.

"Pack up! Pack up!" came the order. Soon we were on the move once again, up, down, up, down. We came to a couple more farms, then some swamps.

I remember saying to Martin that day for about the five hundredth time, "I just don't think I can keep doing this much longer. I can't take this anymore."

And he answered, like so often before, "You know, Gracia, I just think we're going to get out of here soon. I think this is all going to work out. After we're home, this is going to seem like such a short time to us. Let's just hold steady."

At about twelve or twelve-thirty we could see a rain front moving in. The Abu Sayyaf began looking for another place to stop. We crested a mountain and started down the other side toward a little stream. The slope was very steep—maybe as much as forty degrees. From top to bottom, its length was no more than a city block, with low vegetation covering it. We brought out our hammocks once again.

It was June 7. "You know, tomorrow is my brother Paul's birthday," I said as we worked to get the hammock set up.

"Oh, yeah, that's right," Martin replied, with a long look at me.

Neither of us said any more. We both knew what the other was thinking: *Wouldn't it be nice to be out for that, so we could give Paul a call?* But by now, there was no point in verbalizing such wishes. We let the matter drop.

We also put up our *tolda,* as it looked like the rain would start at any moment. Ediborah was having trouble again finding suitable trees.

"Can I help you?" Martin asked.

"No, I think I just found a place. I'll be okay." She was up the hill and a little to our right.

We sat in the hammock a minute. Martin was in a reflective mood. He said, "I really don't know why this has happened to us. I've been thinking a lot lately about Psalm 100—what it says about serving the Lord with gladness. This may not seem much like serving the Lord, but that's what we're doing, you know? We may not leave this jungle alive, but we can leave this world serving the Lord 'with gladness'; we can 'come before his presence with singing' [Psalm 100:2]."

We prayed together then, something we did often. There was nothing else to do; we were totally dependent upon the Lord. We thanked the Lord for bringing us this far safely, and of course we begged him to get us home and back to our kids. We told him we wanted to keep serving him with gladness.

Martin had a toenail that had become ingrown. He borrowed a knife from the guys nearby and worked on his nail for a while. It gave me the creeps to watch him. But he said it started to feel better.

We returned the knife to the guys and then decided to lie down for a nap. It was starting to rain. We had just closed our eyes when a fearsome barrage of gunfire cut loose from the crest of the hill. The AFP? Surely not! It was raining, and they never fought in the rain.

"Oh, God!" I said. I wasn't swearing; I was honestly praying. My instincts, after sixteen previous battles, told me instantly what to do: *drop immediately.* I flipped my feet around to get out of the hammock—and before I even hit the ground, I felt the *zing!* of a bullet slamming through my right leg.

I rolled down the steep hill maybe eight feet, dazed. I looked up and saw Martin on the ground, too, so I quickly crawled to his side. He was kind of twisted, with his legs underneath his body. His eyes were closed. He was wearing a white Suzuki shirt with blue sleeves. Then I saw it: the blood was beginning to soak through his shirt from his upper left chest. *Oh no!* I thought. *He's been hit, too.*

Shots continued to ring out. The Abu Sayyaf were just getting themselves positioned to start firing back. Martin's breathing was heavy, almost a soft snore. He lay quietly on his back and partly on his side; he was so still that I refrained from yelling about my wound, which is what I normally would have done.

"Mart!" I heard Ediborah yell from where she was, just one time. Then nothing more. It was the last word she ever said.

I thought to myself, *If the Abu Sayyaf see that I'm wounded but still alive, they'll drag me down the hill, and I'll have to walk while wounded.* So I deliberately tried to lie still and look dead. Martin had taught me to focus my mind in a firefight, to hang on tightly to my emotions, and I knew that now, more than ever, I needed to do just that.

Once in a while, he moaned softly. I didn't say anything to him but just focused on being still. The shooting continued. Grenades blew up. Each moment was going to be my last, I was sure. *Lord, if this is it, just make it happen quickly for me,* I prayed. The battle raged. The pain in my leg was not as severe as the terror in my heart. I forced myself to keep lying still.

Several minutes passed. Then without warning I felt Martin's body become heavy and sort of sag against mine.

Is he dead? I wondered. I had no experience by which to judge. *Maybe he just passed out.*

The shooting gradually became more sporadic and then finally stopped. At the top of the ridge I heard shouting in Tagalog, the language of the AFP. No sounds came from the bottom, however, which told me that the Abu Sayyaf had fled down the streambed.

I didn't want to startle anyone who might be nearby, so I slowly moved my hand to signal that I was still alive. Immediately an AFP soldier spotted me. He and his partner ran down and tried to pick me up, one by lifting my shoulders, the other my ankles. I cried out in pain. So they let me down again, and both took a shoulder to pull me back toward our hammock and *tolda.* In the wetness they couldn't get a good grip on me, and their feet were slipping as well.

I looked back at where Martin still lay. The red spot on his shirt was larger now. His complexion was pasty white. And then I knew—the man I loved more than anyone in the world was gone.

::::

I wanted to stop the world in that moment, to reflect on my dreadful loss, to mourn the senseless death of my wonderful husband. Unfortunately, circumstances demanded otherwise. I had to think about getting myself off this mountain alive.

I gazed upward at our *tolda*. It had been riddled with bullet holes. As we had feared for so long, the AFP had come upon us with all barrels blazing.

"Did you get Sabaya?" I asked.

"Yeah, we think so. The one with the long hair?"

"No—that's Lukman. Sabaya was under the green *tolda* over there. Check that one."

A search revealed that he had gotten away.

The soldiers yelled up the slope for more help in moving me. Somehow we reached the top of the hill.

There I remembered the green backpack. It was still back by our hammock and it had all the notes we had written, the letters to the children, the stories. "Go get that green bag," I said. "I've got to have that."

The soldiers looked at me like I was crazy.

"Go get that green bag!" I insisted. "It has letters from Martin to our children. It will be the only thing they have left from their dad. You have to get it!"

One of the soldiers said to me, "Oh, Martin's okay. . . ."

I stared back at him. "Martin is *dead*. All the kids are going to have left is what he's written to them in the green bag. *Please* go get it!"

At that, one of them disappeared over the ridge. In a minute, he came back with the precious bag. I reached out to touch it, but they wouldn't let me. "We have to go over it for intelligence," someone said, which I thought was ridiculous.

There was some arguing about when I would get the papers inside. I locked eyes with one soldier whose English was pretty good. "Do you swear you'll get those letters to me?"

"Yes, ma'am, I will."

By this time, the medic was starting to cut off my wet *pantos.* I leaned back to close my eyes. Suddenly I was so exhausted, I just wanted to close my eyes and drift off into sleep.

"Oh, no, don't go to sleep," I heard someone say. "Stay awake."

The medic looked at me with a big smile and announced in heavily accented English, "I am the medic, and you are my first patient!" His hands were shaking. He proceeded to wrap some cloth around my wounds and then pronounced cheerfully, "Okay, you're all right! Do you need anything else?"

I stared blankly at him. "Do you have a Tylenol?" I asked him.

"Sure, okay." He didn't even have medicine with him, so he began asking around. Somebody came up with some mefenamic acid, an anti-inflammatory drug, which I took.

Somebody else brought dry clothes for me. Soon I was told, "A helicopter is coming for you."

I looked up at the rain still coming down. "A helicopter can't come right now," I said. "The ridges aren't clear, and it's raining."

They looked at me as if to say, *What do you know, lady?* They didn't realize I was a pilot's wife who had tracked the weather for hundreds of flights in my life. I knew it wasn't safe for a helicopter to operate under these conditions.

"No, no, for you the helicopter will come," someone answered.

"No! Please don't call one," I pleaded. "The pilot can't see what he's doing, and I don't want anyone else to lose their life today. Let's just wait." Nevertheless, the helicopter was already on its way.

The soldiers were clearly upset, realizing that in their rescue attempt, they had shot all three hostages. Several of them were smoking to calm their nerves. *I can't go to sleep, and I can't fall apart here,* I told myself. *I've made it this far.* I tried to remember Martin's words from so many times before: "You can do this, Gracia. You've got to go home whole."

Eventually, the lieutenant in charge came over to talk with me.

"Mrs. Burnham, I know that you're probably very angry with us," he said. "But we were just doing our jobs."

"I know," I replied. "We never forgot who the bad guys were and who the good guys were. I don't think of you as the bad guys."

In a moment, I continued. "How did you find us?"

"We've been following you all day. We saw your tracks where you crossed the logging road last night."

I knew it! We hadn't been careful enough.

I told them how hungry we were after so many days without food.

"Yeah, we saw where you ate your breakfast this morning at the farm. We just kept tracking you."

A little later, I heard the *chop-chop-chop* of a helicopter rotor. The ridges had cleared, and a little patch of blue was starting to peek through the clouds. "Now close your eyes, because it's going to be very windy," someone said. "We don't want you to get anything in your eyes."

Soon they were carrying me in a *malong* to the floor of the chopper. There I opened my eyes. I looked at the pilot, hoping he was an American, but I couldn't tell. Several of the soldiers wounded in the battle were already sitting on the seats. They strapped me down and closed the door.

But wait! What about Martin's body? Was I just going to be whisked away and leave my husband on this soggy hillside? *This can't be. . . .* I leaned back and sadly realized that in my physical condition, I had no other choice. We pulled away into the sky, leaving my best friend lying in the rain.

CHAPTER 20

THE EMBASSY

(June 7–10, 2002)

In less than thirty minutes, the Black Hawk set down at an airport in Zamboanga City, and my world instantly changed from rugged jungle to paved runways, modern terminal buildings, electricity, running water, toilets with privacy, professional-looking signs—it almost made my head spin. The helicopter door slid back, and immediately I saw American troops. An ambulance was waiting with an honest-to-goodness stretcher. Within minutes I was on a bumpy road heading for Camp Navarro General Hospital, which had been set up several months before to serve the U.S. military advisers and other staff.

When we arrived at the hospital and the ambulance door opened again, I was suddenly surrounded by people, everyone talking all at once. In the distance I noticed a beautiful American servicewoman. Her dark hair was pulled back and she was dressed in fatigues. She smiled at me, and I smiled back. As medics whisked me into the facility, I saw a whole row of U.S. troops with automatic rifles standing guard. The guys seemed so huge! After 376 days of living with short Filipinos, I was struck by their size. I began to realize that all this security was just for me.

Once in the examining room, the doctors moved in, one after another. All kinds of activity swirled around me. The American servicewoman never left the foot of my bed. When things grew calm for a moment, she introduced herself: "I'm Major Reika Stroh. I'm going to stay with you until you don't need me anymore." She began to stroke my arm and play with my fingers. I lay back and thought how nice it felt.

Who had planned ahead to provide this special service? I wondered.

Soon I was ushered into X ray. Once again, I glanced sideways to see the security detail still standing guard. The attention was almost overwhelming.

The X rays found that no bones had been chipped or broken and no arteries had been hit by the bullet; it had passed through the flesh from the back of my thigh out the front. I needed surgery to close the two wounds, but it was a simple enough procedure that it could be done right away at this facility.

They gave me a shot of anesthesia; I closed my eyes and drifted into unconsciousness.

When I awoke, it was dark. Major Stroh told me that although the surgery had gone well, some shrapnel had to be left behind. My leg wasn't in a cast, but a thick wrapping engulfed it from near my hip down to my knee.

I was well enough to leave and the American authorities wanted to fly me to Manila, she explained. "The whole mission of this plane and its crew has been to sit on the tarmac and wait for you and Martin to come out of the jungle," she told me. "They'll finally get to finish their mission."

Once we got back to the airfield and my stretcher was safely clipped to the wall of the huge C-130, Major Stroh said, "General [Donald] Wurster is here to meet you." I had seen a picture of this U.S. Air Force brigadier

June 7
3:00 A.M.: The phone rings in Kansas. U.S. Ambassador to the Philippines Francis Ricciardone tells Paul and Oreta that their son is dead and their daughter-in-law is wounded.

June 7
3:30 A.M.: President Arroyo calls the Burnhams to confirm the news.

general in a *Newsweek* magazine while we were in the jungle, so I knew that he was the commander of the joint task force in the southern Philippines. I wasn't alert enough to grasp everything he said, but he told me that he was glad I was finally out, and that I was going to be okay. He said something about my being brave and then added, "Here, I want you to have something."

He pressed the general's star from his cap into my hand.

"Oh, thank you very much," I said, overwhelmed with his thoughtfulness.

As soon as he left, I turned the star over to Major Stroh for safekeeping. "Are you hungry?" she asked. "We saved some of what we had for supper. Would you like some?"

Of course I did! But as soon as I took a bite, I began to feel nauseated. I realized that my stomach was simply not up to this yet.

The trip to Manila took less than an hour. There the U.S. ambassador, Francis Ricciardone, a distinguished-looking man in a suit, came onto the plane to say, "We are so glad you are here. Welcome to Manila. We're going to take you to the embassy." Within minutes I was in another ambulance headed through the nighttime streets of the capital.

Later I found out that, in order to protect me from the curious press, two decoy ambulances had already been sent toward Malacañang, the presidential palace. Meanwhile, we went the back way to the embassy and were there within ten or fifteen minutes. They had obviously planned all this in detail, and everything went like clockwork.

As we pulled through the security gates there on Roxas Boulevard, I gazed out at the palm trees and the beautifully manicured lawns and remembered when I had been to these buildings years before for passport matters. But this time, I saw rooms I'd never seen before. They wheeled me into a cozy two-bedroom suite with tasteful furniture and attractive art on the walls. There was food in the refrigerator, and in the closet I found some of my own clothes, items the New Tribes people had brought down from Aritao months before in hopes that someday I'd be here to wear them.

Although it was late on a Friday night, Ted Allegra, the embassy's chief of American citizen services, was waiting for me. A wonderfully gracious man, he briefed me on everything that was going to happen, including a visit with President Arroyo. Then he asked me, "What are *your* wishes?"

"I want to get out of here as soon as possible. Or if I can't go home soon, I want my family to come and join me here."

"Your sister Mary is already on her way to escort you home. How about if we get you on your way by Monday morning?"

I was thrilled and told him so.

Ted then told me that he had called both my parents and Martin's, and that the AFP had managed to retrieve Martin's body from the hillside. "We're going to fly him to the big military hospital in Okinawa for an autopsy," he gently explained. I was relieved to know that he was finally in American hands.

"Is there anything else?" he asked.

I wondered if there was any way to contact Ediborah's children. "I know they don't live here in Manila, but I'm the only one who can tell them how their mother lived and died," I told him. "I'd also like the chance to talk with my coworkers from New Tribes Mission."

Ted looked at me a little oddly and said, "Well, I

want you to know you are not a prisoner here at the embassy . . . but you may not leave."

I looked back and said, "Then I guess that means they'll all have to be invited here."

Ted sat there a minute and then said he'd try to make the arrangements.

When he left, I reached for the phone to call Martin's parents, having calculated that it would still be Friday morning in Kansas.

"Hello . . . this is Gracia, calling from Manila. I just wanted you to know that I'm fine."

"Hi, Gracia." I heard the voice of my mother-in-law on the other end of the line. "Doug is here with us, too." We talked for a minute and then I couldn't wait any longer.

"Can I talk to the kids?"

"They're not here—they've been with your folks in Arkansas for a few days, now that school has let out. Your brother and his family took everybody to the lake. But we've already been in touch with them, and they're driving back here to Kansas today."

I would have to wait just a bit longer to hear their voices. I was so disappointed.

But before we hung up, I knew I had to move ahead to the painful subject of Martin's death.

"I'm so sorry that Martin didn't make it out," I said to Oreta.

"We're sorry, too, but we're glad you're okay," she answered.

I proceeded to give them details of the last encounter,

June 7
4:30 A.M.: Mary Jones, having received a call during the night, passes the word to her parents in Arkansas, who must then tell the children.

wanting them to hear it from me instead of the press. They were terribly sad, of course.

We talked about a tentative funeral date. Suddenly, I felt very tired. I looked at the clock and realized it was three-thirty in the morning! As we hung up, I promised I'd call again once I got some sleep.

A Filipino nurse arrived and cleaned me up a little bit. The feel of clean, warm water on my skin was such a soothing treat.

She gave me a bit of cranberry juice and helped me change into my pajamas. I looked at this bed, with its spotless sheets and comfortable mattress, and thought, *No hammock tonight! And no one is going to chain Martin ever again.*

I finally sank down and turned out the light, but rather than sleeping, I found myself reliving the scene of Martin's death. I replayed in my mind those awful moments when we were both lying there wounded on the hillside in the rain. *What if I'd spoken to him and tried to wake him up? What if I'd rolled him over so the bleeding wouldn't have filled up his lungs so fast? Would he still be alive?*

I began to berate myself for not doing something, anything. But deep inside, I knew that no matter what I might have tried, the outcome would have been the same. Martin had lost massive amounts of blood and had been struggling to get his breath. Now he had gone directly into the Lord's presence . . . and I was left here in this nice bed in Manila—alone. This would be the first of an endless string of such nights to come.

Together we had imagined so many times what it would be like to be released and flown to Manila. We had talked about going to Mega Mall together, seeing our friends, going out to dinner, and celebrating. We certainly never wanted to imagine a scenario like this one.

I had just drifted off to sleep when sounds of gunfire erupted through the embassy. I quickly sat up in bed and began to scream. My heart was racing, but with my injured leg, I couldn't get out of bed to hit the floor.

The nurse came running.

"Who was shooting?" I demanded.

"There was no shooting," she assured me. "You're fine. Trust me—there was nothing."

She sat there with me until I got my bearings enough to realize my mind was playing tricks on me. I lay back down.

The next thing I knew, it was morning. I saw a Gideons Bible on the bed stand and I stretched over to pick it up.

What a privilege to hold this book in my hands once again! I turned on the lamp and opened to the Psalms. I began reading:

> *Deliver me from my enemies, O God;*
> *   protect me from those who rise up against me.*
> *Deliver me from evildoers*
> *   and save me from bloodthirsty men.*
> *See how they lie in wait for me!*
> *   Fierce men conspire against me*
> *   for no offense or sin of mine, O Lord. . . .*
> *But I will sing of your strength,*
> *   in the morning I will sing of your love;*
> *for you are my fortress,*
> *   my refuge in times of trouble.*
> *O my Strength, I sing praise to you;*
> *   you, O God, are my fortress, my loving God.*
> *(Psalm 59:1-3, 16-17)*

Soon the nurse was at the door. "What are you doing? It's only 6 A.M."

"I found this Bible here, and I'm reading it."

"Don't you think you ought to get some more sleep? You went to bed awfully late."

So to make her happy, I turned the light off and lay back down. After a few minutes of not sleeping, though, I turned the light back on and kept reading, this time from my favorite passage:

> *Therefore, since through God's mercy we have this ministry, we do not lose heart. . . . For God, who said, "Let light shine out of darkness," made his light shine in our hearts to give us the light of the knowledge of the glory of God in the face of Christ.*
>
> *But we have this treasure in jars of clay to show that this all-surpassing power is from God and not from us. We are hard pressed on every side, but not crushed; perplexed, but not in despair; persecuted, but not abandoned; struck down, but not destroyed. . . .*
>
> *Therefore we do not lose heart. Though outwardly we are wasting away, yet inwardly we are being renewed day by day. For our light and momentary troubles are achieving for us an eternal glory that far outweighs them all. (2 Corinthians 4:1, 6-9, 16-17)*

I then began to pray. *Oh, Lord, thank you so much for my getting out . . . and that my leg is going to be okay. Thank you for the joy of having your Word in my hands once again. Please go with me through these next difficult days, and make my life a blessing.*

::::

After breakfast, I was desperate to get back on the phone and try to reach my kids, but Ted Allegra told me it was too early—that they might not yet have arrived in Rose Hill from Arkansas. Meanwhile, he had a whole list of people who needed to see me that day: the ambassador, the doctor, even President Arroyo, who was scheduled to come around nine in the morning. I could see the staff already cleaning up the place for her arrival.

But as the morning wore on, we learned that President Arroyo's trip had been delayed and that she wouldn't arrive until evening.

"Then let's try to call my kids," I said. A speakerphone was provided, and I eagerly dialed the number. I knew it would be about nine o'clock Friday evening in Kansas.

"Hi, everybody—it's Gracia!"

The room was full: Paul and Oreta, my mom and dad, Martin's brother Doug and his family, his youngest sister, Felicia, and her husband—and Jeff, Mindy, and Zach.

"Mom, you ought to see our front yard!" Jeff said.

"Why?"

"There's news media all over! Television cameras and everything. I even called the cops on some of them when they got too pushy."

"Wow, that's amazing," I replied. "Hey, who else is there with you?" Others chimed in. "How are you feeling?" someone asked.

"Well, I'm here in the American Embassy in Manila, and actually I'm feeling okay. They did surgery on my leg yesterday afternoon down in Zamboanga, and it went pretty smoothly."

"When are you coming home?"

"How does Monday morning sound? Soon enough?" I kept talking, trying to update them on the travel plans I'd made with Ted Allegra.

I hated to break the upbeat mood of the conversation, but I knew I needed to talk to the kids about their dad. I had read somewhere that when a loved one passes away, people want to know the details of exactly what happened, even if it's hard to hear. Like with Martin's parents, I wanted my children to hear it all from me, not from someone else. I asked if they were ready to hear about how their dad had died.

"Yeah, Mom, go ahead and tell us." So I plunged into the story. The rawness of the event was impossible to gloss over, of course.

I could hear sniffling on the other end of the line. I knew they were crying—this wasn't easy for anyone. When I finished the story, Felicia and several others left the room.

"Mom, are you going to have a nervous breakdown?" Mindy asked. "Everyone is expecting one."

"Oh, honey," I said, "I had my breakdowns in the jungle. Actually, I wasn't very strong there. But your dad sure was. I learned so much from him this past year."

Then she asked, "Are you going to make us move from here?"

Up to that point, I hadn't really thought about our next step. But I could tell from Mindy's tone that moving would not be popular. If my kids wanted to stay in Kansas, that's what we'd do.

"No, we'll live there," I said. "I'm not going to make you pull up and move again. We've been through some hard times, and we are really going to be a family again. From now on, we'll make our decisions together."

After I spoke with the kids, I had the chance to talk to others in the room. In her classic southern "Missourah" drawl, my mom said, "We are thrilled to hear from you, Gracia. We are happy and very sad at the same time, but it's so nice to hear your voice."

My dad, ever protective, jumped in to say, "Gracia, you're probably very tired now and need to stop talking." I told him no, that on the contrary I just wanted to talk and talk.

The kids seemed to feel the same way. As Zach excitedly told me about throwing Aunt Beth off the jet ski at the lake the day before, the other kids cut in to say what a wild driver he was!

At the same time, I kept hearing my folks repeat, "It's so good to hear your voice." They were afraid, I guess, that I would be too broken up to carry on a conversation. Instead, we were reconnecting in a wonderful way.

In retrospect, I think the phone call was especially bittersweet for Martin's family. I know they were glad I was alive, but at the same time they were also grieving the loss of their son and brother. It had to be extremely difficult for them. As for my kids, I think it simply helped to hear that I was okay.

That went well, I thought as we hung up. I was encouraged by their resiliency. Maybe what I'd said about rebuilding our lives as a family could be true after all.

As the day wore on, my room filled with a steady stream of visitors. One conversation ran into another, it seemed. I received several phone calls about Martin's body. The autopsy had been finished, and they wondered if they should leave his beard as it was or shave it off. I had no idea what to say. After several phone calls to his parents in the U.S., we decided to leave his beard on. He was so thin by the time he died, and I didn't want to scare the kids. I thought with his beard gone, it would just show how sunken his cheeks had become. I still don't know if I made the right decision there, because the kids had never seen him with such a long beard.

I spent the rest of the day meeting people, answering questions, and making decisions. At one point Major Stroh came to sit on the bed beside me and start the first of many debriefing sessions for intelligence purposes. I talked on and on about what life had been like the past year, how the Abu Sayyaf had treated us, and the various emotional peaks and valleys we'd been through. She diligently took notes on a pad, but when I got to the part about Martin discovering his handcuffs no longer worked, I suddenly lost control.

"No!" I yelled. "You can't write that down! It'll make him look bad. He was so afraid people would think he was a chicken or something for not trying to escape! Don't tell anybody what I just said!" I was shrieking as I began to sob.

She put down her pen instantly and just sat quietly. Tears began to fill her eyes, too. She reached over to give me a big hug. We wept together, until finally I could calm down and regain my composure. I apologized for yelling at her, and we continued.

Later that afternoon, a State Department counselor arrived. Gary Percival specialized in hostage situations and was a really neat Christian guy. "You're going to get hit with a lot of press and a lot of people wanting you to do things you don't want to do," he told me. "You're also going to have to deal with people who love you and haven't been able to do anything for you for a year but wished they could. Now will be their big opportunity— whether you want what they have in mind or not. They won't consciously mean to run your life, but that's what it will amount to.

"You are going to have to decide how much you want to do, what you want to do, what you can let others do for you, and how to say no nicely to the rest." I hadn't thought about any of this, but I was grateful for the advice.

We talked for a long time. When I became teary-eyed as I shared parts of my story, he just sat there—unlike everyone else, who always ran to get me a tissue. Finally, Gary commented, "Do you notice I'm not getting up and getting anything for you?"

"Well, I hadn't really noticed."

"I'm going to let you ask for what you need. If you need a Kleenex, you can ask me for a Kleenex," he said. "You haven't had to make very many decisions for more than a year, and now you may not know how. I'll help you if you need help. But you have to express it."

I thought back to this advice more than once in the days and weeks ahead. The other thing Gary told me was, "It is not your job to make everybody happy now that you are out. Just from being with you for these few hours, I can tell that you want everything to run smoothly, you want everybody to feel good, you don't want to disappoint anyone." This guy obviously had my number! "Your job now is not to make everybody happy with you. Your job is to do what is best for you and get on with your life.

"For example, you don't owe the media anything. Feel free to talk to them—in fact, it's probably good if you do. But don't feel like you're obligated to them. Just write out a good statement to make when you leave here, and another one for when you land in America, and you'll be set."

Later on, three of our mission leaders came to see me: Bob Meisel; Jody Crain, the field director; plus Macon Hare from the home office in the States. It was so good to see them and talk together.

Just before President Arroyo was set to arrive, it dawned on me that I hadn't yet prayed about the visit. In the jungle, Martin and I had prayed about every little thing. We had thanked God for every drink of water. Now here I was, only twenty-four hours into the midst of plenty, with a nice bed and medicine, and I could already see my whole attitude and thought process changing.

Martin's sister Cheryl, who lives in the Philippines, had come to be with me. I turned to her and said,

"Would you sit down here and pray with me about President Arroyo's visit?" She held my hand and we prayed together. I can't tell you how good that felt.

President Arroyo finally showed up about nine that evening, complete with a video crew. I hadn't realized what a small person she was. I'm only five foot two, and she was noticeably shorter than I.

She was beautifully dressed. I knew she had had a long, hard day, and I was honored that she still came to see me so late. She brought a basket of orchids with other gorgeous flowers, as well as a basket of fruit. She sat on the couch near my chair, and at first, as the cameramen were maneuvering to get the angles they wanted, it seemed kind of awkward. She didn't quite know what to say, and neither did I.

"Tell me how you are feeling," she began.

"Fine—really, I'm doing very well," I answered. "My leg is going to be all right, they say."

What do I say now? I wondered.

Without thinking, I said the first thing that came to my mind. "You know, you might be interested in the fact that the Abu Sayyaf really don't like it that a woman is running this country, because they don't think much of women. Personally, it seems to me you're the first president who has ever said no to them. Maybe that's part of why they're upset that the Philippines would let a woman be president."

"No, I hadn't realized that," she said, keeping her composure.

I glanced over at Ted Allegra, who looked like he was about to have a heart attack.

Oops! That wasn't a very good way to start, was it?

I took a breath and said, "Um, would you like to hear about my husband, Martin, and how he died?"

"Yes, I would."

I began the story of our walking all night, getting to the hillside, setting up our hammocks, and then hearing gunfire start from the top of the hill. I went through it all. She was genuinely listening. By the end of the story, we were just sitting there facing each other and talking like two friends.

I told her I wasn't mad at anybody, and I wasn't blaming anybody—except the Abu Sayyaf. I assured her that we had never forgotten who the bad guys were.

Sometimes at night when I couldn't sleep in the jungle, I used to lie in the hammock and think of all the unkind things I would say to President Arroyo someday—about how her military was on the take, and how they were too proud to stand aside and let the Americans lead the rescue effort. I'd made up my little speech. It wasn't nice. My natural self wanted to blame someone.

Then I would try to tell myself either that it wasn't her fault, or that even if it was, she was responsible to God, not me, for her actions.

At this meeting, none of my venom came even close to the surface. I didn't feel like chewing her out after all. I knew the army felt very bad for what had happened. I didn't need to make anyone feel worse.

::::

On Sunday, I fulfilled my wish and called my brother, Paul, to say happy birthday. We had a wonderful talk. He told me later, "When I first heard that Martin had been shot to death, I got very angry and bitter. But when I heard how well you were coping, something healed in my heart."

Around noon, my New Tribes Mission friends began to arrive—probably thirty of them altogether. Ted Allegra let them in six or eight at a time so I wouldn't be overwhelmed. What a special time we had, talking and crying and even laughing together. Everybody seemed to want to touch me and make sure I was okay.

Later in the day, I got a chance to meet Ediborah's four children, her mother, and her brother, all of whom President Arroyo had specially flown to Manila. We spent maybe an hour together, and I told them stories about the year and how brave Ediborah had been. I told them she had been a good cook and had even built the cooking fires when the guys were too lazy to do it. She had always looked good and smelled good. Her English had been excellent, I said, which was such a help in keeping us informed.

The family members were somber, of course, still grieving their loss. I did the best I could to comfort their hearts.

Of course, I was not about to leave the Philippines without a visit with my dear friends Angie and Fe. The girls had been waiting their turn for hours. They finally came walking through the door, cautiously at first, and then we fell into each other's arms for long, long hugs.

They looked so good! Beautiful haircuts, makeup, clothes that fit—we laughed about that. No more baggy clothes to hide our figures!

Buddy and Divine (Angie's brother-in-law and sister) were there, too. They told me about the injuries they'd sustained as we were escaping from the Lamitan hospital and about their recovery. Angie and Fe got down on their knees beside my chair and we talked and talked. They told me someone had spotted Hurayra in the Zamboanga passport office, probably trying to head for Malaysia. That sharp-eyed person had tried to chase Hurayra but had lost him in the crowded street.

How good it was to see these girls I had come to love dearly, now smiling, talking, and rebuilding their lives. They had been through so much! We were survivors, and we celebrated until Ted announced that their time was up. He was afraid I was wearing down. But by now, I didn't want to be protected—I wanted to keep talking to my friends.

Later that evening, my sister Mary and her husband, Lance, arrived. What a thrill! She just came marching in and took over in her usual Mary way. She sat me down on the bed and then pulled out my wedding ring! She had ended up with it and hadn't yet given it to Mindy, in hope that I would someday be released. Mary had been saving it for me. I put it on as we sat there . . . my most prized possession!

Mary and I went through some of my stuff in the closet and figured out what I needed. The nurses had gone out to the market to buy some baggy pants that would fit over the fat dressing on my wound so I'd have something to wear home.

"Is there anything else I can do for you?" she asked.

"Well, how would you like to shave my legs? It's only been about four months now!"

"Sure!" So we headed for the bathtub. What a riot. As I recall, Mary, Cheryl, and two nurses all tried to help.

Mary was eager to update me on her pregnancy, now four months along. She told me she had been using my situation as a wonderful excuse. "Whenever I don't want to clean house or do the dishes, I tell Lance, 'Oh, I couldn't possibly do that—my sister is a hostage!'"

We talked late into the night as we packed up for the flight the next morning.

::::

When we got to the airport early that Monday, the ambassador was there to greet me. Soon it was time for me to face the reporters.

I pulled out my notes, as Ted and Gary had advised, and made my statement.

Good morning. Martin and I had so many dear friends here in the Philippines. You know who you are. Our friends in Malaybalay, in Brookes Point, in Darapida [our barrio in Aritao], in Manila—we love you so very much, and we thank you for the precious memories that you gave us during our fifteen years here. Martin loved this country with all his heart.

We want to thank each and every one of you for every time you remembered us in prayer. We needed every single prayer you prayed for us during our ordeal in the jungle.

We know there are countless of you who don't even know us who prayed and offered support also, and we thank you, too. We especially want to thank the military men, the Filipinos and the Americans, who risked and even gave their lives in order to rescue us. May God bless these men in their ongoing efforts.

During our ordeal, we were repeatedly lied to by the Abu Sayyaf, and they are not men of honor. They should be treated as common criminals. We support all efforts of the government in bringing these men to justice.

I return to the States this morning to rejoin my children and to put my life back together. Part of my heart will always stay with the Filipino people. Thank you.

And with that, I was wheeled into the jet way for a Northwest Airlines flight to Tokyo, which would connect in Minneapolis with a flight bound for Kansas City. Looking out the window for my last glimpse of the Philippines, I saw several dozen AFP soldiers enthusiastically waving good-bye to me from the tarmac. I knew I was closing the door on a sixteen-year era of my life. Everything was now about to change.

CHAPTER 21

GOING HOME

(June 10–17, 2002)

The flight from Manila to Tokyo takes four hours. It immediately became apparent that more than a few fellow passengers knew I was aboard. As I was wheeled down the aisle, well-wishers reached out to touch me—some of them smiling, others in tears. The phrase I heard over and over was "I'm so sorry."

After another twelve hours in the air, we finally began our descent into Kansas City. As I looked out the window, I thought back to something Martin had written months before in the jungle in anticipation of this moment:

> Highest priority when getting home is to reconnect w/ the kids. Need to recognize and respect the role that others have had in their lives and not snatch them away. Our parents will also need some time. There are going to be a lot of demands on us, and setting priorities is going to be difficult. Sometimes we're going to do it wrong. Keep going.

What wisdom he had voiced!

A mixture of joy and apprehension swept over me. It was going to be so fantastic to see Jeff, Mindy, and Zach again! Even in my excitement, however, I was a little nervous. There would no doubt be some awkwardness once we were all together again. I had never worn the title of Single Mom before. I hadn't even thought about what that would be like. I was bound to "do it wrong" sometimes. I knew that I could only ask God for guidance and not be too hard on myself.

I wasn't even out of the jet way when I got my first glimpse of Zach, pacing back and forth. The instant I got out into the open, a burst of glee went up, even though there were strangers everywhere. I stretched my arms up from the wheelchair to squeeze Zach.

"I love you, Mom!" he cried, squeezing me back.

As I reached for Jeff, then Mindy, I exclaimed, "Oh, thank you, God! We're back together!"

I clung to Mindy and then I looked at her. She suddenly seemed very grown up. "I didn't know if I would ever hug you again," I told her.

"Me neither, Mom."

My mom and dad and Paul and Oreta were also there. It was so good to see them all again. We were quickly ushered into a separate room for just a few minutes. Along the way, I spotted friends from high school and college scattered in the crowd. I waved at them; it was so cool. I couldn't believe they were there.

After a moment or two of reconnecting with my family, it was time to face the media once again. Zach wheeled me out into the crowd of flashes and microphones. In light of the story I'd heard on the phone about his driving skills, I wasn't sure he should be the one to push me around with my leg sticking out. But he did fine.

Once again, I pulled out my card to make sure I said the proper things, and no more:

Good afternoon. It's good to be home. I want everyone to know that I'm fine.

Several minutes ago I was reunited with my children and my family, and I think this must be one of the happiest moments of my whole life.

We want to thank each and every one of you for every time you remembered us in prayer. We needed every single prayer during our ordeal in the jungle.

We know there were countless of you who don't even know us who prayed and offered support also. And we thank you.

I would like to thank Representative Todd Tiahrt and Senator Sam Brownback for helping my family and being such a support during this difficult time.

During our ordeal we were repeatedly lied to by the Abu Sayyaf, and they are not men of honor. They should be treated as common criminals. We support all U.S. government efforts in assisting the Philippines in ridding that country of terrorism.

A very bad thing happened to Martin and me when we were taken hostage. But we want everyone to know that God was good to us every single day of our captivity. Martin was also a source of strength to all the hostages. He was a good man, and he died well.

Again, it's good to be home. Keep praying for me and my kids as we begin to rebuild our lives. And thank you.

I was glad I'd written this out ahead of time. But even though I'd taken precautions like this, there were still a lot of inaccuracies in the media accounts of our story. The one that really upset me originated with the Associated Press and was picked up by *Time* magazine. They quoted me as saying of Martin's death: "That is God's liking. That is probably his destiny."* I would never say such a thing. In fact, this sounds more like an Abu Sayyaf comment than anything else. I wrote *Time* to protest the blatant misquote and got back a letter passing the buck to AP. The magazine refused to run a correction.

::::

We left the airport that day and were taken in a shuttle bus to a separate office building to meet the rest of our

*Verbatim, *Time,* 17 June 2002.

family. The only nonfamily member in the room was Rep. Todd Tiahrt, who had flown in from Washington for the occasion. "Congressman Tiahrt, it's a pleasure to meet you," I said, shaking his hand. "Did you happen to fly over Basilan on New Year's Eve?"

He looked a bit surprised and said yes.

"We saw you!" I said, and I briefly told him the story. He was amazed and pleased. It was fun to watch his face. He told me he was glad I was home and sorry he couldn't have done more to get Martin out safely.

I turned then to the family; we had so much catching up to do! We were all talking fast and furious, of course.

There was laughter but also tears, especially when I told a few stories about Martin's bravery and the struggles I had with God during my ordeal.

The more the conversation and celebrating continued, the more a slight divergence of mood settled in. Although my side of the family had lost a beloved son-in-law, they were primarily ecstatic at having me back again. The Burnhams, while glad to see their daughter-in-law, were having to face the aching reality that this scene contained no firstborn son and never would.

Oreta eventually came to me and quietly explained what was occurring. I hadn't picked up on it until then, but I definitely understood what was going on. I wheeled myself over to Felicia, who stood away from everyone else and seemed to be struggling the most. I held her hand as I said, "Felicia, I don't know how you must be feeling right now. It must be hard to come to terms with Martin not being here. But the honest truth is, I said good-bye to Martin over and over and over, every time the guns started up. He's gone now—and I can't stay sad. You didn't have him for the past year; you didn't get to say good-bye like I did. He was snatched from you, and I know it will be very different for you."

She gave me a hug, and we cried a bit together. In that moment I realized that I wasn't going to be able to please everyone in every circumstance. I had to just do the best I could and, as Martin had written, "keep going."

In time we moved out into the afternoon sunshine, where a big charter bus was waiting to make the two-hundred-mile drive to Rose Hill. Everybody was talking at once. The kids wanted to tell me stories about everything from football season to the friends they'd made in Rose Hill to the Christmas musical at school.

As we left the Kansas Turnpike and got close to home, the sun was just setting. I began noticing squad cars with flashing lights at every intersection.

"What are these policemen doing here?" I asked my father-in-law.

"They're for you, to make way for the bus," he replied.

As soon as we got into town, I saw that the streets were lined with people! They were waving flashlights and holding signs of welcome. Others had candles. Yellow ribbons and balloons were everywhere. I just couldn't believe my eyes. I thought to myself, *Martin would be so honored to see how this town has turned out for us.*

When we got close to Paul and Oreta's house, streets were clogged with TV-station uplink trucks, and reporters were already talking into their microphones. I was helped off the bus and into a wheelchair. I waved at everybody across the street and called out, "Thank you!" as I blew kisses. *Those young, screaming girls must be Mindy's friends,* I thought as I smiled. As we headed inside the house, my heart was overwhelmed with people's kindness.

To be honest, I don't really remember much about that first night home—I was too jet-lagged. I can't even tell you who was there. I just remember being surrounded by people who really cared about me.

My family screened the visitors pretty stringently over the next couple of days, not wanting to wear me out. I heard somebody say, "Getting in to see Gracia is like getting into Fort Knox!" I ended up circumventing the system a time or two, sneaking some people into my room for visits when everyone thought I was sleeping.

My mom and dad stayed right next door at the Hansons' house. My brother, Paul, was there from Kansas City as well to help me start thinking through various financial matters, among other things. The living room was full of flowers and gifts and potted plants. The phone rang constantly. People brought food. It was amazing.

I looked once and noticed a woman in the kitchen who was not a family member; she was just quietly cleaning up, putting food away, and making coffee. It took me a while to realize it was Marilyn German, wife of one of the New Tribes Mission executives from Florida. She was such a servant. She hadn't waited to be asked; she just showed up and went to work for at least three or four days.

On the second morning, I asked Felicia to be my fashion adviser and buy me an appropriate dress for the funeral. I also asked her to do my hair and makeup for the next few days because I was obviously out of practice. She got a beautician friend of hers to stop by and put highlights in my hair.

::::

The next few days were a flurry of activity as we made necessary phone calls and planned the arrangements for Martin's funeral.

I knew the speaker Martin wanted: his friend from college days, Clay Bowlin, now senior pastor of Northwest Bible Church in Kansas City. We used to pray for Clay every Sunday morning in the jungle, knowing it was Saturday night back in the States and he would be making his final preparations to preach.

Martin's cousin Kirk Hinshaw would play the piano, and Dan Smith, a soloist Martin had heard at Clay's church just before returning to the Philippines a year before, would sing.

I had assumed we'd have a small, quiet funeral at Rose Hill Bible Church, which seats maybe 200 or 250. Then somebody said, "Okay, now Central Christian has graciously offered their facility."

This is one of the biggest churches in Wichita, with a huge sanctuary. "It's kind of a big place, don't you think?" I said.

"Well, we're expecting about four thousand people."

I couldn't believe they were serious. Martin had been such an unassuming, normal guy. *He would be shocked at a crowd that size!* I thought to myself. But in fact, when Friday morning came, we found that we did need the space.

While others were making the various preparations, I knew I had a job that only I could do, and that was to get my kids ready for all this. They'd never really been to a wake or a funeral before.

It seemed that the only place we could really be alone to talk was in the car. I couldn't drive, obviously; I could hardly get into the car with my leg the way it was. But Jeff had his driving permit. So we all went down to Sonic, the local drive-in, for their famous Cherry Lime-ades. There we were able to sit in the car and talk awhile.

"Tomorrow night will be the viewing at the funeral home," I explained. "As you know, Dad really lost a lot of weight, so when you see his body, he's going to look really thin. And he'll have the beard you saw in the pictures from captivity. This will be the one and only time to see him, okay? At the funeral, the casket will be closed.

"The first hour will be just for us family members. After that, other people will come, and you don't have to stay for the whole time if you don't want to. It's just a time for making contact with lots of friends who have cared for us and prayed for us."

We negotiated a bit over what to wear to these events, like any mom and her sons would do. My sister Mary bought a really pretty dress for Mindy, and Felicia had helped me pick out a black dress with a black-and-white flowered jacket. Soon we were all set.

When we arrived at the funeral home, I was pleased to see that Smith Mortuary had put together an excellent video tribute to Martin, with pictures all the way from boyhood to college days, our early years in the Philippines, shots with the kids, shots with his airplanes. The video told the story of his life and what it had meant, and it made us cry.

Martin did not look like himself. If I had it to do again, I would bury him in blue jeans and his favorite flannel shirt. Here he was all dressed up in a suit—and he never wore a suit. When we were home on furlough, he wore a jacket or suit coat only if he was going to speak in a church. He was just a very simple, plain guy.

I was shocked at how thin he looked—only 125 pounds, they said—and how old. I sat there in my wheelchair feeling so badly that all this had happened to him—a man who wanted the best for others and had given up the "American dream" to make a difference in a poor country. It didn't seem fair.

There was a bruise on his forehead that they hadn't been able to fix with makeup. *How did he get that?* I wondered. Had he gotten it falling out of the hammock? I didn't know.

But what I missed most was the laughter in his eyes. That's what *made* Martin—the twinkle in his eyes, the upbeat attitude that said, *No problem is ever too tough to overcome, no ordeal too grim to endure.* He had confidence; he was a doer, and he had fun in the process whenever possible.

The kids gathered around me and we cried together. They said, like family members so often do, "It doesn't look like Dad."

"You're right," I replied. "In fact, he's in heaven with the Lord Jesus, who he loved. This is just his body that's not working anymore."

I laid my hand on his hard chest and thought, *Poor Martin. You went through so much. You were so brave, and you kept me going so I could return home. I'll always love you.*

Soon people began to arrive—cousins of Martin whom I had met only a few times, friends from school, even a group of FBI agents from Kansas City who had been working on our case for months. They seemed so very nice. Many Rose Hill people came—even whole families—and said, "You don't know us, but we feel like we know you. We've been praying for you."

At one point, I looked around the room and realized our whole New Tribes team from the mid-1980s was there: Brett Nordick, who had flown on Luzon; Perry Johnson from Palawan; and Steve Roberts, our chief mechanic. "This was a good group!" I bragged that night, remembering all the wonderful times we had shared. The only team member missing was Martin.

It was late by the time I got to bed. The kids and I had decided to all sleep in the same room for a while. So Mindy and I took the bed, while the boys slept on the floor. I could lie only on my back because my leg was elevated on pillows.

We lay awake talking. "How are you guys doing?" I asked. We all agreed we were coping as well as could be

expected. Soon they were asleep, while I lay there thinking once again about Martin—sad he was gone but oh,
so glad that his ordeal was over and he was now in the
very presence of Jesus.

::::

"Are you ready, Gracia?" my father-in-law said in a low
voice as he prepared to push my wheelchair into the
church Friday morning.

"Yes, I'm ready," I said.

Everything else was in order, it seemed. The TV
trucks outside Central Christian Church were already
getting their signal from the pool cameras we had allowed to be set up in the sanctuary. The dignitaries were
already seated: former Kansas senator and majority
leader Bob Dole, now representing the U.S. State Department; Senator Sam Brownback and his wife; Congressman Tiahrt and his wife; U.S. Ambassador to the
Philippines Francis Ricciardone; his counterpart, Philippine Ambassador to the U.S. Albert del Rosario; and
others. Behind me stood the line of Burnhams and
Joneses who would follow me in and fill up one large section of seats; the rest of the cavernous church seemed full
already.

As we entered, the entire audience stood without being asked. I saw friends on all sides—from the mission,
from college, from our supporting churches, from places
far away whom I never would have expected to fly in to
be there. On the end of one row I spotted my friends
Joyce and Kay, who had encouraged me to accept that
first date with Martin so long ago.

Once my wheelchair was parked at the front, Zach
took his place immediately to my left, then Jeff, then
Mindy, followed by Oreta and Paul, then Felicia and her
husband, Clint. Behind us came Doug and Teresa with

their children; they took their places in the second row.
The whole family processional took a long time while
Kirk continued to play "The Old Rugged Cross." The
familiar words could not have been more fitting for Martin: "I will cling to the old rugged cross / And exchange it
some day for a crown."

One by one, various speakers and singers came to
the podium, each one offering an eternal perspective on
Martin's death. Central Christian's senior pastor, Joe
Wright, commented that people often express their con-
dolences at a time such as this by saying they're sorry for
the loss. "We haven't 'lost' Martin," he observed. "We
know where he is. And someday, because of the promise
of God and the sacrifice of Jesus Christ on the cross, we
can join him and be reunited."

Oreta's brother, Rev. Galen Hinshaw, gave Martin's
obituary, which included not only dates and places but
personal insights. The crowd couldn't help but melt
when he got to letters written by the two older kids for
this occasion.

The first letter was from Jeff:

*My dad was a very special person to me. He would take
the time to do special things with me. We used to take
plane rides together. He flew me to Palawan from our
home in Aritao. We were in a Cessna 180, so it took
around six hours.*

*Once we were in Palawan, we visited all the tribes
there. He said that one day I could fly for these people.
He was going to teach me to fly as soon as I turned 15.*

*He bought me a motorbike when I was 13. He
taught me to drive it and would help me work on it
when I would crash it, or when the motor needed work.
I'm going to miss our times together.*

Mindy had written:

My dad was the most generous person I have ever known. Even though we weren't a rich family, every time I wanted or needed anything, he would do his best to get it for me. He was a big family man. He never missed a chance to get away from work and take our family on a vacation.

He would sing songs to me and change the words, putting my name into it. He would sing them to me when he came home from work and at bedtime.

Rev. Oli Jacobsen, chairman of New Tribes Mission, compared Martin to the apostle Paul's associate Epaphroditus, who more than once "came close to death for the work of Christ" (Philippians 2:30).

"He was one of our best pilots, and one of our best test pilots as well," he said. "As he trained others, his notable characteristics were his patience and his attitude of 'you can do it.' One of our missionaries called him 'Mr. Cool.' But he was much more than a pilot. To his fellow missionaries, he was a servant of servants."

When Clay Bowlin stood up to speak, I leaned forward. I didn't want to miss a word.

"Why did this happen this way?" he asked, hitting on the very question that had been gnawing at all our minds.

"I don't know. God doesn't always look at things the way we do. Isaiah 55 teaches us that God's ways are higher than ours, and his thoughts beyond our comprehension. There's a phrase in Deuteronomy 29:29 that fits this occasion: 'The secret things belong to the Lord our God.'"

For the next thirty minutes or more, Clay had our rapt attention as he gave an eloquent tribute to Martin's life and work. He told college stories; he honored Martin's role as a husband and a dad; and in the end, he presented the gospel of Jesus Christ as clearly as possible. His most memorable line, the one quoted by news outlets afterward, was this: "Gracia was rescued from the jungle by a helicopter; Martin was rescued from the jungle on angels' wings."

We didn't want to end the service on a morbid note. There would be no filing past an open casket. In fact, we set the opposite tone altogether by bringing out a Southern gospel quartet to sing a song fit for a pilot: "I'll Fly Away." Toes tapped and people smiled as they prepared to leave the church after nearly two hours. It wasn't majestic or somber; it was instead upbeat and natural—just like Martin.

My heart was so full as I was wheeled out of the church. I wanted to stop and talk to so many people, but I couldn't. All that would come later. The family headed directly to a small country cemetery east of Rose Hill for a private burial.

My kids loved watching the Wichita police clear the way for us, blocking intersections and racing from the back of the line to the front repeatedly, light after light. We drove by a big Wal-Mart with employees out front holding signs: "We Support the Burnhams" and "God Bless You Guys" and "Welcome Home, Gracia." Again, I was amazed.

Pastor Robert Varner of Rose Hill Bible Church conducted the graveside service, and then we soon headed to the middle school gymnasium, where the various civic clubs had prepared a huge spread of food for anyone who wanted to come. Somebody got me something to eat, but I hardly had time to touch it, because for the next several hours I was busy greeting people.

::::

That night, the Burnham family gathered for a meal at the church. A little later, my side of the family showed up to do one of our favorite things: sit around with guitars and sing. I was amazed at how much Jeff's playing had improved over the past year. As the evening started to wind down and I got reflective, I thought that maybe I was truly weird in feeling that I had honestly "enjoyed" the funeral. I had seen so many people I loved. And the music had been excellent. Martin would have especially loved that.

When it was time to go to bed, we had trouble getting Jeff to stop playing his electric guitar. "Enough already, Jeff. It's late!" I finally announced. As we lay in bed, the kids and I talked about various things—nothing deep, just the events of the day. I reminded myself that I wanted to enjoy every day—whether sad or happy— with these kids. From now on we'd be together.

The next morning, Doug and Brian, Martin's brothers, plus Clint, Felicia's husband, made a flower bed in the side yard for all the potted plants and flowers we had received at the funeral. We put a stone angel we had received as a gift right in the middle.

Meanwhile, my family started packing up to leave. Several of them, however, stayed around for Zach's baseball game. Wheelchair or not, I was determined to be there. This was the kind of thing I had dreamed about for a year in the jungle—getting back to normal living and being a mom to my kids once again. The pageantry of the day before was fine, but the joy of watching my son play right field was every bit as meaningful.

My nephew Nathan transported me to the field, along with his mother, Beth. My cousin Sandy and her daughter Erin were there. So was my good friend from the Philippines Val Petro—the one who had taken the kids for "just a week" while Martin and I went to Palawan. Her husband, Bob, had passed away from a heart problem while we were in captivity. That led us to talk about heaven.

"You know, I just kind of imagine that when somebody arrives in heaven," she said, "they make this announcement: 'Arriving at gate 42 in five minutes, Martin Burnham. Please proceed to gate 42 if you want to greet him!'" she said.

"Yes!" I said. "What a reunion those two had."

She continued, "I can just see Bob standing there and Martin saying, 'Bob! What are you doing here?!' Bob, of course, would already be in the know about Martin's situation."

Val and I talked about what we were going to do with ourselves now. She was thinking of moving to Indianapolis to help a new church get started. I told her I was going to stay in Rose Hill to raise my kids.

After the game, Nathan, Beth, and I drove back out the dirt road to the cemetery to see Martin's grave again. Looking at all the flowers, I felt great sadness at having to say good-bye to him. But I reminded myself that, just like the other good-byes in my lifetime, this was temporary.

I can't wait to see Martin again—and I will.

::::

The next day was Sunday—an ordinary Sunday to millions of other people, but not to me. This was my first chance in more than a year to go to church. I absolutely could not wait.

So many Sundays in the jungle I had sat on the ground thinking of the high privilege of gathering with other believers to worship God. To sit in a pew (actually, in my case, they parked my wheelchair in the center aisle), to sing again, to pray, to listen to the Word of God—it was exquisite.

Doug Burnham led the worship that morning. We began to sing:

> *My hope is built on nothing less*
> *Than Jesus' blood and righteousness;*
> *I dare not trust the sweetest frame,*
> *But wholly lean on Jesus' name.*
>
> *On Christ, the solid rock, I stand;*
> *All other ground is sinking sand,*
> *All other ground is sinking sand.*

My mind flashed back to the mangrove swamp on Basilan, where with every step we sank down into the ooze, where I longed for solid ground to walk on. I knew we had survived only by depending on Christ, the solid Rock of our faith and hope.

Doug also led us in Martin's favorite gospel song, "Wonderful Peace." This again unleashed a flood of memories for me—singing it in the dark as another day ended and we desperately needed God's calm for our troubled souls. How great to sing this song with a church full of people all worshiping the one true God!

The Scriptures that day were taken from James 1:2-4:

> *My brethren, count it all joy when ye fall into divers temptations; knowing this, that the trying of your faith worketh patience. But let patience have her perfect work, that ye may be perfect and entire, wanting nothing.*

We also read from 1 Peter 1:6-7:

Wherein ye greatly rejoice, though now for a season, if need be, ye are in heaviness through manifold temptations: That the trial of your faith, being much more precious than of gold that perisheth, though it be tried with fire, might be found unto praise and honour and glory at the appearing of Jesus Christ.

I sat there thinking, *Well, that's just what has happened to me. My faith has been tested, and I'm more sure of what I believe now than I ever was before. God has given me joy and peace in the midst of trials.*

It was the neatest morning, worshiping the Lord and greeting the folks who mean so much to me.

There was one other gathering I knew I wanted to attend: the 6 A.M. prayer meeting on Monday morning. These men had been crawling out of bed and driving down to the church six mornings a week for more than a year now, just to intercede for Martin and me. I had to join them and say thank you.

I set the alarm for 5 A.M. Because I had to carefully consider every move I made as I hobbled around on crutches, everything took longer. Just getting past my two sleeping sons on the floor was tricky.

I was dressed and presentable a little while after 5:30. I made my way into the living room and gently eased down onto the couch. When Paul came out, he helped me outside and aided me as I hoisted myself up into the van. My dad joined us from next door, where they were staying.

At the church, I was wheeled in through the side door into the room where the men, Ralph, David, Pastor Robert, Les, and Mike, were already gathered around the

long white table. I smelled coffee. They parked me conveniently at the end of the table.

So this was how it had been every single morning.
These dear friends had held us up before God in
prayer—and I knew that all over America and the world,
for that matter, pockets of other people, prayer groups,
and families had also been meeting to pray for us.

With tears in my eyes and a quiver in my chin, I began to speak. "Thank you so much for this act of love,
which you've done over and over again for Martin and
me. You got me home."

And then we started to pray.

CHAPTER 22

REFLECTIONS

(Summer 2002)

Looking around that circle of godly men, thinking about them driving to the church morning after morning regardless of the winter darkness, the summer heat, whether it was raining or snowing, in spite of busy schedules at work or home, I couldn't help but wonder: *Why did their many prayers—and those of thousands of other people—get only a partial answer?*

As my brother-in-law Doug honestly said to the media, "It's not the kind of reunion we were hoping for. We're one short."

After all, if quantity makes the difference in prayer, we certainly had quantity on our side. Six or so men praying six mornings a week for fifty-three weeks— that's more than nineteen hundred prayers. Add to that the intercessions of all the Burnham and Jones family members, our supporting churches across ten states, the entire New Tribes family of some 3,100 missionaries in twenty-five nations, all those who logged on to the Web site PrayThemHome.com, Martin's and my pleadings with God by night and day. The total is incalculable.

I don't doubt the truth of "Ye have not, because ye ask not" (James 4:2). But it sure doesn't seem to apply in this case; we all asked God over and over and over for protection and safe release. No one can say that our petition was inadequately brought before the Lord.

On the very next page in the book of James, it says, "The effectual fervent prayer of a righteous man availeth much" (5:16). Martin reminded me of this Scripture once when I was especially discouraged in the jungle. We were sitting on the ground during a rest break after hard hiking, listening to gunfire in the distance, and I was moaning, "We're totally forgotten. Nobody's doing anything to help us. Nobody's even praying for us anymore."

My good husband replied, "Gracia, you are wrong. Many people are still praying for us. And even if everyone else has stopped, our two dads are carrying on, I promise you. Remember what James 5 says about the prayer of a righteous man? We have two of the best."

He was exactly right, of course. The prayers of Paul Burnham and Norvin Jones alone would have met the requirements of this verse.

Obviously, the answer lies not in the number of prayers or the particular wording used in those prayers. There has to be another factor in the mix.

So what is it?

I can't claim to know for sure. There is an awful lot of Scripture that still mystifies me. During one of my many conversations with God in the jungle, I remember arguing with him about John 15:7, one of the verses I had memorized as a child: "If ye abide in me, and my words abide in you, ye shall ask what ye will, and it shall be done unto you."

I said, *Lord, you would have an excuse if the verse included an extra clause . . . 'ye shall ask what ye will,* and if I agree with you, *it shall be done unto you.' But it doesn't say that!*

These things are hard for all of us. And in my case, it's not just an academic exercise. I lost a husband over this.

Perhaps it's useful to notice that while the verse in James says fervent prayer "availeth much," it does not say it "availeth *everything.*" Why?

Because the Abu Sayyaf—and all of us—still retain the power of personal choice, the option of standing stubbornly against the will of God. And that obstinate stance is, apparently, something an almighty God is not willing to bulldoze. Of course, he could have fired heavenly lasers into the brains of Janjalani and Musab and Sabaya, forcing them to wake up one morning and say, "Okay, Martin and Gracia, this has been long enough. Feel free to hike off whenever you like." But that would have made them puppets instead of independent human beings with free will of their own, for which they will be eternally responsible.

I find it helpful to think about this analogy: Asking God to free us despite the Abu Sayyaf's rigidity was perhaps like ordering the U.S. Marines to come get us despite a prohibition in the Philippine constitution against foreign troops ever again fighting on Philippine soil. This is a rock-solid law born out of four centuries of colonialism, first under Spain, then the United States.

Did the Philippines accept outside military advisers? Well, yes, although even this triggered protests in the streets of Manila. Direct combat? Never.

Since returning home, I've learned just how badly the American military wanted to launch a special operation for us! I've been told how they sat around conference tables in Zamboanga City just itching for the opportunity. They would, of course, have done the job far differently. They would have moved into action at, say, two in the morning instead of two in the afternoon, wearing night-vision goggles and all the rest to snatch us out safely.

A few months after my release, this is exactly what happened in the west African nation of Ivory Coast, when rebels took over several northern cities and threatened a school for missionary children. The Ivorian government in essence said to the French and American generals, "Go for it. Feel free to evacuate your citizens, and any collateral damage you do to the rebels along the way is all for a good cause in our opinion." Within hours the students and faculty were roaring down the highway toward safety, waving the Stars and Stripes out of bus windows.

But nothing like that happened in our case. The local authority said no, and the Pentagon felt it could not trample upon an ally's national sovereignty.

Apparently, God runs into this impasse time after time. Having granted the human race a measure of self-determination, he would be hard-pressed to steamroller it when people misuse it. So it was with the Abu Sayyaf, and continues to the time of this writing, as their bombings and other violence keep showing up in the headlines.

::::

It makes for a messy world, doesn't it? Especially when radical members of a religion that accounts for one-fifth (more than one billion) of the planet's population feel called to advance their cause not only by persuasion but also by force and even terror. The extremist mind-set, as I experienced at close range for a full year, is not an easy thing to manage.

My experiences in captivity have made me think long and hard about an appropriate response to the challenge of the aggressive wing of Islam. I wouldn't presume to make any recommendations about public policy, but to my fellow Christians I feel compelled to say: We need to find ways to defuse the raging resentment and hatred that fuel "holy war" and introduce a God who does more than demand rituals—he truly loves us.

I am fully aware that millions of Muslims in the world are not bent on jihad. They are going through hard times themselves, performing their religious obligations over and over, hoping that somehow, someday, they will be acceptable to Allah.

For every hair that sticks out from under a woman's *terong*, I was told, she will spend a certain number of years in hell. People oppressed by such rules—not just Muslims but billions of people in the world who are desperately trying to stack up enough good deeds to outweigh their bad deeds so God will be happy with them— need our prayers. They need to know what it feels like to be forgiven. They need us to show we care.

When I was back in junior high, a popular song among Christian youth was "They'll Know We Are Christians by Our Love." It was the post-Woodstock era, the time when everybody tossed around the notion of love as the cure for all ills. I heard some adults ridiculing the song as naive and simplistic.

But in fact, that is exactly what Jesus said at the Last Supper (see John 13:35). People in today's world, whether Muslim or not, will not pay attention to Christians because we can explain our theology in crystal-clear terms. They will not esteem us because we give to charity or maintain a positive outlook on life. What will impress them is genuine love in our hearts.

Martin used to remind me of this while we were in the jungle. At one point, some copies of *Reader's Digest* appeared and we read them until they fell apart. Of course, Martin and I liked the joke sections. There was one joke about a teacher who in English class asked the students to write a story using descriptive words. Johnny turned in a paper that said, "The castle was big." The teacher returned it to him, saying, "Big is not a descriptive word. You can do better." The corrected story said, "The castle was big, and when I say big, I mean BIG."

We got a laugh from that, but a few days later Martin said, "I've been thinking about that story. Jesus said that if you want to be great in God's kingdom, be the servant of all. And when he said all, he meant all. He didn't say be the servant of everyone but terrorists. Jesus also said to love your enemies. Do good to those who hate you. Pray for those who despitefully use you and persecute you." And that's what we started doing—praying for our captors, who were despitefully using us.

We have a chance to show the love of Christ to the world. I think Martin managed to do this successfully in the jungle. I'm not sure I did very well myself. I hope nobody calls me a hero, because I know the facts about the bitterness that blazed in my heart that year. I still have lots of maturing to do.

When you stop and think about it, the Abu Sayyaf are not the only "bad guys," are they? We all have pockets of darkness inside ourselves. Recognizing how much I carry inside of me was one of the most difficult parts of my entire ordeal in the jungle. I already knew I was a sinner, of course. It's one of the first things I learned as a child in Sunday school. But I was also a missionary, a pastor's daughter, a lifelong "good girl." Weren't people like me supposed to be able to react to adversity with strength and grace and kindness and courage? Why wasn't I showing more of those traits?

I knew, for example, that I was supposed to forgive my captors, but the truth is that I often hated them. I despised them not only for snatching me away from my family and the simple comforts of a life I loved, but also for forcing me to see a side of myself I didn't like. There was a Gracia I barely knew existed: fearful Gracia, selfish Gracia, bitter Gracia, angry-at-God Gracia. That wasn't the only me, but it was a bigger part of me than I wanted to accept.

Every once in a while, Martin and I talked about the fruit of the Holy Spirit as listed in Galatians 5 and how much we wanted to see love, joy, and peace in our lives.

"All I see is sadness and grief and sorrow," I'd say. "How can we produce the opposite?"

We learned that the fruit of the Spirit could not be drummed up by ourselves. We couldn't force joyfulness or loving action or a peaceful mind. The Holy Spirit had to grow those things within us.

I begged the Lord at times, "Please just give me some peace. I can't find it in my own heart. I can't find long-suffering. I feel anything but gentle right now. Please work some gentleness into my life. Give me some joy in the middle of this horrible situation."

And he did.

Now that I've come home to focus on my children for the next few years, I am determined to keep serving the Lord "with gladness," as Martin emphasized that last rainy afternoon we spent together. Some people in America want me to be offended and angry and bitter with the government for not doing this or that. Others want me to be depressed and morose—the poor, whimpering widow.

I can't be either of those. What good would it do?

What happened to Martin and me was no one's fault except that of sinful human beings, the kind we came to the Philippines to help. This ordeal went with the territory. I refuse to let this dampen my joy or detract from the love that God means to flourish in my heart.

Do I miss my husband? Absolutely. Every time I hear an airplane overhead, I can't help thinking about him—and I live next to Wichita, Kansas, the aircraft capital of the world. Boeing, Cessna, Raytheon (formerly Beech), Bombardier Aerospace Learjet, McConnell Air Force Base are all here. They constantly remind me of what Martin loved to do and did so well.

But no amount of pining is going to bring him back. I choose instead to rejoice in his memory and to keep it alive in my kids. One Friday night in August 2002, they were all at church for vacation Bible school and I wanted to go to the closing program. By now my leg wound had healed enough that I decided to walk the one block to our church rather than drive.

On the way I looked up into the wide Kansas sky, and for some reason, a deep happiness swept over me. I heard myself saying out loud, "Oh, Martin—you were the best! You were the best!" I don't know whether or not people in heaven can hear our comments here on earth. They probably have better things to do with their time. But if Martin was listening, I just wanted him to know how I felt. He was simply wonderful.

The special people God gives us along the way make us stronger to face the trials of an ugly world. Obviously, I never expected to face something of this magnitude. But I thank the Lord for helping me to endure it. I honor the legacy of a wise and godly man who kept me going, trail after trail, gun battle after gun battle. I value the efforts of all who worked so hard to get me out alive. And I resolve to keep living in the embrace of God's gladness and love for as long as he gives me breath.

Wherever I go these days, whether to the local grocery store or across the country to speak, the question is usually the same: "How are you doing now, Gracia? What's happening in your life?"

I'm glad to report that my leg wound healed very quickly. Within a few weeks I was off the crutches and back to normal walking. Nowadays when the weather turns cold, my leg aches a bit, but otherwise I don't even think about it.

In fact, I've had more trouble getting the tropical amoebas out of my digestive tract. One medicine made me severely nauseous, so I stopped taking it. Eventually someone gave me a dietary supplement, Optiflora, that has helped a lot.

In the jungle I used to console myself with every woman's fantasy: *I'm sure I must be losing an impressive amount of weight.* Well, would you believe that by the time my leg was strong enough for me to stand on a scale, I weighed the very same as the day I'd been captured! I was so bummed.

It turns out that all the exertion up and down the hills carrying mortars had converted a fair amount of fat into muscle, which weighs more. I had certainly lost some inches, but no pounds.

The joy of my newfound mobility was immediately put to use. One summer morning about nine-thirty or ten, I got a sudden craving for a sweet potato. So I walked the three blocks over to the IGA and bought one, brought it home, boiled it, then sat down to slather it with butter and brown sugar, and had my feast! My kids thought I was crazy, but I didn't care.

A far more serious need at the beginning was finding a place in Rose Hill to live. Of course, Paul and Oreta Burnham, Martin's parents, would have let us live with them forever. But I knew we needed to be on our own eventually.

I told the kids, "Be looking for 'For Rent' signs. We have to find our own place pretty soon, you know." In the back of my mind, I also thought that maybe we could buy a modest trailer house.

Then came a letter from a local man named Steve McRae. He said he wanted to do something in Martin's honor, and he'd thought about planting a memorial tree—only he realized we didn't even have a yard in which to plant it.

So that led him to a larger question: Could the community come together and build us a whole house? Would I be interested in that, he wondered.

Oh, my. This was far beyond my wildest dreams. A few days later I met with Steve and a builder, Mark McKenna. The project began to take shape. Before I knew it, plans were drawn for a brand-new, nine-room home to be built on a corner lot in the middle of town. People began donating supplies, cash, and time for what was dubbed "Gracia's house." It was overwhelming.

As the word spread, even out-of-state people began calling to offer help. A group from Oklahoma wanted to build cabinets; a Christian radio station in Champaign, Illinois, organized a shower of Sears gift certificates; the president of Oak Express told me to go to his store in Wichita and pick out whatever I liked; a crew from Texas came to take charge of cleanup efforts as the carpenters finished.

While all this was happening, a local family offered

us temporary use of a second home they owned. It even had apple trees and pears trees in the backyard. Friends helped us collect odds and ends of furniture, and we set up housekeeping. We loved it.

The phone rang constantly at our place, of course. One day I picked it up and was shocked to hear, "This is the White House operator calling. Stay on the line for the president of the United States, please." What?!

I could hardly catch my breath before I heard a familiar voice say, "Hello, this is President Bush. Welcome home to the U.S."

"Yes, uh—thank you, Mr. President!" I mumbled.

"I'm so sorry that Martin didn't make it out, but I'm glad you did. How are you feeling?"

"I'm fine," I replied. "A lot of people who love me are helping me these days."

"How about coming here to visit at the White House?" he said. "Bring your kids, and your parents, and Martin's parents. I especially want to give those kids a hug."

So that's what we did. As it turned out, the FBI wanted me to testify before a Washington grand jury investigating the Abu Sayyaf. So while I was holed up in a courtroom racking my brain all day for names and dates and details, the rest of my clan got to see the sights of our nation's capital. But I also found time to meet some wonderful people, particularly in Representative Todd Tiahrt's office, who had worked so hard on my behalf.

Just as we arrived in his office, my son Zach got one of his infamous nosebleeds. We ducked into a little bathroom and tried to get it stopped. By then, his shirt was a mess. Chuck Knapp, the congressman's communications director, ran downstairs to the gift shop and brought back a House of Representatives shirt for Zach to wear the rest of the morning! Not long afterward, we were on our way to the White House.

When we first entered the Oval Office, it was definitely an emotional moment. The president came over, greeted us, and shook everyone's hand. That caused my mother-in-law to choke up a bit, and Mr. Bush graciously put his arm around her shoulder as he began giving us a little guided tour of his office: the desk that dated back to Franklin D. Roosevelt's time, the big rug in the middle with the presidential seal on it, and so forth.

Of course, we posed for pictures together. Then he said (at least as I recall his words), "I just want America to be a safe place, a place of freedom for our children as they grow up. And the only way that will be true is if we fight terrorism now. I'm going to do everything I can so our children can grow up in the kind of nation we've grown up in."

He also had a bit of welcome advice for Jeff, Mindy, and Zach. "Do you kids know how you can be a success?" he asked with all seriousness.

They shook their heads, waiting for him to answer.

Then he cracked a smile as he replied, "Obey your mother!" We all laughed together.

"Thank you so much for everything you tried to do for Martin and me," I said.

"Well, you're quite welcome," he said. "And there's something you can do for me. Pray for me every day, because I really need it. If a person working in this office doesn't realize their need for God's wisdom, they just really don't understand what's going on."

And with that, we left.

A week or two later came a Jones family reunion in Arkansas. I put everybody to work helping me open the thousands of sympathy cards that had arrived, and writing thank-you notes. We had a whole assembly line going with all the envelopes, stamps, and everything.

My family also helped me through the trauma of

July 4. After all, I hadn't been out of the jungle a full month yet, and the sound of even a modest firecracker would make me hit the ground in panic. I couldn't yet control my instincts after so many gun battles. So my family found a camp in the Ozarks that was far from any town. That evening, the fireworks celebrations could only be heard faintly in the distance. I kept telling myself, *That's far . . . that's far. . . .* Those were the actual words that we and the Abu Sayyaf used to say about most of the AFP's artillery bombardments. Somehow I got through the night.

Soon enough, the school year began back in Rose Hill. I elected to homeschool Zach, whom I sensed needed extra time with Mom, even though I was working with Dean Merrill on this book at the same time, and the days were extremely full. I carried around a minicassette recorder and taped my story everywhere I went—waiting in the car for a football practice to end, sitting in the Wal-Mart parking lot, you name it.

Tyndale House, this book's publisher, hired a wonderful publicist named Nancy Guthrie to help manage the incessant media requests. Nancy pushed for nearly all interviews to be done in Rose Hill so I wouldn't have to travel. The one exception, of course, was the *Dateline NBC* interview with Katie Couric, which had to be taped in their New York City studios.

Even the FBI agents were kind to come my way as they pursued their inquiries. I'll never forget the day I was being debriefed by two agents and two State Department men. At a certain time in the afternoon, I bluntly said, "Okay, guys, that's it for today. I have to go be a mom now and watch Zach's baseball game."

"We'll go with you!" they announced. "We love baseball."

And so we all went together. What a sight on the

bleachers of the Rose Hill baseball diamond: four G-men in dark suits, white shirts, and dark ties yelling at the top of their lungs every time Zachary came up to bat.

On October 26, 2002, my sister Mary had her baby girl in Ohio. What a happy time for their family and us all. Zach decided midway through the year that he'd like to transfer to public school alongside his siblings, where he adjusted well.

But other, ordinary days along the way have been, frankly, tough. As I said earlier in this book, I never planned on being a single mom. At times I have been overwhelmed. I've gotten to the end of the day and realized it contained far too many unkind words, messed-up schedules, and frustrated feelings.

Still, when telling me good night, one of the kids would say, "You know, it hasn't been a very good day, has it, Mom? But this still sure beats what you guys went through in the jungle, right?"

Yes, indeed. No matter what happens, I can still lie in bed at night and say to myself, *I had food today. I had water. I have a roof over my head. I have friends ready and willing to help me. I have a vehicle for running errands. It's going to be okay.*

The vehicle was a particular case of God's blessing. Right after the funeral, a neighbor of Paul and Oreta's gave me a van to use for a while. Martin and I had occasionally talked in the jungle about what I should do if for some reason I came home to the kids without him. He gave me a speech on what kind of car to buy and how much to borrow from the bank.

I was still trying to remember what he had said when, one day, Parks Motors in the nearby town of Augusta called to say, "Guess what—the Dodge dealers association of Kansas has decided to give you a van. In fact, it's sitting here right now on our showroom floor.

Come on over and have a look at it. If you don't like the color, we'll reorder."

I was speechless! With no effort on my part, I was suddenly the owner of a brand-new Grand Caravan with all the bells and whistles.

When I had first arrived home from the Philippines, I had occasionally pictured Martin up in heaven, pulling on God's sleeve and saying, "Don't forget to look after Gracia and the kids. See what they need. Do you think you could provide that for them?"

Now I realized that the God of the universe doesn't need Martin Burnham reminding him what to do. He knows me and what I need. He loves me. He bought my salvation. Now when I think of heaven, I picture God pulling on Martin's sleeve and saying, "Watch this! Look what I'm going to do for Gracia now. . . ."

I felt this especially strongly when in February 2003 we moved into the new house. It is far more than I ever dreamed. I held three days of "open house" to thank the community for all their work. And I told the Lord, "Thank you for this beautiful place that we can call home. I want you to use it—and us—for your glory."

I also told the kids, "This place is marvelous—but don't get too used to it, okay? If God wants us back in a hut in the Philippine jungle, we're gonna go." They readily nodded in agreement.

The Lord continues to supply our needs. So far I've been able to concentrate on my mothering without financial worries. The three kids get a Social Security check, of course, due to their father's death. I'm still considered a New Tribes Mission representative, and some of our longtime donors continue to support us. My occasional speaking honoraria and book sales pay the cost of secretarial help to manage the phone calls and mail, which can be heavy.

Occasionally, fourteen-year-old Mindy will blurt out, "Mom—are we broke?"

"No, we're not," I'll reply. "But we do need to be careful."

All in all, it's a good life. I'm content. Notice, I didn't say "thrilled," as if I'd just won a lottery and could now fulfill my dreams. The truth is, while this life is okay, I loved my old life. I loved my career as a missionary. I loved the Philippines. I loved my husband. He was truly my soul mate, the person I clicked with, laughed with, bore children with. And all that was taken from me.

The only thing that has remained the same in this new life is my children. I accept the present situation because I affirm by faith that God is making it good. But I've lost the good life I had. You don't just pack up those memories and stick them in a box on a closet shelf in your heart.

I make a daily decision to trust that this new life I've been given is God's plan for me. He is for me, not against me. He can make this life good, even though it's different.

Were it not for my kids, I would just as soon have died along with Martin on the hillside that afternoon. Martin is the one who got the good end of the deal. But at the same time, I'm so glad that Jeff, Mindy, and Zach have a parent. I would hate for them to be orphans. I want to be excited about each new day that God gives us together instead of dwelling on what I lost.

When people recognize me on the street or in a store, which happens often here in central Kansas, they are always very kind as they ask how I'm doing. After one such conversation, Zach said to me, "Mom, when are we going to be normal? When will we get back to like it used to be, when nobody knew us, nobody called you to go anywhere or do anything?"

I said, "You know, Zach, I don't think that's what God has for us right now. I think God has called us to this special time. I don't understand it all, but let's just follow Jesus. Let's allow what we're in right now to be 'normal' for us, and be happy in it, okay?"

He nodded.

Inside our home, we've declared a little jihad—on our knees. The kids and I continue to pray for the Abu Sayyaf. Whenever we read in the newspaper about them taking more hostages or blowing up more buildings, we ask that each of them would have the chance just once to hear the gospel of Jesus Christ in an understandable manner in his own language, so he can make an intelligent choice.

In the jungle, I used to say, "Martin, what is this all about? How can these people be so cruel and hard-hearted?"

And he would answer, "I think God is gracing these guys with one more day of life. He's giving them one more chance to turn to him, to finally get it right."

One time the kids and I were in Kansas City for a Steven Curtis Chapman concert in which he featured Steve Saint, the son of missionary martyr Nate Saint, who died in Ecuador in 1956. He and four other missionaries were trying to take the gospel to the Waorani, a primitive tribe where 60 percent of all adult deaths were the result of getting speared. Steve had brought along an elderly Waorani man named Mancaye, one of his father's killers who had become a believer. They showed a moving documentary video called *Beyond the Gates of Splendor.* Jeff got to sit beside Mancaye during that showing. We also got to visit with him backstage.

A little dream was born in my heart in that moment. *What if someday one of my kids would get to stand beside an Abu Sayyaf member who had come to know the Lord?*

Wouldn't that be incredible? I don't know if that will ever come to pass. But we can pray about it.

One day, Jeff and I were driving into Wichita—he has his driver's license now—and he said, "Mom, do you remember when we were on the mission field, and donations would be low in a month so that we couldn't even afford to go to the market—but it didn't matter, 'cause we were making a difference? Now here we are in Kansas, and we seem to have everything we need. But I'm not sure we're still making a difference."

I looked over at my firstborn son and said, "Yeah, I hear you. I guess we just need to ask God to help us make a difference right here in Rose Hill. This is where we are for now, and God needs us to make an impact right in this place."

Come to think of it, that's all he expects from any of us.

About the Authors

GRACIA BURNHAM is the widow of Martin Burnham and the mother of Jeff, Mindy, and Zach. Gracia and Martin worked as New Tribes missionaries in the Philippines from 1986 to May 2001. Until their capture, Martin was a missionary pilot, delivering mail, supplies, and encouragement to other missionaries and transporting sick and injured patients to medical facilities. Gracia served in various roles supporting the aviation program in the Philippines and also homeschooled their children.

DEAN MERRILL, coauthor with Gracia Burnham on this book, is vice president of publishing with the International Bible Society. The former head of publishing at Focus on the Family, he has authored and coauthored numerous books, including the best-seller, *Fresh Wind, Fresh Fire,* with Jim Cymbala.

The Martin & Gracia Burnham Foundation

*seeks to extend
the Good News of Jesus Christ
through its support of missions
around the world.*

Gracia Burnham
Founder and Director
www.GraciaBurnham.org

*For more information on the variety of ways
in which you may donate to the foundation, please contact:*

The Martin & Gracia Burnham Foundation

c/o Christian Community Foundation in Kansas City
11599 Ridgeview, Suite 103
Olathe, KS 66061
(816) 474-8800
www.ccfkc.org

*The saga of the yearlong captivity of
Martin and Gracia Burnham*
captured the world's attention.
People were amazed that they could endure such hardships
and even more that they could respond to their captors as they did.
What caused Martin to thank the guards
who chained him to a tree at night?

In the final days Martin and Gracia spent together
their thoughts focused on a passage of Scripture that says:
"Serve the Lord with gladness: come before His presence with singing."
(Psalm 100:2, KJV)
Martin said, "We might not leave this jungle alive,
but at least we can leave this world serving the Lord with *gladness*.
We can serve him right here where we are, and with *gladness*."

Such attitudes are not generated by human effort.
They are a direct result of the grace of God in the lives of his people.
It is this life-changing message that
the Martin & Gracia Burnham Foundation
seeks to share with the world.

The foundation's goal is to provide funding
for special needs in the areas of
missionary aviation, tribal mission work,
Christian ministries to Muslims, and
the often-neglected persecuted church around the world.

The horrendous ordeal is over for Martin and Gracia Burnham.
Though Martin is now with the Lord,
his message is far from being extinguished.
You can help continue the legacy of faith that Martin embraced
and extend the good news of the wonderful love, faithfulness,
and saving grace of Jesus Christ
to a world that desperately needs to know him.